MW01033226

ARROW THROUGH THE HEART: THE BIOGRAPHY OF ANDY GIBB

By

Matthew Hild

ARROW THROUGH THE HEART: THE BIOGRAPHY OF ANDY GIBB

The promotional photographs and publicity materials reproduced herein are in the author's private collection (unless noted otherwise). These images date from the original release of the films and were released to media outlets for publicity purposes.

Front cover photo: Andy Gibb performing at the Carlton Celebrity Dinner Theater in Bloomington, Minnesota, on November 11, 1983. Photo taken by Mike Zerby and used with the permission of the Minnesota Historical Society.

Back cover illustration: Painting of Andy Gibb by Chris Minoldi, 2021, provided courtesy of the artist

Published in the USA by
BearManor Media
1317 Edgewater Dr. #110
Orlando, FL 32804
www.BearManorMedia.com

Softcover Edition
ISBN-10:
ISBN-13: 978-1-62933-920-7

Printed in the United States of America

Table of Contents

Acknowledgments

I could not have written this book if people who knew and worked with Andy Gibb had not been willing to share their memories with me. Many of them had never publicly shared those memories before, and I am grateful to them for finally doing so. Some filled in small bits of Andy's story, while others knew him well and shared a lot of information and insights, but they all were helpful as I tried to piece together the story of his life and career.

In alphabetical order, I would like to thank: Marion Adriaensen, Howard Albert, Lenard Allen, Malcolm Balfour, Michael Barbiero, Russell Battelene, Peter Beckett, Dick Bright, Joey Carbone, Charlie Chalmers, James Dayley, Scott Glasel, Kenny Hodges, Bud Horowitz, Sarah Irvine, Ann Jillian, John Kozyak, Julie LaMagna, Peter Leinheiser, Jeff Lodin, Rick Lotempio, Jerry Manfredi, Tony Messina, Michael Miller, Andy Murcia, Joey Murcia, Olivia Newton-John, Trevor Norton, Bill Oakes, Scott Paton, Jim Photoglo, George Recupito, Kim Richards, Cathi Robbins, Rick Robbins, Nicole Romine, Pam Rossi, Joe Shane, George Terry, Chuck Throckmorton, Jeff Witjas, and Lenore Zann. Journalists Mick LaSalle, Joel Selvin, and Michele Willens also shared some memories and insights. Tai Babilonia and Wally Kurth also shared some recollections of Andy on Twitter.

Scott Paton kindly provided me with recordings of interviews that he conducted with Andy Gibb, Barry Gibb, Hugh and Barbara Gibb, and Karl Richardson and Albhy Galuten during 1977 and 1978 while he was working for the radio shows *American Top 40* and *The Robert W. Morgan Special of the Week*. None of these interviews ever aired in their entirety. Kenny Hodges generously sent me a recording of an interview that he conducted with Andy on June 1, 1986, in Orem, Utah, when Andy was there to appear on the Children's Miracle Network Telethon.

Thanks also to Michael Caprio, Andrew Curry, Jayjay Epega, Lesley Gibb Evans, Sheila Kennedy, Marìa Fernanda León, Michael McCartney, and Taylor Patterson. For assistance in finding the negative of the cover photo and obtaining permission to use the photo, thanks to Jennifer Huebscher, Jenny McElroy, Jennifer Wagner, John Wareham, the photographer Mike Zerby, and the Minnesota Historical Society. The portrait of Andy Gibb on the back cover was painted expressly for this book by Chris Minoldi, and I am grateful to him as well as Deborah Cristina and Tony Messina for their help in making that happen. Last but not least, I must thank Ben Ohmart and BearManor Media for believing in this book and publishing it.

Prologue

"Mr. Gibb, can I have your photo?"

The year was 1986, and as *San Francisco Chronicle* music journalist Joel Selvin recalled, Andy Gibb was in town for a weekend to serve as the grand marshal of a charity rally for the March of Dimes, an organization for which the singer made many charity appearances from the late 1970s through the mid-1980s. He had just walked out of an office at Kezar Stadium, surrounded by security officers. Andy shooed them aside, spread his arms out, and smiled for the photo.

The photographer quickly took the shot and then approached Andy. "Here, this is for you," he said as he handed Andy some papers. Andy was puzzled. "What's that?" "I've just served you," the photographer replied.

The photographer, H. Allen Gilstein, was not a member of the press. Gilstein was a private detective, acting, in this instance, as a process server. Andy was badly in debt, and many of his creditors had run out of patience. One of them had promised Gilstein $500 (equivalent to over $1,200 in 2021) if he managed to serve Andy. Hoping to seize the opportunity, Gilstein had phoned Selvin, who suggested the ruse that the private eye utilized. When Selvin arrived at his office on the following Monday, he found "a magnum of champagne and a photograph of Andy Gibb on my desk."

This short but dramatic episode would have been unthinkable five years earlier. From 1977 to 1981, Andy Gibb, who made pop music history by reaching number one on the record charts with his first three singles, sold 20 million records, and when his popularity as a recording artist began to slip, he transitioned into television, hosting the popular syndicated musical variety series *Solid Gold*, and theater, landing a starring role on Broadway in *Joseph and the Amazing Technicolor Dreamcoat* in the fall of 1982. But just as a winning combination of attributes—his talent, charisma, boyish good looks, and the assistance of his brothers, the Bee Gees (especially Barry)—propelled Andy to sudden superstardom at the age of nineteen, so did a perfect storm of demons cause a downfall that was almost as spectacular as his rise to the top. Andy was insecure about his success, believing that he owed much of it to Barry; he was tormented by not being able to see his only child, a daughter born in January 1978 out of a brief teenage marriage; and in an era when cocaine use was rampant among pop and rock stars, Andy often indulged. Finally, his much-publicized romance and, in March 1982, breakup with television star Victoria Principal sent him into a downward spiral. He lost his jobs on *Solid Gold* and Broadway due to missing too many shows.

By 1984 his career was floundering, and his addictions were damaging his health. He entered the Betty Ford Center in 1985, but he continued to struggle. In 1986 he sought treatment again, this time without the press coverage that had accompanied his first attempt at rehabilitation, at a clinic in Santa Barbara. He also joined Alcoholics Anonymous. Andy was now clean and sober and eager to rebuild his broken career, but he was so hopelessly in debt that he would have to declare bankruptcy before he could make any serious efforts to do that. In the fall of 1986 he returned to Miami Beach, which he had left for California six years earlier in a bid for independence from his brothers (particularly Barry), to try to get back on his feet.

Shortly before he returned to the Sunshine State, Andy sat for an interview with the legendary DJ and radio host Cousin Brucie Morrow for the television program *PM Magazine*. For all the incredible highs and lows he had experienced, Andy was still only twenty-eight years old, and he sounded hopeful about his future. "In my heart," he declared, "I really want happiness, serenity, peace of mind, and I want to keep growing, you know. Just growing, and I think more than anything else I want to give, give a lot."

Tragically, he wouldn't get the chance. At the beginning of 1988, Andy left Florida for England, where he settled into a cottage on his brother Robin's estate about sixty miles outside of London, and signed a recording contract with Island Records. He seemed optimistic and excited, but by the time he turned thirty on March 5, his insecurities were taking hold of him again, and an inflammatory heart condition that had plagued him for years began flaring up badly. His brothers Maurice and Robin both had frightening premonitions about him. "It was like a nightmare except that I was awake," Robin told a reporter in 1989. "It frightened the living daylights out of me. Everything started to close in on me. I felt I would not be able to escape, like I was trapped in a box. I was claustrophobic and gasping for breath. A few days later [on March 10], Andy was dead."

Chapter ONE

Words and Music

"You can't talk to Andy Gibb without talking about the Bee Gees." Canadian radio host and DJ Bob Durant made this assessment after interviewing Andy on his "Night Music" radio show in 1985, while Andy was in Toronto for a nightclub engagement. In that one sentence, Durant captured one of the central facts of Andy's life: while many people's destinies are shaped to some extent by their families, for Andy the influence of his family was overwhelming.

Andy and his four siblings were born into a musical family. Father Hugh Leslie Gibb was born in the industrial city of Manchester, England, on January 15, 1916. While his siblings plied trades such as engineering clerk and typist, Hugh learned to play the drums and gravitated toward a career in music, which by his own later admission made him "the oddball" in his working-class family. By 1940 he was leading the Hughie Gibb Orchestra. That profession enabled him to avoid military service in World War II; instead, as his son Maurice would joke more than half a century later, "he did the soundtrack to World War II" as his band toured across northern England and Scotland.

Barbara May Pass was also born in Manchester, on November 17, 1920. She, too, was a musical performer, albeit on a more local scale than Hugh, singing as a dance band vocalist in Manchester. She met Hugh in a ballroom in that city where his band was performing. The pair began dating and tied the knot in Manchester in May 27, 1944. Their relationship would not cross from personal to professional. As Barbara laughingly recalled in a radio interview in 2005, "He would never let me sing in the band. He said one in the family was enough. He didn't realize what was going to come."

Over the next five-and-a-half years, Hugh and Barbara had four children. Daughter Lesley was born in Manchester on January 12, 1945. Son Barry was born on September 1, 1946, in Douglas on the Isle of Man, which is located in the Irish Sea between Great Britain and Ireland. By then, Hugh's orchestra had a regular engagement at the Douglas Bay Hotel. Fraternal twin sons Robin and Maurice also entered the world in Douglas, on December 22, 1949.

By 1955, Hugh's luck had run dry on the Isle of Man, and so the family returned to Manchester. Here the children began to show mischievous tendencies: Lesley and Barry began skipping school, while the twins, especially Robin, developed an alarming propensity for setting things on fire. One friend recalled Robin setting a TV and radio shop on fire. "Robin," Hugh allowed in an interview in 1979, "was a bit of a firebug."

The family endured a hardscrabble existence; both parents worked, with Hugh sometimes holding two jobs, but neighbors recalled the Gibb kids appearing to be underfed. By now the three boys, influenced in no small part by Hugh's collection of Mills Brothers records, had begun harmonizing together. By 1956, they were performing with two friends as a group called "The Rattlesnakes," and they began earning small amounts of money for gigs.

The family was still living in Manchester when Andrew Roy Gibb (his middle name was in honor of one of Hugh's brothers) was born there, at the Stretford Memorial Hospital, on March 5, 1958. He would be the last of Hugh and Barbara's children, although the pair would raise Lesley's first child, daughter Bernice, who was born on September 29, 1964. Beri, as she would be called, and Andy grew up together, and after Andy became famous he often created confusion among fans about the Gibb family tree by referring to her as his sister.[1]

1 Bernice often spelled her nickname "Berry," but sometimes spelled it "Beri." Books about the Bee Gees usually use the latter, probably in part to avoid confusion between "Barry" and "Berry." Bernice passed away on April 15, 2021.

Andy would not spend much of his infancy in England. In the summer of 1958—Andy would later say he was five months old at the time—Hugh and Barbara and their five children boarded the *Fairsea* as third-class passengers, with one-way tickets, on a five-week voyage to Australia. In 1980 Andy told television host Mike Douglas that the family made the move "mainly for the reason that . . . my brothers had the bug to get into music . . . and the family as a whole wanted a fresh start." Robin also used the phrase "a fresh start" in recalling the family's motivation for the move, while adding that his parents were having a tough time supporting the family in England. Other accounts suggest that the three older boys "still getting into trouble" for matters like minor theft also factored into the decision.

The Gibbs arrived in Australia on September 1—Barry's twelfth birthday—and made their new home in Redcliffe, a suburb located on the Moreton Bay about 25 miles northeast of Brisbane. Hugh soon found employment as a "bush photographer." Robin would later explain that his father "used to go out into the small towns and photograph people's families." Soon Barry and the twins were singing on a Brisbane radio station and between races at the Redcliffe Speedway Circus. There they met speedway manager Bill Goode, who was sufficiently impressed with their talent to introduce them to Brisbane disc jockey Bill Gates, who was equally taken aback by the young brothers. At this point, Gates later recalled, "The actual naming of the group took place at the Redcliffe Speedway. Barry pointed out that his initials, Bill Goode's, and mine were all B.G. so the name 'B.G.s' almost wrote itself." (Another "B.G.," of course, was Barbara Gibb.) Bill Goode and Barry soon decided on "Bee Gees" as the proper spelling of the name. The Bee Gees continued to perform on local radio and in pubs and clubs, and in 1960 they made their television debut in Brisbane. At the beginning of 1963, the Bee Gees signed a recording contract with Australia's largest independent record company, Festival Records, and began recording songs written by Barry and releasing them as singles.

By this point, Andy was about to turn five years old, and he was already declaring that he wanted to grow up to be either a doctor or a member of the

Bee Gees. "He sings in perfect pitch with the boys when they're practicing," Barbara noted, "and we'd like him, one day, to join the group." In fact, according to Bee Gees biographer Simon Spence, Barbara had even suggested that the Bee Gees add four-year-old Andy to their lineup. A home movie made by Hugh around this time shows the four brothers walking outside, with Andy almost literally in tow as Maurice grabs his hand. In March 1963, Andy's parents enrolled him at the Clovelly Infants School in Sydney, where the Gibbs had just relocated to further the Bee Gees' career. Two years to the month later, Andy would move on to the Dacgyville State School, also in Sydney.

In 1966, the Bee Gees made their big breakthrough in Australia. "Spicks and Specks," written by Barry, became a top five hit there in November of that year. On January 3, 1967, the Gibb family (except Lesley, who stayed behind with her Australian husband Keith Evans) boarded the *Fairsky* (a similar name to that of the ship that had taken them down under over eight years earlier) to return to England. "You had to really leave Australia," Robin later explained, "[and] either go to the UK or America to go any further. We knew, by the time we left, that we could only go so far—and then we had to get out." The Gibbs had not become wealthy in Australia. "We were a family who had literally no money," Barry recalled in 2020. "We probably rented twenty houses during the seven years or so that we were in Australia. I think, without overemphasizing it, my father just didn't pay the rent. We were that family in the middle of the night with the suitcases."

Returning to England apparently proved surprisingly sentimental for young Andy, considering that he had been an infant when the Gibbs had left. When the *Fairsky* settled into port at Southampton on February 6, 1967, Andy, as he later recalled, "went running down the gangplank, nine years old, you know, and I left at five months old, so I'd never even seen it. I was running down there and kissed the ground and [saying] 'England, England,' you know, and my brothers all kissed the ground. After a few months we wondered why, but we did it." Within days the Gibb family settled, for the time being, into a furnished house in Hendon, just northwest of London.

Eighteen days after the Gibbs returned to England, the Bee Gees signed a comprehensive five-year management contract (which also included record and publishing deals) with impresario Robert Stigwood. A native of Australia, Stigwood had recently become a partner of Brian Epstein, the famed manager of the Beatles, in the latter's NEMS Enterprises. After Epstein died on August 27, 1967, and the Fab Four refused to work with Stigwood, the latter, according to the London newspaper *The Guardian*, "would walk away from NEMS, with a golden handshake, to set up the Robert Stigwood Organisation (RSO)." RSO would achieve tremendous success during the latter half of the 1970s; the Bee Gees would be at the center of that success, but Andy would also figure quite prominently in it himself.

The Bee Gees made the leap to international stardom with their very first release after signing with Stigwood, the Barry Gibb-Robin Gibb composition "New York Mining Disaster 1941 (Have You Seen My Wife, Mr. Jones)." The single made it to number fourteen on the *Billboard* Hot 100 and reached number twelve on the British charts. By early 1968, the Bee Gees had racked up four more top twenty hits in the United States: "To Love Somebody," "Holiday," "(The Lights Went Out In) Massachusetts," and "Words." Andy would later make the last of those songs a staple of his concerts throughout his career, telling a reporter in 1985, "It's amazing, that song. If a show is going bad, for any reason . . . once I sing 'Words,' it's plain sailing through the end of the show. 'Words' has never let me down yet. It seems to stop the show."

"(The Lights Went Out In) Massachusetts," written by all three Bee Gees, became the group's first number one hit in the UK, and by 1968 Andy was noticing his older brothers' stardom, even though he later claimed to be unfazed by it. "Well, it didn't change my life that much, because I was only ten years old and I knew they were in the business," Andy recalled ten years later. "And I had always known they were in the business, not being anything extra special to me. And at ten years old you don't think about show business, you don't think glitter, you don't think that you have four or five hundred kids outside the front door because your brothers are big stars. I'd just walk in after school, pass the five hundred kids at the front door, go in the back door, my brothers would all be sitting, watching television with the curtains drawn. Girls banging on the windows and that was their whole life, you know." While young fans did indeed camp outside the family home, it is entirely possible that Andy was exaggerating, a tendency that he shared with his brothers in telling stories. (In fact, just one year earlier, in 1977, Andy had told an interviewer, "It was not uncommon for me to come home from school and see two hundred kids standing by the door.")

By 1969, Andy's brothers had moved out, but Andy told a fan magazine that year that Barry still visited about twice a week. The family's oldest son and youngest son had become close despite the eleven-and-a-half-year difference in their ages. "I think he's my favorite brother," said Andy. "He's so kind and generous, and when he comes to visit us he plays with me. I've only got to ask for something and he'll buy it for me. I think he's too soft-hearted, people can talk him into things and he hates hurting anyone." People who knew Andy would later describe him in similar terms. Andy also happily reported that Barry had bought him a horse, which Andy named Gala, for his eleventh birthday, and that the two brothers took rides in Barry's Bentley, adding that "he doesn't let me have a go at driving it, though!" Andy did get to have fun with the horse, however—he was soon engaging in show jumping. "He was the youngest member of the team" at eleven, his father recalled. A childhood friend of Andy's recalled him making a visit to her family's house in Beaconsfield on the horse, which "promptly tried to get through our side gate into the garden," tearing the gate off the hinges in the process. Her father "wasn't very impressed," of course, and Andy himself was "mortified." Hugh and Barbara paid for a new gate.

While Barry apparently has never gone on record as saying that Andy was his "favorite brother," he practically admitted it in an interview for a VH-1 *Behind the Music* episode about Andy in 1997. "Maurice and Rob were twins so they always had each other. Andy was someone I could always talk to and who always could talk to me," Barry recalled, "because both of us sort of had a sense of isolation in growing up, so we were extremely close." In 2014, Barry said of Andy in an interview for *Rolling Stone*, "We were like twins. The same voice, the same interests, the same birthmark." Barry told another interviewer, "I lost my best friend when I lost Andy."

While Barry and Andy were getting along well in 1969, the Bee Gees were falling apart. Robin left the group in March of that year to pursue a solo career; Hugh publicly suggested that Andy might replace Robin in the group at some point in the future. Of course, that did not happen.

More than fifty years later, Barry seemed to blame Robin for the split: "When we had our first number one, 'Massachusetts,' Robin sang the lead, and I don't think he ever got past that; he never felt that anyone else should sing lead after that. And that was not the nature of the group. We all brought songs in; whoever brings the idea in sings the song." With the exception of Robin's single "Saved By the Bell,' which was a big hit in the UK (but not in the US), the brothers couldn't replicate the Bee Gees' success as solo artists, however, and they reunited in the summer of 1970. They immediately turned out back-to-back singles that became huge hits in the US (but not in the UK), "Lonely Days" and their first number one hit on the *Billboard* Hot 100, "How Can You Mend a Broken Heart."

Meanwhile, one year after giving Andy a horse, in March 1970 Barry gave his youngest brother his first guitar for his twelfth birthday. By now Andy had decided that he wanted to be a Bee Gee, not a doctor. He wanted to be like Barry. In the *Behind the Music* episode, Maurice recalled that Andy "emulated Barry a lot. He thought a great deal of his older brother. He had sort of a hero worship for him." Observers outside the family shared this opinion. Longtime Bee Gees drummer Dennis Bryon, who met Andy in 1973 (and played in Andy's band in the mid-1980s) later described young Andy as "Barry's little shadow," noting that "he followed and mirrored every move his elder brother made."

In early 1971 Hugh and Barbara, along with Andy and Beri, moved to the island of Ibiza, off the east coast of Spain. Here Andy would begin his career as a singer and musician. He landed his first gig through Tony Messina, the young manager of an establishment called Debbie's Bar in the resort town of San Antonio. Messina hailed from Australia, and as he would recall fifty years later, Andy "had heard that there was an Australian with a bar." One day shortly after the Gibbs' arrival on the island, Andy came in and introduced himself to Tony. "Hey, my name's Andy Gibb. Do you know the Bee Gees?" (Andy meant did Messina know who they were, which he most certainly did, and not if he actually knew them, which he did not.) Andy started bringing Bee Gees albums to the bar for Tony to play, and soon he told Tony that he sang and played guitar himself. "So," Andy told journalist Stan Soocher in 1978, "I started singing in a tavern on Ibiza called Debbie's Bar on St. Patrick's Day when I was thirteen. I sang Paul Simon's 'The Only Living Boy in New York' and 'Feelin' Groovy,' and the Bee Gees' 'Words.'"

Tony's memory of Andy's debut would differ slightly. Upon Tony's suggestion, the manager of a larger bar called Nito's booked Andy. "That's where he first sang publicly . . . and he was a hit," according to Tony. "That bar was packed every night. He just loved doing it . . . [it] was just a magical time."

Andy later recalled that Swedish tourists made up most of his audience, and that "the majority . . . 90 percent, were girls between sixteen and twenty-four years old. Ah yes, that was really fun. But I certainly became more aware vocally of what I could do and what I was suited to do, playing music." On occasion, the Bee Gees would show up and sing with him onstage. Some of those who saw Andy perform in Ibiza would remember him telling them that in a few years he would become the fourth member of the Bee Gees.

Andy also began writing songs at this time. He later recalled falling "head over heels in love" with a sixteen-year-old Swedish girl and writing a song about her. He told Barry about the song and Barry wanted to hear it. Andy demurred at first, telling his oldest brother, "No, no, not for you of all people. You've written good songs—you know what good songs are." But Barry insisted and Andy relented. "And when I finished," Andy remembered, "he said that he was amazed, that I'd proven to him that I could write. Then he told me the important thing was to keep writing." Andy would follow this advice for about the next seven years.

As Andy became more interested in performing and writing songs, he became less interested in school. None of his brothers had completed their secondary education, as Andy would somewhat defensively point out in interviews when the subject of his limited education came up. Even before he began performing in bars and clubs in Ibiza, he had emulated Lesley and Barry in skipping school. "I'd send him off to school but he'd sneak off to the stable and sleep with his two horses all day," his mother recalled. "He'd wander back home around lunchtime smelling of horse manure, yet he'd swear he had been at school. Oh, he was a little monkey!" Andy also faced a problem at school that Lesley and his brothers had not. "I never thought I was different from anybody else. I tried my hardest but I never was accepted at school," he told an interviewer in 1977. "I was marked as the Bee Gees' brother. The last school I went to was a modern public school that had a lot of children from poor homes. You can imagine what they felt like seeing me picked up at school every day in a Rolls Royce. I was getting picked on all the time. I hated going to school so [at age thirteen] I just quit."

Young Andy emulated his brothers not only in quitting school at an early age but also in getting into trouble. While he may have once again been engaging in his penchant for telling exaggerated stories, he later said that at the same time he was having difficulty at school in England, "I was moving about with my own gang, the skinheads, wearing steel-toed army boots and kicking in shop windows." Given that Andy was small—he only grew to a height of 5'6$^{1/2}$" and was slender—this seems unlikely, but from what he later told friends, it was apparently true. He also said that he and his "skin-head" friends would go into a crowded soccer stadium and throw a hammer into the air. "And wherever it lands, it lands. We were really very nasty." But again, there were some big differences between Andy's childhood and those of his brothers. Tom Kennedy, who worked for the Bee Gees for many years, recalled that Hugh and Barbara would let Andy "have a limo to go around London with his pals and twenty quid to go to the cinema. It was unheard of in those days!" Kennedy also recalled that Andy "used to try to get me to buy him beer when he was underage," perhaps an aftereffect of having been given beer while performing at bars in Ibiza.

Andy's spoiled, undisciplined upbringing may well have contributed to his inability to cope with adversity as an adult. As his mother admitted in 1997, "He never grew up, *never* grew up. He was just like Peter Pan. He was just like a little boy all his life. He was a baby all his life." Or as Kennedy, who remembered Andy fondly, put it, "I suppose if he had had a little more discipline in his life, he might still be with us today."

Tony Messina agreed that Andy was spoiled. "Whenever he needed anything, he'd go to his mum and he'd get it. That's all he was used to his whole life." Andy "was driving a Jeep at thirteen." It was, of course, the largesse of Barry, Robin, and Maurice that made it possible for Hugh and Barbara to spoil Andy. "And they were spoiled, too," remembered Tony. "Hughie was like a playboy." But Tony found Hugh and Barbara to be nice people, and he thought Andy "was one of the most generous, kind persons that you could meet."

In the summer of 1973 Hugh and Barbara, reportedly "feeling uncomfortable under the repressive Franco regime," left Ibiza with Andy and Beri in tow and returned to the Isle of Man, where they had last lived almost two decades earlier. Only the family and a few close friends knew the real reason why the Gibbs left Ibiza. Andy had begged his parents to buy him an MG Midget. Within forty-five minutes of getting behind the wheel of the sports car for the first time, Andy later told his personal manager James Dayley, he hit a man who was riding a bicycle. "I think he lost both his legs in the accident," Andy told Dayley about four years later. "I don't know if he even survived or not," Andy added as he broke into tears. Andy told Dayley that he had run home from the accident, told his parents what had happened, and that they gathered what items of value they could in the house and then boarded themselves, Andy, and Beri onto a plane, never to return to Ibiza. Some of the few friends of Andy's who ever heard this story believed that his guilt over the accident may have contributed to his later problems.

The hasty departure from Ibiza did not hinder Andy's budding career, though, as he was able to perform regularly at the Isle of Man's two main clubs. In fact, living closer to his brothers proved to be a boon to his progress. On August 22 and 24, 1973, Maurice took Andy into Nova Sound Studio in London for Andy's first recording sessions. On the first date, Andy (with Maurice's assistance) recorded "Windows of My World," which is believed to have been written by Maurice and Andy. Two days later, Andy recorded Maurice's composition "My Father's A Rebel." "Windows of My World" had a country feel much like some of the songs on Andy's first, mostly self-composed debut album, *Flowing Rivers*, which would be recorded in 1976. These two recordings would never be released but would surface among collectors after the tapes were sold at an auction in 2004. Joseph Brennan, an authority on the recordings of all the Gibb brothers, has noted that at age fifteen, "Andy already sound[ed] exactly like he did later."

While Barry was the brother who had done the most to encourage Andy to follow in the Bee Gees' footsteps, it was nevertheless not surprising that Maurice helped him make his first recordings. According to Tony Messina, Maurice, "a fun-loving guy," ultimately came to have a friendlier, warmer relationship with Andy than Barry did. "He [Maurice] and Andy were always kidding around. You didn't see [Andy having] the same interaction with Barry or with Robin," although Tony thought that Andy wanted "more of a brotherly thing" with Barry.

Nevertheless, Barry had plans to add Andy to the Bee Gees. In the late winter and early spring of 1973, Andy had traveled with the Bee Gees on their North American tour, one that did not go particularly well given the group's declining popularity. "He's basically on this tour watching us and studying us," said Barry, "so he knows what to do when he joins us, which will probably be in about a year." Hugh concurred.

Andy made a strong impression on his new neighbors on the small Isle of Man. Disc jockey Bernie Quayle of Manx Radio, the isle's national commercial radio station, recalled that Andy, "though he wasn't licensed, had a sports car" and "at sixteen years of age was racing around the island. He just had this wonderful joy of living." (Of course, virtually nobody on the Isle of Man knew about Andy's car accident in Ibiza.) Andy competed in motocross on the Isle of Man as well.

As his sixteenth birthday approached, however, Andy was feeling lonely and depressed; the Bee Gees had gone (without him) to America for another concert tour in early February 1974 and did not return until a couple of weeks after his birthday (March 5). Andy seemed to be realizing that his dream of becoming the fourth Bee Gee would not be coming true. Noting that "I almost joined the group a couple of times" but such plans had "always fallen through," he declared, "The only way I think I'd get to join now is if one of the group left. I'm sort of a ready-made understudy. I can do any of their voices and sound just like them, particularly if I do their material." When Barbara found him crying one night in February 1974, she suggested that they "go out and buy some amplifiers and get some good players and we'll start our own group." Andy agreed and it was done. It could be said without much exaggeration that Barbara Gibb formed Andy's first band. She named it, too: Melody Fayre, after the Bee Gees' song "Melody Fair" (1969). When one of the band members, drummer John Stringer, objected to the name, which he thought "soppy," Barbara let him know that he had no say in the matter. Barbara would be the band's manager, and Tony Messina, who had been working for Maurice in London as his personal assistant, soon rejoined Andy on the Isle of Man as the group's roadie and sound man.

While Stringer, lead guitarist John Alderson, and bassist Jerry Callaghan were impressed with Andy's lineage—especially when Barry showed up to help them complete a set list (which included multiple Bee Gees and Elton John hits) and give them pointers—they also soon came to appreciate Andy's talent and attitude. Alderson found Andy to be "very energetic . . . and 110 percent into it. It was very easy to buy into what he was doing." Alderson also remembered that Andy would not tolerate band members using drugs or alcohol before or after their shows, and that Andy himself not only showed no interest in marijuana at a party once, but did not even know how to roll a joint for a stoned young man who asked him to do it for him. Alderson made another observation about Andy that others had and would: "He talked a lot about Barry. Barry was his idol."

By June 1974, Melody Fayre began performing publicly. The band's concerts, which sometimes were attended by Barry and Maurice (and occasionally featured Hugh sitting in on drums for a song or two), were soon proving to be a hit. "They were good performances," Stringer recalled more than three decades later. "It just worked. We seemed to gel together as a band, and the crowds liked it. We were full every night, and we got applause for every song. We got encores. It went really well." By the end of the summer, Barry and Hugh decided that Andy was ready for the next step on his path to stardom. "Barry and my father suggested I go out there to Australia," Andy recalled in an interview in 1978. They told him to "start working there and get some records released."

Barbara wholeheartedly agreed. "Barbara was really very pushy with trying to get Andy into something," according to Tony Messina. "She was the one who got the whole Australian thing going with Kevin Jacobsen, who was the CEO of ATA Records." Jacobsen and his brother, the popular Australian singer Col Joye, had helped the Bee Gees get their recording career started nearly a dozen years earlier. "She got the okay from them [Jacobsen and Joye] to bring Andy over, [and] they signed him up." The all-encompassing deal included recording, music publishing, and management contracts. When Robert Stigwood brought Andy to the United States and into the RSO fold, he had to give 20 percent of Andy's music publishing, 5 percent of his management, and 2 percent of his record sales to Jacobsen and Joye. Furthermore, Andy's recordings for RSO Records would be released by ATA Records in Australia. The contracts with Jacobsen and Joye also gave Hugh and Barbara a cut of Andy's earnings, as would his contract with RSO.

Andy arrived in Australia with two members of Melody Fayre (Alderson and Stringer) and Messina days before the Bee Gees themselves did for a September-October tour of their former home country. Andy and his entourage soon found themselves staying in the same luxurious hotel in Sydney as the Bee Gees and riding in limos. In September Maurice once again took

Andy, along with Alderson and Stringer, into a recording studio, in this instance the ATA Sound Studio in Sydney. The trio was supplemented by a bass player and a cello player, and Maurice on organ, to record Andy's composition "To a Girl" (although as Stringer remembered it, Maurice and John Alderson helped Andy develop the melody). Col Joye served as producer. All parties involved intended for this dramatic, lilting ballad to be Andy's first single—Andy even performed the song on *The Ernie Sigley Show*, his television debut—but the recording never got released. "The only reason they wouldn't release the single was because it was about six [or] seven minutes long," according to Stringer, who added, "A bit of a shame because it really was a good song." (An audio recording of Andy's performance of the song on the television appearance, however, which now can be heard on YouTube, clocks in at just under four-and-a-half minutes.)

Andy had expected to serve a lengthy apprenticeship down under. "I went to Australia with the intention of staying for about five years, maybe even more," he told journalist Peter J. Boyer in 1977. "My brothers were there for nine years before they made it famous. So I went there with the intention of getting experience." But there were some important differences between Andy's situation in 1974 and that of his brothers in 1958. For one, Andy was sixteen, whereas the Gibbs had arrived in Australia in 1958 on Barry's twelfth birthday, before Robin and Maurice had even turned nine. And Barry, Robin, and Maurice had had to make their own contacts and be "discovered." No one took them upon their arrival to sign with a record company and go into a recording studio. Moreover, the Bee Gees, despite their then ongoing career slump in the US and UK, were still huge stars in Australia in 1974; Andy got immediate attention there as their younger brother. Of course, Andy's status as the Bee Gees' younger brother also had "disadvantages, because before I had any success that I could call my own, I had to live under that shadow, 'the youngest brother of the Bee Gees.' In fact, when I performed in Australia, the billboards used to say 'Tonight, Andy Gibb'—about two inches in size—'youngest brother of,' and in three-foot letters 'BEE GEES,'" he recalled laughingly in an interview in 1985.

"And so, but I also knew that it had to be that way, because I was not known."

Things began happening quickly for Andy in Australia. He made numerous television appearances, not only on music shows but also on talk shows and quiz or game shows, to the extent in fact that Alderson and Stringer, who were not being kept on retainer, soon found themselves not getting enough work and eventually returned to the Isle of Man. They allowed Andy to find a new band before they left, and he (or Jacobsen) placed an advertisement looking for musicians in a local paper. Jim Towers of the Cordon Bleu booking agency in Sydney saw the ad and recommended a four-man rock band named Zenta. The band consisted of vocalist Glen Greenhalgh, guitarist Ric Alford, bassist Paddy Lelliott, and drummer Trevor Norton.

After an audition in which Zenta played a few songs, Andy hired the quartet to play with him in live performances. Zenta would not accompany Andy in his next recording sessions in Sydney in mid-1975, however; instead Andy was backed by session musicians, mostly from a band called Crossfire, described by Australian music journalist Jeff Apter as a "jazz-rock combo." Andy recorded twelve songs, all of them self-composed except for the Barry Gibb-Maurice Gibb composition "Twinky" from 1969, which the Bee Gees had never released. None of these dozen recordings were released, although later recordings of four of the songs ("Words and Music," "Westfield Mansions," "Flowing Rivers," and "In the End") would come out between 1975 and 1977. ("Westfield Mansions" was never released outside of Australia and New Zealand, though.) Later in the year, Andy returned to Sydney's ATA Sound Studio to re-record "Words and Music" and "Westfield Mansions," with Col Joye again serving as producer. In November 1975 ATA Records released the two songs as a single.

Much like Barry at the same age, Andy was proving to be a precocious talent as a songwriter. Tony Messina would later reflect that Andy "was on a roll as a songwriter in Australia . . . [he] was into his creative juices. Just listening to the 'Flowing Rivers' song, you can tell exactly how he was feeling . . . how he was moving on, how he was coming along." Songs that Andy wrote in

Australia from 1974 through 1976 would make up the majority of his debut album, *Flowing Rivers*, which was released in 1977. Col Joye said in an interview in 2020 that Andy, during his time in Australia, "did his homework and he became a good performer." Andy, in Joye's estimation, ranked alongside his brothers as "a natural talent."

As Joye recalled, Andy didn't live a pampered life while performing in Australia. On one occasion, Andy and the band borrowed Joye's wife's car to drive to Adelaide—some 850 miles from Sydney—and back just to perform one show. "They played the show," Joye said, and then "the promoter shot through with all the money." Andy and his bandmates were only able to make it about halfway back to Sydney before they were out of money and in need of gasoline, food, and someplace to spend the night. Andy called Joye from the town of Deniliquin. Joye, a well-known singer in Australia, told Andy to go to the police station and have the sergeant call him. Joye then explained the situation to the sergeant and asked if he could "put them up for the night." The sergeant replied, "Oh yeah, the cells are empty, yeah, they can stay here." Andy and the band members spent the night in jail cells, and in the morning the sergeant gave them money for gasoline, which Joye paid back by mail. When Trevor Norton heard this story in 2021, he had no recollection of it, which would suggest that it occurred while Melody Fayre was still with Andy.

Sydney residents Jacqui Reed and her twin sister, who were one year older than Andy, first saw him perform at Chequers, a well-known nightclub in the city, shortly after the release of his single. They would see him perform numerous times, and soon they got to know him offstage as well. Andy still had a small following at this point. "It didn't seem to bother him so much the small crowd," Reid recalled in 2011. "He was just grateful to be out there performing his music. It was fresh and original and Andy was so inspired. . . . It was easy to like him. His enthusiasm was infectious and there was a vulnerability about him; not exactly gullibility but more he was embracing the idea of something new and the novelty hadn't worn off yet."

During Andy's second period of residence in Australia, he reacquainted himself with the sibling who had remained behind when the rest of the family had returned to England in 1967: sister Lesley, who lived in Sydney with her husband, Keith Evans, and a family that ultimately included seven children. (Lesley had returned to England briefly in the spring of 1969 to rehearse with Barry and Maurice and then replace Robin in a televised Bee Gees concert in London.) Lesley had since become a successful breeder of Staffordshire Bull Terriers. Around the same time that Andy was launching his recording career, he attended a dog show with Lesley, who introduced him to seventeen-year-old Kim Reeder, whose family also bred Staffordshire Bull Terriers. Andy and Kim started dating, and soon he was spending much of his free time at her family's home. "He sort of latched onto our family in those early days like a lifeline," Kim recalled after Andy had died. Kim was Andy's first real girlfriend. Before Andy met her, according to John Alderson, he had "always [been] very shy with girls, almost to the point of being silly at times. I don't remember him going out with any girls at all."

Barbara Gibb, meanwhile, accompanied Andy to Australia in 1974, returned to the Isle of Man, and then she and Beri (and, later, Hugh) moved back to Australia in the fall of 1975. Barbara, in particular, wanted to be near Andy and keep an eye on him and his progress. Trevor Norton remembered riding in a car with Andy in Australia one day, before Barbara had come back down, and seeing about twenty letters on the dashboard, all unopened. Glen Greenhalgh asked Andy, "What's all these letters?" "Oh, they're from my mum," Andy replied. "Well aren't you gonna read them?" Glenn asked. "Oh yeah, I will one day," Andy nonchalantly answered. Norton recalled that Greenhalgh then began opening the letters and reading them aloud while Andy drove.

When Barbara moved to Australia, she didn't move into the same home as Andy (or vice versa). "Andy lived in a unit in Station Street, West Ryde," Norton recalled. "Barbara lived in a house ten minutes away in Gladesville." (West Ryde and Gladesville are both suburbs to the northwest of Sydney.) Not long after Barbara got settled in, Andy took the members of Zenta to her house to meet her. Beri and Lesley were there, too. "They all seemed like a very happy little family to us all," said Norton. But Lenard Allen, who was one of Andy's backup singers in the mid-1980s, witnessed a conversation between Andy and Barbara over breakfast during a tour that suggested that Andy felt some resentment towards her. Andy, Lenard recalled, was asking Barbara to do some favors for him, as if she were his "personal assistant." "She kind of glared at him . . . and said, 'Can't you hire people, Andy? Don't you have enough people already around you?' And he said, 'Listen. You never had time for me as your child until I was famous. And now that I'm famous, you want to be around me. But before that, you only wanted to be around my brothers. So I think you can just maybe show me that you care and do what I ask of you.'"

Andy's debut single, meanwhile, did a respectable job of getting his Australian recording career underway, although the claim made in some later articles and books that "Words and Music" had been a smash hit in Australia was untrue; it only reached number seventy-eight on the Australian pop singles chart. In 1981, Andy told Los Angeles DJ and radio show host Robert W. Morgan, "I had one single out in Australia and it never did anything for me at all." This was another of Andy's exaggerations, though, for the single reached number twenty-nine in New Zealand, and it fared better on some of Australia's local charts. After Andy performed "Words and Music" on the weekly Australian ABC-TV show *Countdown*, it reached number twenty-six on the Queensland chart and the top five in Canberra, the capital of Australia.

Andy and Zenta landed a pair of high-profile bookings as an opening act around this time, too, for two globally popular British bands of the day, the Sweet and the Bay City Rollers. The promoter of the Rollers' Australian tour, Garry Van Egmond, later said that the band's management soon became disgruntled because Andy and Zenta were delivering better performances than the Scottish teen idols were, although Andy would later tell a reporter that someone pelted him in the forehead with a tomato at one of those concerts. (Actually, according to an audio tape of the concert that Norton has, it was an orange. Andy can be heard saying with what sounds like some bemusement, "Somebody's got a rotten orange they've been throwing at me.") Andy opened for the Rollers in December 1975; two years to the month later, he would be co-headlining with them at the Boston Garden at radio station WRKO's annual Christmas benefit concert.

Having released his first single, Andy took another significant step forward in his Australian "performing apprenticeship," as Barry later called it, in May 1976 when he played the role of Buttons in a Newcastle production of *Cinderella*. Andy also continued to record his own songs with Col Joye as producer at the ATA Studio in Sydney. None of these recordings would be released, but Andy would soon re-record four of the songs ("In the End," which he had recorded in 1975 as well, "Come Home for the Winter," "Let It Be Me," and "Starlight") in Miami for his debut album. Andy also recorded at least one cover version at ATA. "At one point, Ray Stevens came to Australia with my manager's promoter," Andy said in an interview in 1978. "I met him and wanted to record a song of his, 'Can't Stop Dancing,' which the Captain and Tennille later hit with. I tried it with two producers, didn't like it, and ended up producing the session myself. I played all guitars and keyboards, but it was never really finished and I don't know where the tapes are." Andy told the *Sydney Morning Herald* on July 11, 1976, that "Can't Stop Dancing" would be released as his second single on July 21, but like most of his Australian recordings, it never saw the light of day, even though ATA Records pressed some copies.

The reason why ATA made the last-minute decision not to release "Can't Stop Dancing" may have been the sudden realization that Andy would not be in Australia to promote it (even though he had performed it once already on an Australian television show). Barry Gibb and Robert Stigwood had been keeping their eyes on Andy's progress in Australia from afar. "Andy needed to work his way in and not just go on the coattails of his brothers, which he didn't want either," Stigwood recalled decades later. He had seen Andy perform in Australia and "thought he was sensational." By June 1976, Stigwood and Barry had decided that Andy was ready to leave Australia and launch his career in the United States. The Bee Gees had revitalized their own career with the 1975 album *Main Course*, which included "Jive Talkin'," a number one hit in the US and a number five hit in the UK. For the remainder of the

1970s, the Bee Gees would be as hot as any band before or since: their last six singles of the decade, from 1977 to 1979, all reached number one on the *Billboard* Hot 100, and by the summer of 1976, Barry was ready to help Andy have some hits of his own.

Barry called his youngest brother from Anchorage, Alaska, after a Bee Gees concert, telling him the news: "I want to produce your records and Robert wants to manage you . . . plus he wants to sign you up for the label." Andy had figured on spending more time honing his skills in Australia, but, "Obviously," he said in 1978, "I wasn't going to refuse an offer from RSO Records. They don't come along every day, you know." But at the time, recalled Trevor Norton, "I could see he was in a bit of shock in a way."

The summons to come to America forced Andy into a decision, though. He didn't want to leave Australia without Kim Reeder. According to what Andy later told James Dayley, Kim told him that she wouldn't leave Australia with him unless they got married, and that she wouldn't wait for him if he left without her and returned later. Andy decided to marry her. "He said we'll just have to get a wedding arranged, and that's all there was to it," she said more than twenty years later. She said that Andy telephoned her "every two minutes" until she agreed to a date. Kim said that she "felt very safe" with Andy, though, and that he had "a great sense of humor so it was always a lot of fun."

Andy's parents and brothers thought it was a bad idea; Barry and Maurice had both married at the age of nineteen and each of those marriages had been short-lived. Moreover, according to Dayley, Hugh and Barbara "didn't like Kim." Andy's bandmates were also skeptical. "To me and the [rest of the] guys in Zenta, Andy and Kim were like cheese and chalk," Trevor Norton remembered. "Andy was afraid of her father. I would have to go with him to Kim's place at times because her father was so abusive towards Andy that he was afraid her father would hit him." Norton also cringed at Kim's treatment of Andy. "One night before a show," he said, "Kim and her [identical] twin sister Kerrie decided to play a mind game with Andy. Kim said, 'Andy can't tell the difference between Kerrie and me.' That night they had dressed exactly the same and Kerrie played Kim. Andy fell for it and it made him feel one inch small in front of everyone in the band. It was so embarrassing for him. It was hard to pick them apart when they dressed exactly the same. It was disgusting and everyone thought what a bitch she really was. They [Kim and Kerrie] laughed in his face so loudly. It was like a boxer hitting the canvas and we were trying to lift him back up. If she really loved Andy, the thought of doing such an act would have never even entered her sick mind."

Nevertheless, Andy and Kim married in Sydney on July 11, 1976. The *Sydney Morning Herald* reported the wedding the next day, under the headline "Bee Gees' brother weds, but he wants to stay solo," along with a photograph of the newlyweds exiting the Wayside Chapel. None of the Bee Gees came to Australia for the wedding.

Andy asked one more person whom he had met in Australia to accompany him to America. Although his suddenly impending departure had made it a moot point, Zenta had actually just quit his band after Glen Greenhalgh had unsuccessfully demanded higher wages for the group. Nevertheless, as Trevor Norton told an interviewer nearly forty years later, "He [Andy] wanted me to go with him; he *really* wanted me to go with him over there. It didn't really appeal to me because I thought, 'Well, he can get any drummer he wants [in America], any drummer in the world'... it just wasn't for me to do that... I *really* didn't want to go."

Norton sensed that he wasn't the only one. "In a way, he [Andy] didn't really want to go, but he knew he had to go."

Chapter TWO

Thicker than Water

"There's fame and there's ultra-fame and it can destroy. You lose your perspective, you're in the eye of a hurricane and you don't know you're there. And you don't know what tomorrow is, you don't know if what you're recording will be a hit or not. And we were kids, don't forget." So reflected Barry Gibb in 2020, recalling when he, Robin, and Maurice became pop stars in 1967. His comments, as Barry would undoubtedly admit, could just as well apply to his youngest brother, who a decade later would find himself in the eye of an even bigger hurricane, and as a solo artist with no one with whom to share the glory and the pressures. In 2014, Barry expressed regret for having encouraged Andy to follow in the Bee Gees' footsteps. "He would have been better off finding something else," Barry said with more than a quarter century of hindsight. "He was a sweet person. We lost him too young."

In 1976, though, Barry was optimistic about Andy's future. "I thought, 'Well, if anyone can do it, if anyone can make Andy a star, it's Robert Stigwood,'" he recalled in 1997. Barry himself would play at least as big a role in Andy's rise to stardom, however, as Stigwood. When Stigwood invited Andy and his new bride to his Bermuda estate for a three-week honeymoon, Barry joined them. Stigwood had heard Andy's Australian recordings, most of which were of songs written by Andy alone, and he liked them—six of the ten songs on Andy's debut album were among those that he had written and originally recorded in Australia. Nevertheless, Stigwood didn't think that any of them would be hit singles, and he wanted Barry or Barry and Andy to write a couple of surefire hits. Stigwood also introduced Andy to James Dayley, a young assistant of his (only two years older than Andy) who would soon become Andy's personal manager, a position that he would hold until about the middle of 1978.

Reunited for the first time in at least a year with the older brother that he idolized, Andy introduced Barry to Kim, but soon the brothers got down to business. They went into a bedroom alone with their guitars to collaborate, but as Andy would tell an interviewer, "When Barry writes, it is very hard to collaborate with him, because he is so quick." Andy could only sit and watch in astonishment as Barry wrote "I Just Want to Be Your Everything" on the spot in about twenty minutes (although he didn't finish the lyrics until later that night). Andy felt confident that the song would be a hit for him: "I thought, 'Wow, what a hook!' It was right in there." Barry then started writing another song, but this time he asked Andy for some input first. "He said, 'Help me think of a great title,'" Andy told Robert W. Morgan in 1981. "I said, 'How about "Thicker than Water?"' I did not say, 'Love is,' just 'Thicker than Water.' He said, 'That's great!' Then he came up with [and here Andy sang to Morgan] 'Love is higher than a mountain, love is thicker than water.' Then he just went on from there, but the title was totally my idea." Barry gave Andy co-writing credit on "(Love Is) Thicker than Water," generously if Andy's account of how the song was written is accurate.

While in Bermuda, Andy and Stigwood agreed to a five-year management, recording, and publishing contract. That the contract was for that long of a term (just like the Bee Gees' first contract in 1967) showed that Stigwood believed that Andy would have a long-term future as a hitmaker. In fact, Stigwood apparently delayed the execution of the contract until March 1977, one month before the release of "I Just Want to Be Your Everything," since the contract expired in March 1982. Little could the impresario have imagined what would happen to his relationship with the Bee Gees, and what would happen to RSO Records and Andy Gibb, by then.

Business aside, the newlyweds were able to enjoy their honeymoon, doing some of the same things together in Bermuda that they had in Australia, such as riding motorbikes, swimming, boating, and fishing. Stigwood was a gracious host. "We ate five course dinners," Kim recalled. "Robert Stigwood imported nothing but the best and he cooked the food himself. He's a pretty good chef."

Next the newlyweds and Barry were off to Miami, where Andy would record demos of the two new songs. Andy and Kim then returned to Australia. Andy visited Trevor Norton, still trying, to no avail, to get Norton to come to America with him. "Andy would return back to Australia a few times in 1976-77," Norton remembered. "He would contact me and we met up every time."

Andy and Kim's homecoming in Australia proved to be a brief one. Stigwood and others at RSO heard and liked the demos, and in September 1976 Andy and Kim came back to Miami. Barry recruited Albhy Galuten and Karl Richardson, who, along with the Bee Gees themselves, had produced the Bee Gees' new album, *Children of the World*, to produce Andy's album. Barry would only co-produce "I Just Want to Be Your Everything" and "(Love Is) Thicker than Water," but he would serve as executive producer for the entire album. In fact, before Andy even started recording, Barry already had produced the backing tracks for both of those songs, leaving Andy only to overdub his lead vocals. Barry also sang backing or harmony vocals on both finished records. Guitarist Joey Murcia, one of the musicians whom Galuten had recruited to play on the album, would reminisce shortly after Andy's death that "Barry wrote those songs for Andy. We cut those hits in one day, with Barry singing. Then six months later we heard Andy on the radio."

Murcia, who was ten years older than Andy, was impressed when he met him and started working with him. He thought Andy was "just a beautiful little kid . . . heart as big as gold . . . incredibly young and infatuated with the music business." Even as a newly signed, eighteen-year-old recording artist, Andy did not take his session musicians for granted. "He really went to bat for us [the session players] with the record company," said Murcia. "We were just studio guys, but Andy wanted us in on the royalties and on the road with him later." At the time of Andy's death, Murcia was living in Key Largo, where he was performing in clubs. "Andy enabled me to buy my property in the Keys," he told a reporter. "I'm living here thanks to his generosity."

Richardson and Galuten also quickly came to think highly of the youngest Gibb brother. "Andy was a gift out of left field," Richardson recalled in 2020. "I never knew he existed until one day he shows up fresh from Australia." To Galuten, "Andy was just so full of just, I don't know, fire and brimstone, or piss and vinegar. He was just so excited and young and fired up about it. It was absolutely fantastic."

Recording took place at Miami's Criteria Recording Studios, where the Bee Gees had made their last two albums, in October 1976. Andy recorded six songs that he had written and recorded (twice, in some cases) in Australia: "Words and Music," "Starlight," "Flowing Rivers," "Come Home for the Winter," "Let It Be Me," and "In the End." Andy wrote two songs for the album in the United States—"Dance to the Light of the Morning" and "Too Many Looks in Your Eyes"—which by some accounts should have included a co-writing credit for Albhy Galuten, although James Dayley remembered Andy writing the latter in its entirety at a hotel after a quarrel with Kim. Dayley also said that when Andy was singing the song at Criteria, with Kim sitting on a couch, he was singing "right to Kim, I mean, every word, he was looking right at her . . . [and] pouring his heart out to her." Kim ignored him, however, as she looked at a photo book of Staffordshire Bull Terriers. "It literally just about brought tears to my eyes," Dayley recalled.

Even though Andy's marriage was clearly already in trouble, the recording process went smoothly. Furthermore, recording at such a high profile studio as Criteria brought a serendipitous stroke of good fortune to Andy: the Eagles were finishing their *Hotel California* album at the same time that he was recording his album. The Eagles were also staying in the same hotel as Andy and Kim, the Key Biscayne Hotel. "Albhy Galuten played my tracks for the Eagles," Andy told Peter J. Boyer in the spring of 1977, "and apparently, they were flipping out and getting off on the stuff. One night while we were in New York on some business, Joe Walsh came into the studio and put in a guitar lick in 'Thicker than Water.' He came in again to do another track a couple of days later."

Describing Walsh's contribution to what would be the album's second single as merely a "guitar lick" was an understatement. Music journalist Grant Walters offered a much better description four decades later: "Walsh's intriguing, searing guitar solo brings the four-minute song to a dramatic climax just a quarter of the way into its elapsed time. When the intensity subsides, Andy's honey-drizzled voice plays almost at a whisper on top of Tubby Ziegler's hi-hats. At two-and-a-half minutes, the chorus-verse negotiation is finished, and the song slides into a gently rolling coda of nonchalant 'da da da's.'" Andy did not specify which additional song Walsh played on; some accounts say that it was "I Just Want to Be Your Everything," but no guitar work that sounds like Walsh can be clearly heard on that recording. (In fact, according to Joey Murcia, he and Tim Renwick were the only guitarists on that track.) From listening to the album, it sounds like Walsh may have overdubbed some licks onto "Flowing Rivers."

According to James Dayley, Andy's debut album almost featured further contributions from other members of the Eagles as well. "They laid down some vocal tracks on Andy's record," said Dayley. "We were really pumped." But the Eagles' manager, Irving Azoff, wouldn't hear of the Eagles harmonizing on Andy's record, and so their vocals were removed, although Walsh's guitar contributions remained.

After the album, which would be titled *Flowing Rivers*, was completed, Andy and Kim left Miami for Los Angeles. Kim had not particularly liked Miami, and she later said that Andy acted differently when he was around his family, that he became more possessive and was not quite the sweet young man she had known in Australia. The couple rented a small apartment in West Hollywood, as did, in the same building, James Dayley, who recalled that RSO provided Andy with a $500 weekly advance (worth a little over $2,300 in 2021). This was necessary because Andy's album would sit, in record industry lingo, "in the can" for a while. RSO had to plan a promotional campaign and North American tour for Andy, and lawyers needed to procure the British citizen who had come from Australia the right to work and stay in the United States. (The Immigration and Naturalization Service would classify Andy as "an alien of distinguished merit and ability" on July 8, 1977; he would be granted permanent residence on May 10, 1979. He never, however, became a U.S. citizen.)

Andy and Kim's marriage would collapse during their short residence in California. After Andy died, Kim would say that he fell in with the wrong people in Los Angeles. "The hangers-on in the rock industry are like piranhas," she lamented. "They hang around stars and offer drugs as a way of making friendships. I suppose they think the stars will become dependent on them for drugs." (Yet, Andy wasn't a star yet.) She said that his behavior changed drastically. "All of a sudden Andy wanted to go to the mountains by himself." She said that his cocaine addiction, which became public knowledge in the early 1980s, began at this point. "He became ensconced in the drug scene. Cocaine became his first love. He became depressed and paranoid. He wasn't the man I married," she told a reporter just after his death. She would say repeatedly that she had told him that she was pregnant and that he needed to clean himself up. "I left Andy because he wouldn't stop taking drugs," she said in 1993.

Andy's friends from that time, however, would debunk Kim's claims. "That's all fantasy," said James Dayley. "He was smoking pot when he was with Kim. He wasn't doing cocaine." Dayley, who saw Kim and Andy "constantly fighting," also said that Andy didn't learn that Kim was pregnant until about a month after she had left him. Tony Messina said much the same thing. Messina got the call to leave Australia and come to America when Kim left Andy. For nearly the next three years, Tony spent more time with Andy than anyone else did during that period. "I'm pretty sure he probably didn't [know Kim was pregnant when she left]," Messina said in 2021. Messina recalled that Andy seemed both surprised and "really in a bad state" when telling him that he had found out about the pregnancy. Messina also said that when he rejoined Andy in America, Andy was not using cocaine. Some of Andy's friends have suggested that the torment of being unable to see or have a real relationship with his child contributed to his later reliance upon cocaine.

According to Dayley, Kim left Andy, flew home to Sydney, and then back to Los Angeles at least three times before she left him for the final time. On one of those occasions, Dayley was convinced that Kerrie had come to Los Angeles pretending to be Kim. Andy drove with her in his Pontiac Firebird to San Francisco, where Dayley was spending that particular spring weekend in 1977. Upon the couple's arrival, Kim greeted Dayley "like she had never greeted me before. Open arms. Kim was *always* very closed. And suddenly it's like, 'Oh, James, hi, how are you? It's great seeing you!'" She then gave Dayley "a big bear hug." Dayley was taken aback. "I'm thinking, 'This isn't Kim. It's her sister.' Because Kim *never* offered me a hug. *Ever*. And I think that she recognized it. She recognized the fact that I knew something wasn't quite right." Dayley later voiced his suspicion to Andy, asking him, "Are you sure that was Kim and not her twin sister?" Andy replied, "I think I know my own wife, mate." But of course, Kerrie had fooled Andy before in Australia.

Andy and Kim also returned to Australia together a couple of more times before their marriage ended. On Saturday, January 29, 1977, Andy performed at the Arcadia Vision Valley music festival about twenty-five miles outside of Sydney with a band that Trevor Norton hastily assembled for the occasion. (In addition to Norton, another member of Zenta, which had disbanded, also played with Andy at the festival, bassist Paddy Lelliott.) Hugh and Barbara attended the concert. Andy and Kim went back to Australia together again shortly before the release of his debut album. Andy had Trevor visit him at the Sebel Hotel, where he and Kim were staying, and the next day he introduced the band Norton had recently joined (Thundaband, which soon became Night Shift) to Kevin Jacobsen and Col Joye. The band, Norton recalled, "landed a one-year recording contract with yearly options at Festival Records . . . a short cut thanks to Andy Gibb, Kevin, and Colin who we were all very grateful for."

Norton also witnessed more disturbing behavior by Kim towards Andy. Just before Andy and Kim returned to the United States, Andy invited Norton and his girlfriend to the Sebel Hotel. They went to Andy's room.

"We had a bit of a chat for a while then Andy said he had to go and pick up Kim," Norton recounted. "'Oh okay,' I said. 'I will be back in about half an hour, feel free to use room service, whatever you want. See you soon,' Andy said. Hmmmm. We looked at each other and said, 'Oh well we will just wait.' We really didn't know what to do." While Andy was gone, Kim phoned the room. When Norton answered, she asked him, "What are you doing in my hotel room?" "Andy asked me to wait here until he returns with you," Norton replied. Kim screamed at him, "If you do not get out of my hotel room now I will call security and have you thrown out!" Norton, who was "in disbelief at what Kim had just said to me," was momentarily speechless. Kim screamed at him again. "*Get out of my hotel room now, Trevor!*" He and his girlfriend left the hotel.

"The next morning," remembered Norton, "Andy called me on the phone. 'Man, why did you leave yesterday?' 'Kim didn't tell you?,' I replied. 'Tell me what, man?,' Andy replied. I told him exactly what happened." Norton then heard Andy say to Kim, "*What?* Did you tell Trevor to get out yesterday or you will call security?"

"There was a hell of a lot of muffled arguments and screaming that I could hear over the phone," Norton recalled. "Then Andy came back to the phone and said, 'I will have to call you back, man, I am sorry.' 'Okay, mate, no worries,' I told Andy. I was thinking, 'What is this all about? What is the problem with Kim?' About two hours later there was a knock at my front door. I opened the door and Andy is standing there. I was surprised. I am pretty sure he was flying out that day. 'Man, I apologize for what Kim did. I don't know what her problem is.' 'Me too, mate,' I replied. Andy said, 'Look at this,' as he rolled up both sleeves of his shirt. He had at least three very bad bite marks on each arm. My eyes almost popped out of their sockets. I could not believe my eyes. They were red, blue, and deep."

"I apologize for Kim, man, I am very sorry," Andy told Trevor. "It's okay, mate, no worries," Trevor replied. "I felt so sorry for him; I really did not know what to say to him," Norton said nearly four-and-a-half decades later. "Andy said, 'I'm sorry, man, I am heading back today; I will be in touch with you, okay?'" Trevor replied, "Okay, mate, you take care, okay?" "Yes man," Andy replied. Trevor said, "Good luck, Andy." "Thanks, man," Andy replied, and then he left. "He was very upset," Norton recalled, "and he had every right to be. That was the last time I seen Andy." Andy subsequently had someone from Kevin Jacobsen's office bring Trevor a copy of *Flowing Rivers* weeks before it was released, and he phoned Trevor shortly after that, but that was the last time Trevor ever heard from him.

Kim and Andy's relationship disintegrated just as he stood poised on the edge of stardom. In April 1977, six months after Andy's recording sessions, RSO Records finally released his American debut single. What Andy would describe in an interview in 1985 as a "great big beautiful rollercoaster ride" was about to begin. Kim, meanwhile, left Andy and returned home to Australia for good in June. Dennis Bryon, the Bee Gees' drummer, was sympathetic. "They were both so young," he reflected in 2020. "I did think to myself then, 'How long can this last?' Because the [music] business is so hard, and for a wife it must be very, very difficult."

Robert Stigwood had originally planned on releasing "(Love Is) Thicker than Water" as the first single from Andy's October 1976 recording sessions. He changed his mind at the last minute—just three days before the single was scheduled to come out—and released "I Just Want to Be Your Everything" instead. Andy later suggested a reason for Stigwood's change of heart, explaining that "['I Just Want to Be Your Everything'] was a big hit within the industry before it was even released. Acetates went around to people at different companies, and they rang us up, saying, 'This is amazing. Everybody at our label is singing that song here.'" Each of the three major record industry trade publications of the day—*Billboard*, *Cash Box*, and *Record World*—reviewed the single in its April 23, 1977 issue. All three reviews were favorable. *Cash Box* chose "I Just Want to Be Your Everything" as a "Pick of the Week." *Record World* put the single in its "Sleepers" category, declaring that "the youngest Gibb brother—he's eighteen [actually he had turned nineteen the month before]—has inherited the family tenor range, and with a sure pop touch should take this tune penned by brother Barry right up the charts."

The release of Andy's first album, *Flowing Rivers*, soon followed. *Billboard* reviewed it in the May 14 issue as one of the week's "Top Album Picks." "Youngest of the Gibb brothers debuts with an album imbued with the Bee Gee sound—hardly surprising since Barry Gibb is listed as executive producer," the review began. "Andy has an appealing and expressive singing voice that lends itself well both to uptempo disco material and lush ballads."

Aside from "I Just Want to Be Your Everything," though, the resemblance to the "Bee Gee sound" was to the earlier, pre-1975 Bee Gees, most notably "Words and Music," which Andy had written in 1974. Other than the debut single, nothing else on the album could be characterized as "disco." Peter J. Boyer, writing for the Associated Press, described *Flowing Rivers* as "a sort of mix-match album featuring vibrato vocals *à la* Bee Gee and the rich, strong country-rock flavor of the Eagles." Andy said that he "was influenced by the Eagles' sessions just from having them nearby and hearing their songs all the time," but a number of his Australian recordings had a country-rock sound, including the original version of "Flowing Rivers," which had one more verse than the American re-recording did. Andy often cited folk-rock singer-songwriter Don McLean as his "biggest influence." McLean would thank Andy when the two met on the set of *Solid Gold* in 1981.

By late July 1977, it was time for Andy to bring his music to live audiences in North America. Joey Murcia's recollection of touring with him came from the *Shadow Dancing* tour of 1978, when Andy headlined in stadiums and large arenas. In 1977 he performed mostly at fairs and nightclubs, and, after opening for April Wine at two concerts in Canada, he opened for Neil Sedaka, a friend of the Bee Gees, for the next month. Murcia and other musicians who had played on Andy's album were among the most sought-after studio players in Miami, and the cost of hiring them as a road band ($1,000 a day per musician, according to Murcia) would have far exceeded the budget for this tour. When Melody Fayre had disintegrated in Australia with the return of John Alderson and John Stringer to the Isle of Man, Andy hired a band that already existed (Zenta) to back him in concerts but not on his records. He would do the same thing in America in 1977, hiring a band that already existed to play with him on tour.

That band consisted of Richard Page and Steve George as vocalists and keyboardists, Peter Leinheiser on guitar, Jerry Manfredi on bass, and Russell Battelene on drums. "We were already a band, we were rehearsing original material," recalled Battelene in 2021. "We all knew each other, we were all from Phoenix." The band had its own songs but did not have any leads on a recording contract or even a name yet. One day Leinheiser was driving home from a gig in the Los Angeles suburb of Downey to his home in West Hollywood and heard, twice in a roughly half-hour drive, "I Just Want to Be Your Everything" on the top forty station 102.7 KIIS-FM. The record struck him as a surefire number one hit. When he got home, he called the station and asked about the record. He was told that it was by an artist on RSO, Andy Gibb. Leinheiser thought he'd heard the name Andy Kim (of "Rock Me Gently" fame). The person at the radio station corrected him: "No no no, Andy *Gibb*, like the Bee Gees." The next day, Leinheiser called RSO's office on Sunset Boulevard and learned that Andy would be going on tour soon but didn't have a road band yet.

The band's manager, George Ghiz, contacted James Dayley. The band got a copy of *Flowing Rivers* and learned Andy's songs, and Ghiz arranged for them to audition for Andy. "We went down there [to George Harrison's Dark Horse Recording Studio] as a band and played with Andy," Battelene recalled, "and he hired us." "It was just kismet," according to Leinheiser. "We just nailed the grooves, and [Page and George] nailed the backgrounds" vocally. After the band played three or four songs with Andy, they stopped, and Leinheier asked Tony Messina, "How many other bands are you going to audition?" "You're the first," Tony replied, "and you're the last." This must have simply been Tony's way of letting the band members know they had the job, since, according to Dayley, several dozens of bands had auditioned, none of whom had sufficiently impressed Andy.

Ghiz negotiated the terms of the band's employment with Dayley. Dayley offered each band member $250 a week, which to Manfredi sounded sufficient for the three weeks of rehearsals, but he told his bandmates that they should demand more for touring. Ghiz got Dayley to agree to pay each band member $500 a week while on tour, much to the displeasure, Battelene recalled, of Stigwood, who suggested that Dayley had been had. According to Dayley, though, Stigwood had authorized him to pay each band member up to but no more than that amount. After Ghiz and Dayley reached an agreement, however, the three weeks of rehearsals went by without the band members being paid at all. When Manfredi told Andy at the last rehearsal that he was quitting because he hadn't been paid, Andy seemed shocked. "Call Robert," Andy ordered Dayley, "and get this straightened out now. Immediately." The payments came within twenty-four hours, and from then on, the band members were paid on time.

These musicians were less polished than the older, more experienced session men who had played on *Flowing Rivers*, but they were a tight and cohesive band. Furthermore, the youthfulness of most of the band members made them look like more of a natural fit with Andy onstage. The vocal talent of Page and George significantly enhanced the band's value to Andy (and, despite his grumbling over the band members' salaries, Stigwood, too, since he didn't have to hire anyone else to sing backgrounds and harmonies). The band would accompany Andy not only in concerts but also in live appearances on two television series that brought popular performers into millions of viewers' homes, NBC's *The Midnight Special* and the syndicated *Don Kirshner's Rock Concert*. Andy's tour entourage also included Dayley, Messina, and tour manager Allan LaMagna, who had worked for the Bee Gees in that capacity. Richard Page's cousin, John Lang, who was not a band member but wrote lyrics with them, served as the stage manager. Russell Battelene recalled that Maurice Gibb showed up at at least one show and met the band members.

On the tour, Andy had a regular post-concert ritual. "Every night after a gig, we would congregate in Andy's room, and he would sing Bee Gees songs," Battelene recalled with a chuckle. "That was like the routine . . . initially, everybody's showing up for that, just because he's the boss and let's pay respects, and then pretty soon it started to get a little bit tedious, you know, we might want to step out and do other things." "We always had to check in," Battelene said, laughing again at the memory, "and Andy would be sitting there singing some Bee Gees songs. He just idolized those guys." One of Andy's "catch phrases," Leinheiser recalled, "was 'my brother Barry.'"

Andy garnered mostly good reviews on the tour, which began in July and ended in September, and his star rose rapidly. "I Just Want to Be Your Everything" spent four weeks at number one on the *Billboard* Hot 100 that summer (with the fourth week coming four weeks after it had been knocked out of the top spot) and sixteen weeks in the top ten. No single had accomplished the latter feat since Bobby Darin's famed 1959 hit "Mack the Knife." Andy's debut single became the most played record of 1977 on US radio stations, and it also became a number one hit in Australia, Canada, Chile, and Brazil. When Andy opened for Sedaka to an audience of more than 10,000 at the Colorado State Fair in Pueblo on August 30, a reviewer for a local newspaper wrote that the pop music veteran "was almost upstaged" by Andy, whose thirty-minute set made it "clear that he is only beginning to tap his full potential as a singer-songwriter."

Just over a week later, Andy performed *sans* Sedaka at the Roxy Theater on the Sunset Strip in West Hollywood. Stigwood and RSO Records president Al Coury used the occasion to present Andy, onstage, with a gold record signifying one million copies sold of the single "I Just Want to Be Your Everything."[2] Andy, remembered Julie LaMagna (Allan's wife), was a hit at the small but prestigious venue. "He slayed everybody. They could not believe how good he was." Ed Harrison, reviewing one of Andy's Roxy shows for *Billboard*, wrote, "With time, maturation and his brothers' influences and encouragement, Gibb should sustain a long and successful career."

Andy soon astutely began expressing concern though that his "teen idol" status—he became a fixture on the cover of magazines such as *16* and *Tiger*

2 Incredibly, the website (riaa.com) of the Recording Industry Association of America (RIAA), which has certified and issued "gold records" since 1958, lists the gold record certification of "I Just Want to Be Your Everything" as signifying sales of 500,000 copies, when, in fact, from 1958 through 1988, the requirement for a gold single was one million copies sold.

Beat alongside the Bay City Rollers and Shaun Cassidy—would hinder his chances of long-term success. "I never put myself in a teen idol bracket," he told an interviewer in 1978. "I've always been scared of falling into that category. Because . . . it's not a very long-lived career." (The careers of his aforementioned contemporaries bore this out: all six of the Rollers' US top forty hits came in the span of two years, and all four of Shaun Cassidy's in less than one year.) But Andy also appreciated and even sympathized with his young fans, saying that "they worry me sometimes. They lose their mind and get hysterical—it's really frightening sometimes." He also knew better than to complain publicly about the hysteria and its effect on his privacy and ability to go out in public, even though Kim later said that he already had expressed concern about that on their October 1976 trip to New York City. In 1977, when a radio interviewer asked him if he was ever frightened "when fans . . . try to get at you," he said no and laughingly added, "When they don't, you worry."

Most of these fans, at first at least, had no idea that their new idol had an estranged, pregnant wife thousands of miles away in Australia. As Kim noted twenty years later, "He was on the front of all those teenybopper magazines, and I suppose they had to give the perception that he was available." In October 1977, the supermarket tabloid *The Star* published an article written by Australian journalist Norm Lipson under the headline "Pop idol Andy Gibb's wife says: I'm broke while he lives in luxury." Lipson reported that Kim was living in Sydney with her parents and "struggling on a $45-a-week Australian social security check." "I haven't got a cent," she told the reporter. "Andy refused to give me money and said he would refuse to support me and the twins I am expecting in December." (Only one child would be born to Kim, in late January 1978.) She had filed a lawsuit against Andy in Australia, demanding that he pay her $200 a week. She also blamed the "hangers on" around Andy for their split. "We couldn't move without these people being there and Andy, a really mixed-up fellow," she said, "has been easily led by them." She had tried making phone calls to Andy in America, but, she told Lipson, "Every time I call, one of his protectors picks up the phone and tells me he is not available. I won't be calling again—he knows where to get in touch with me." James Dayley tried on more than one occasion to get Andy to talk to her, but he refused.

When Lipson contacted Andy for his side of the story, Andy told him, "It is a very personal matter and I don't really want to discuss it." He said that he was hopeful for a reconciliation but admitted that it would be difficult with Kim now living in Australia. Andy also admitted to Lipson that he was seeing other women and "slowly trying to get an involvement again." One month later, *People* magazine published an article that told essentially the same story, albeit in less detail. Peter Leinheiser, seven years Andy's senior, remembered Andy telling him once in 1977 that his marriage was crumbling. "He was confused, I know that," Peter reflected. "What would you do, Peter?" Andy asked him.

The end of the marriage also marked the end, for the time being, of Andy's residency in Los Angeles. An "application for alien employment certification" that he signed on October 19, 1977, for submission to the US Department of Labor gave his home address as Miami Shores, where he had settled on an eighty-foot houseboat with what he called "great vibes and an interesting history." (A previous owner, "rumored to be a mobster," explained *People*, "was murdered in the mirrored master stateroom.") Andy told journalist Stan Soocher, "Miami has become home for me because I record there, my parents are there now, and the atmosphere is so relaxed. There is something indescribably special about Miami that you can almost feel in the air." Perhaps Andy figured that it was already such common knowledge that each of his three brothers owned a home in Miami Beach that there was no need to mention it.

By now it had been a full year since Andy had recorded *Flowing Rivers*, although the long chart run of "I Just Want to Be Your Everything" (thirty-one weeks on the Hot 100) meant that the album's second single, "(Love Is) Thicker than Water," was just being released in mid-October. The album itself would peak at number nineteen on the *Billboard* chart that month, and it remained on the chart until the middle of October 1978. Nevertheless, it was about time to get to work on the second album.

Barry, Robin, and Maurice were all in Los Angeles at this time, filming the ill-fated movie *Sgt. Pepper's Lonely Hearts Club Band*, in which they co-starred with Peter Frampton, and for which they had just finished recording their contributions to the soundtrack album. Andy arrived both to visit and to collaborate with them for material for his own album, although he had been writing songs himself. Andy's RSO labelmate Peter Beckett recalled in 2021 that around this time, Andy invited "me and the rest of [the band] Player up to his place. . . . He pulled out his guitar and performed a new song he was working on. He was very gracious, but I do remember thinking he seemed troubled about something." (Player's debut single, "Baby Come Back," would soon become the only non-Gibb affiliated single to be a part of RSO's incredible twenty-one consecutive week monopolization of the number one spot on the *Billboard* Hot 100 from December 1977 to May 1978.)

Being in America, and Miami in particular, as opposed to Australia, influenced Andy's songwriting—he told an interviewer that his self-composed songs on his second album would be "more R&B and Latin influenced" than the "country" songs on *Flowing Rivers*. This change of direction would also be apparent in the first song to be written by all four Gibb brothers. Andy explained the genesis of "Shadow Dancing" in an interview several years later. "My brothers were making *Sgt. Pepper*, the movie," he recalled. "And one night, while we were relaxing, we sat down and we had to start getting tracks together for the [second] album. So we just literally sat down and in ten minutes, we had a group going, [singing] the chorus part. As it says underneath the song, we all wrote it, the four of us." This time Barry came up with the title and presented it to Andy before the four brothers began composing.

Recording of the song began in December 1977 at Wally Heider Studios in Hollywood, which like Miami's Criteria was one of the most renowned recording studios of the day. Karl Richardson, who, as was the case with almost all of Andy's singles, produced the record with Albhy Galuten and Barry Gibb, said four decades later: "I remember what we started with was in L.A., and the band was out, and they stayed at the Chateau Marmont [a famed hotel on Sunset Boulevard] with Andy." The band, dubbed the "Andy Gibb

Hit Orchestra" by Richardson, consisted of Joey Murcia and Tim Renwick on guitars, Harold Cowart on bass, and Ron "Tubby" Zeigler on drums.[3] While many other musicians also played on various recordings that Andy made for RSO Records, these four constituted the core of his band on nearly all of those recordings. "Barry would show up to the studio as an excuse to get away from this movie," Richardson remembered, "and we were in a little Heider room." The record would be completed on more familiar turf. "I remember we went back to [Criteria's] Studio C and did a lot of overdubs. We did the horns with the University of Miami guys. Certainly all the Barry stuff and the background vocals with Johnne [Sambataro] and the guys." According to Sambataro, everyone in the studio, including an excited Robert Stigwood, knew that Andy had another smash hit record on his hands.

Work also began on some other songs for Andy's second album, which would be titled *Shadow Dancing*, at Wally Heider Studios. Andy stayed in Los Angeles long enough to join his brothers at the premiere of *Saturday Night Fever*, which was about to elevate their popularity to even greater heights through their domination of its soundtrack. The premiere party, held at Mann's (Grauman's) Chinese Theatre in Hollywood on December 14, 1977, was taped and became the basis for a television special. Andy lip synced "(Love Is) Thicker than Water" after being introduced by a famous young fan, actress Kristy McNichol. He also received attention for showing up at the event with the attractive, twenty-seven-year-old British actress Susan George, whom he had met when the two appeared in *US Against the World*, an NBC-TV special which was taped on the campus of UCLA on August 27–28.

The Star took Andy's appearance at the *Fever* premiere as an opportunity to continue its coverage of his relationship status. The tabloid reported that "almost ignoring the other guests, Andy and Susan hugged and kissed throughout the evening. They left each other's side for only a moment, when Andy stepped up on stage to perform." The article quoted an unnamed "close friend" of Andy's who confirmed that "Andy is very fond of Susan. She is the

3 The band eventually organized as a legal entity called the "Andy Gibb Orchestra."

first girl he has been serious about since his marriage broke up. The split upset him a lot, and he withdrew a little. He's been much happier since meeting Susan."

Andy and Susan would continue seeing each other for months, and she also accompanied him to the premiere of *Grease*, another Stigwood/RSO (co-)production, also held at Mann's, on June 4, 1978. (This premiere party also became a television special, where once again a famous young fan—this time actor Adam Rich—introduced Andy lip syncing his newest single, "Shadow Dancing.") By then, however, Andy told a reporter that "Susie is a very close friend, but we never touched on a serious relationship. She helped me in my marriage problems when my wife left."

For her part, Susan George would later offer a similar assessment of the relationship: "Andy and I were the best of friends but there was no affair." Some of Andy's friends said otherwise, and she got close enough to him to see him develop an addiction to cocaine in 1978. She tried to help him kick the habit but soon sadly concluded that it was hopeless. "Those nights were terrible," she said in an interview after Andy had died. "I would try my best and, to be fair, so would he. But it became too much . . . in the end, you feel helpless." Like many who knew Andy well, she was puzzled as well as saddened by his inner demons. "It is really hard to judge what causes the unhappiness that led him into drugs. He was such a natural boy—never a bit fazed by all the success. He had tremendous charisma and vitality. He was always very special to me and always will be." Susan did not speak about Andy's drug abuse while he was alive.

After the *Saturday Night Fever* premiere, Andy returned to the east coast. On December 17, 1977, he performed at the Boston Garden on a bill with opening act the James Montgomery Band and co-headliners the Bay City Rollers and England Dan and John Ford Coley. Shaun Cassidy was on hand, too, not as a performer but as a guest emcee. The bill's partial bent toward youngsters probably stemmed from the fact that the event was the annual WRKO radio station's benefit concert for the Kennedy Memorial Hospital for Children. Steve Morse, rock music critic for the *Boston Globe*, reviewed the concert and was impressed by Andy and his new band, which now included some of his studio players, such as Tim Renwick, who played on all three of Andy's full-length studio albums and would also record and tour with Elton John, among others. Morse wrote that "Andy Gibb interjected the smoothest set of the day, and proved he is progressing from teen idol to serious musician. He has a new, funky band . . . and his finale of 'Shadow Dancing,' written with his brother, Barry Gibb of the Bee Gees, was sophisticated rock." Morse could be forgiven for not knowing that all four Gibb brothers wrote "Shadow Dancing," since this was its first public performance and the record had not even been completed yet.

Andy had enjoyed working with the five musicians who had performed with him on his summer tour, and when it ended, he told them that he wanted to keep doing so. But Al Coury told the musicians that their services were no longer needed now that the tour was over. By then, Andy had done some songwriting with two of the band members, Richard Page and Steve George. According to Russell Battelene, one of the songs that the trio wrote was "Good Feeling," which would appear on Andy's second album in 1978, but with Andy listed as the sole composer. "I believe we performed it even a couple of times towards the end of our tour together," Battelene recalled. (Indeed, they performed it at the Roxy.) Page and George figured, probably correctly, that Stigwood, jealously guarding his share of Andy's publishing royalties, had been responsible for cutting them out. "I don't think those guys ever held it against Andy," Battelene said, adding with a chuckle, "for very long." Andy, Battelene recalled, "was great to work with, and he was the sweetest guy, but not really in control of what was going on as far as his career was concerned."

According to Richard Page, the band had had no intentions of remaining a backing band anyway. "That wasn't the idea behind the band," he told a reporter in 1978. The band, which took the name "Pages," wanted to make it on its own. "We felt we had a lot of strong material," Page said, "and the Gibb tour helped open some doors." Peter Leinheiser later said, "It was a great experience, I'll tell you that. Andy was like a little brother to me." A little over one year after Andy and the members of Pages went their separate ways, he invited them to come see the taping of a Bob Hope television special on which he was a guest star, which they did. By then, Pages had signed with Epic Records and released a self-titled debut album. After failing to make much of a commercial impact with that and two more albums, the band broke up. Richard Page and Steve George subsequently formed another band, Mr. Mister, that would achieve brief but major success in the mid-1980s, with a number one album and two number one singles.

Andy finished 1977 by singing his first two singles on the sixth annual *Dick Clark's Rockin' New Year's Eve* television special on ABC. (He had made his American TV debut on Clark's *American Bandstand* in July.) *Billboard* did not publish an issue for the week ending on December 31, 1977, having published a special year-end issue the week before, but competitor *Cash Box* did and had "(Love Is) Thicker than Water" climbing to number 25 with a bullet that week in its ninth week on the chart. Meanwhile, the third major trade publication of the day, *Record World*, named Andy and Shaun Cassidy the joint winners of the "Best New Male Artist" award in its December 31 issue. Finally, when Casey Kasem counted down the biggest hits of 1977 at the end of the year on *American Top 40*, "I Just Want to Be Your Everything" came in at number one.

Professionally, then, 1977 had been a great year for Andy Gibb, almost unimaginably so. At the beginning of the year, he was unheard of in America; by the end of the year, he was a rising superstar and was receiving accolades from critics and within the industry. At the beginning of the year, he had been living on a $500 weekly stipend from RSO; by the end of the year, he had reportedly made $2 million. (Robert Stigwood, with much fanfare, presented Andy with a check for $1 million that he proudly showed to friends before depositing.) In interviews, he expressed excitement about the new album that he was working on as the year ended.

Personally, the year had been less rosy. His marriage, while not yet over legally, had for all intents and purposes ended within a year of the wedding.

His estranged wife was suing him for support and was about to give birth, but it would be difficult for Andy to see his child in Australia with the constant demands on his time that had come with his rapid rise to superstar status, not to mention his strained relationship with his soon-to-be-ex.

Barry Gibb would later acknowledge that pressures, temptations, and other distractions undermined Andy's focus on his music after his first album came out. "That was when he was at his best, at that age, wanting to be successful, not having the success but having the hunger," Barry reflected upon the eighteen-year-old Andy who had recorded *Flowing Rivers*. "The music was all. The music was everything."

Chapter THREE

Shadow Dancing

"I don't know, I can handle it and yet . . . I suppose I must really remember 'cause twenty years old and three number ones is a lot; and I'm just worried about the ten years or all those years ahead until I'm thirty." Andy Gibb expressed these concerns on Robert W. Morgan's radio show in 1978. One can only wonder just what Andy was worried about. It is difficult to imagine, however, that he had any idea what the ten years ahead would hold in store for him.

As 1978 began, Andy's star continued to rise. On January 9, the National Academy of Recording Arts and Sciences announced its annual nominees for the Grammy Awards. Andy made the list in two categories: Pop Male Vocalist (for "I Just Want to Be Your Everything") and Best New Artist. (Andy wouldn't win in either category, but the Bee Gees didn't even get nominated until 1972, winning their first award in 1978 in the Pop Vocal Group category for "How Deep Is Your Love.") Andy also received a nomination from the less prestigious American Music Awards in the Favorite Pop/Rock Song category for his debut single; again, he didn't win, but he performed "(Love Is) Thicker than Water" on the Dick Clark-produced television special. This was Andy's third appearance on a Dick Clark television program, and he would be something of a regular on Clark's shows as late as 1984.

Andy also made another major television appearance in January 1978, although its importance to him would prove to be as much personal as professional. He guest-starred for the first time on ABC-TV's *Donny & Marie* on the episode that aired on January 27; it would be the first of many times that he performed with the Osmonds on television. As was typical for guests on Donny and Marie's variety show, Andy participated in a couple of skits with the two stars. He also gave yet another performance—clearly a lip sync—of "(Love Is) Thicker than Water." The show also marked the first time that Andy and Marie (who had never met before) sang together; somewhat surprisingly, their duet was a rendition of an obscure Chicago song, "Happy Man," from the album *Chicago VII* (1974). The young pair—Andy was still nineteen, and Marie eighteen—clearly had chemistry together.

Of course, Andy wasn't exactly single at the time. He was still seeing and being seen in public with Susan George. Meanwhile, down under in Australia, Kim gave birth on January 25 to a daughter, Peta Jaye Gibb. Kim endured a rough, forty-hour labor in which her obstetrician feared for the baby's survival. She later said that the situation with Andy had hardly helped matters. "There I was, sitting at home with mum and dad, pregnant, believing Andy would be with me for the baby's birth because he'd promised, no matter what, he would be there," she recalled in 1989, "and suddenly the Sydney press were calling me telling me a press release had gone out saying that Andy and I were getting a divorce. The divorce papers arrived two weeks before Peta was due. I don't think I stopped crying until her birth." Aside from the mounting obligations and pressures of his burgeoning career, Andy, by all accounts, disliked conflict and tried to avoid awkward situations. He didn't travel to Australia for Peta's birth, and, according to Kim, he had James Dayley call her for him shortly after the event. Dayley told her that Andy was away fishing. (Dayley, however, couldn't remember making such a call when asked about it in 2021.) Andy "didn't even send me a card," Kim said. In fact, she did not "hear from him for some time" after Peta's birth.

Not surprisingly, Andy started getting bad press when Kim, as newspaper scribe Lynn Van Matre put it, began "complaining loudly from Australia that she and her child were having to struggle along on welfare due to Gibb's lack of financial support." Andy, who by now had publicly blamed the breakup on

Kim—"she couldn't cope with show business," he said—insisted that "funds have been and are still available for her use." But at the beginning of April 1978, Kim came to New York to meet with lawyers. (Her parents mortgaged their house so that she could hire them and make the trip.) When Andy had filed for divorce, he (or his lawyers) had claimed there were no children from the marriage. Kim wanted Peta legally recognized as Andy's daughter, and she also wanted Andy to provide for Peta.

After three weeks, Kim's lawyers and Andy's lawyers reached a settlement. At the time, the London *Daily Mirror* reported that the amount was "believed to be almost $250,000." Kim recalled in 1989 that the amount was $225,000, of which $60,000 was placed into a trust for Peta. (Those amounts would be the equivalent of about $940,000 and $250,000, respectively, in 2021 dollars.) Kim said that aside from the money for Peta's trust fund, however, "There was very little left after all the expenses." "And you know, I really didn't mind," she added. "I'd made my point—Peta was officially recognized. That's all that mattered to me." Kim stayed in New York while the case was being settled, but she never heard from Andy while she was there.

None of these personal matters, despite generating generally negative publicity for Andy, slowed his career momentum one bit. After slowly climbing the *Billboard* Hot 100 for seventeen weeks, "(Love Is) Thicker than Water" finally reached number one in its eighteenth week, March 4, 1978—one day before Andy's twentieth birthday. Andy had watched its progress up the chart with a mixture of excitement and anxiety. "It slowed down . . . we were all a little scared," he admitted. "There's lots of points where all the record people at RSO said they were a little worried that it was stopping. It didn't lose its bullet, but it really heavily lost its jump in sales activity. And then, for an equally strange reason, it just picked up and nothing stopped it. So it was not predictable . . . but it's still a commercial song. . . . We believed in it. . . . I think the momentum of the first record obviously helped the second a little, but it was, again, a different record."

Andy later said, though, that he felt that "(Love Is) Thicker than Water" would not have been a hit had it been released as his debut single, as Robert

Stigwood originally had planned. As it was, Andy's second single knocked the Bee Gees' "Stayin' Alive" out of number one, only to be knocked out of the top spot itself two weeks later by another Bee Gees record, "Night Fever." Some industry observers later said that Al Coury's well known adroitness at working with radio program directors and industry trade magazine chart directors helped "Thicker than Water" reach number one, but it was a consensus number one, reaching the top on *Cash Box* and *Record World* as well as *Billboard*, and the RIAA certified the single as a million seller around the same time that it peaked on the charts. Coury would also be credited by many in the industry for helping the Bee Gees run up a string of six straight number ones on the *Billboard* Hot 100 from 1977 to 1979, but they didn't match that feat on the *Cash Box* or *Record World* charts.

Almost as soon as Andy's second single began its descent from the number one spot, RSO released his third single, "Shadow Dancing," in late March. The single entered the Hot 100 at number 69 for the week ending April 15, 1978. In the following week's issue, *Billboard* reviewed "Shadow Dancing" as one of its "Top Single Picks," describing it as "another infectious tune with a catchy beat that should score the kind of huge success his previous two No. 1 singles did. The song has that inimitable Bee Gees sound with collaboration from all four Gibb brothers." Andy had told Dennis Hunt of the *Los Angeles Times* in September 1977 that "there won't be anything on it [his second album] that sounds like the Bee Gees. That was fine once. Let's face it, the Bee Gees-sounding single got me started. Now it's time for me to find my own sound. Remember, I'm not a Bee Gee." Surely, though, when the four brothers wrote "Shadow Dancing" together, Andy had to know that it would be another "Bee Gees-sounding single."

RSO released the *Shadow Dancing* album in late May 1978. *Cash Box* heaped praise upon Andy in its review of the album, while at the same time pointing out the large teenybopper element of his fan base: "The youngest recording Gibb brother has perhaps the loveliest voice, and it is the outstanding instrument on this LP—one that is sure to add new members to Andy's legion of young female fans."

Barry had more input on this album than he did on *Flowing Rivers*; on that album, he had written or co-written two songs, and those were the only two that he had a direct hand in producing. On Andy's second album, Barry wrote one song by himself ("An Everlasting Love"), co-wrote another ("(Our Love) Don't Throw It All Away") with Bee Gees keyboardist Blue Weaver, co-wrote another ("Why") with Andy, and of course, Barry, Robin, Maurice, and Andy (which was the order in which they were listed in the songwriting credit) wrote "Shadow Dancing." Andy wrote the other six songs on the album with no help from Barry, although the credits listing him as the sole author of all six were inaccurate. In addition to Richard Page and Steve George deserving co-writing credit on "Good Feeling," Albhy Galuten perhaps should have been listed as a co-writer of "One More Look at the Night," for helping Andy, in the latter's words, "find chords." As was the case on *Flowing Rivers*, Barry served as executive producer for the whole album, but joined Galuten and Karl Richardson as a co-producer only on the songs on which he had a writing credit.

In interviews Andy seemed pleased with his second album and his writing efforts for it. "I am so much more confident now after doing this second album," he told Robert W. Morgan in 1978, "dealing with the pressures of proving to myself that the first one wasn't a fluke and that I could write a second album. So now I am a lot more confident."

But the way that Robert Stigwood, or RSO Records, treated the songs that Andy wrote for *Shadow Dancing* may well have undermined his confidence. In an era when most consumers were listening to albums on vinyl records or cassette tapes with a "side one" and "side two," RSO put all four of the songs that Barry Gibb had written or co-written on side one (which, granted, included two songs that Andy co-wrote as well), which left room for only one of Andy's self-composed songs, "Fool for a Night." In other words, five of the six songs that Andy wrote without Barry ended up on side two.

When it came to singles, everyone agreed that "Shadow Dancing," which Andy at least had a hand in writing, was the obvious choice to be the first from the album, just as it was also the first song on side one. The single spent seven weeks at number one on the Hot 100 and became the best-selling single of Andy's career. Rich Fitzgerald, then RSO's vice president of national promotion, told *Billboard* in mid-August 1978 that it had sold 2.5 million copies, and a later report from the label put the tally at 2.7 million. According to Fred Bronson's book *Billboard's Hottest Hot 100 Hits*, "Shadow Dancing" ranked as the fifth biggest hit of the 1970s, one position ahead of "I Just Want to Be Your Everything."

For the second single from *Shadow Dancing*, RSO nearly chose "Why," which in fact was released in some European markets. In the US, though, the label released "An Everlasting Love," which was written by Barry and featured his falsetto backing on the chorus, instead. "(Our Love) Don't Throw It All Away" followed as the album's third single. The Bee Gees had recorded the song in 1977 and then chose not to release it; Barry subsequently offered it to Australian singer Samantha Sang. Barry gave Sang a choice, however, between "Don't Throw It All Away" and a song that he and Robin had written called "Emotion." Sang chose the latter and took it to number three on the Hot 100. ("Emotion" would be revived by turn-of-the-century superstars Destiny's Child, who had a top ten hit with it in 2001.) Barry then wrote a bridge for "Don't Throw It All Away" that the Bee Gees' version (which came out in 1979 on *Bee Gees' Greatest*) did not have, and he offered the song to Andy.

"An Everlasting Love" and "Don't Throw It All Away" both became million-selling top ten hits for Andy, so it's difficult to say that RSO chose the wrong track for release as a single in either case. On the other hand, though, Stigwood (who objected when Albhy Galuten tried to set up a writing session for Andy with John Oates, apparently because he didn't want any outside writers cutting into his publishing royalties) should have had more consideration for nurturing Andy's songwriting abilities rather than just trying to maximize his own immediate profits. Of course, to some extent one could fault Barry as well for stifling Andy's development as a songwriter. Clearly, Barry wanted to help his beloved kid brother have a successful recording career, and Andy was happy to accept that help. In fact, the one Andy Gibb-Barry Gibb composition on *Shadow Dancing*, "Why," came about because Andy had composed the music but couldn't come up with lyrics that he liked, and asked Barry to write them.

Furthermore, to cite Barry's songwriting contributions to Andy's first two albums, and RSO's decision to release songs that were written or co-written by Barry as Andy Gibb singles, as what caused the enormous decline in Andy's songwriting contributions to his third album would be mere speculation. Andy's increasing substance abuse might also be pointed to as a factor that hindered his writing efforts for his third album. In an interview in December 1982, he called cocaine "the worst talent destroyer that I know of."

Nevertheless, a lot of people who knew Andy well—his parents, his brothers, and Stigwood among them—later agreed that he had, as Hugh Gibb put it in 1989, suffered from "too much, too soon" when it came to his rapidly achieved runaway success in America. Barry's significant contributions to Andy's records, then, which Andy was always quick to acknowledge, may have not only stifled his youngest brother's development as a songwriter, but may have even contributed to the problems that ultimately undermined his career and health. Without Barry's help, Andy most likely would not have had, as *People* magazine put it after his death, the "lightning-in-a-bottle" success that proved to be more than he could handle, and he probably would have felt more ownership of whatever success he might have achieved on his own, rather than telling John Davidson in 1981, "I believe I owe it chiefly to my brothers . . . and [in particular] my brother Barry who . . . has always steered my career." James Dayley, who had been Andy's personal manager from about the fall of 1976 to the summer of 1978, later recalled that when he had tried to urge Andy to do more songwriting, Andy replied, "Well, Barry tells me he's got enough songs for *two* albums."

While it would be unfair to assign any blame to Barry for what happened to Andy when all he did was help him, Robin Gibb was all the same probably right when he said in 1989, "Maybe he [Andy] should have gotten confidence without having success first; maybe it would have been better for his first four or five records to have died." Instead, Barry wrote or co-wrote smash hits for Andy, while Andy's own songs were relegated to albums and B-sides of singles. *Billboard*'s review of *Shadow Dancing* listed "One More Look at the Night" and Andy's composition "Melody" as two of the album's five "best cuts," a distinction that the review did not accord to "An Everlasting Love."

At the time, though, it seemed that Andy's handlers—Stigwood and Barry—were making all the right choices. Those choices, however, sometimes frustrated Andy, whom Tony Messina could still recall more than forty years later being "really ticked off" when they overruled his choice of even a B-side on a single. "I don't have any say in anything," Andy told Tony with palpable irritation. Even though Stigwood had signed Andy to a five-year contract, he didn't seem too interested in nurturing his songwriting abilities and self-confidence. From a standpoint of coming up with hits, though, the results were hard to debate. Andy certainly realized this, and in 1979 he told an interviewer, "I think Robert's incredible. He's a modern Midas. I trust him completely. Everything he promises comes true."

In addition to the massive sales of the three singles culled from *Shadow Dancing*, the album reached number seven on the *Billboard* chart, number three on *Cash Box*, and number two on *Record World*. None of these three charts, it should be noted, were perfectly accurate—nor were they immune to manipulation by record labels and artist managers—and decades later, Scott Paton, who worked as a researcher and writer for Casey Kasem's *American Top 40* from 1976 to 1979, suggested that Andy's seven-week run at number one with the "Shadow Dancing" single may not have been entirely what it seemed. The radio show's staff would typically get an advance *Billboard* chart listing on a Wednesday, a couple of days before anyone else did, so that Casey and his staff could produce and record the weekly countdown. On one of the Wednesdays during the reign of "Shadow Dancing" at number one, the early chart had Gerry Rafferty's "Baker Steet" knocking Andy's record out of the top slot. The next day, during or after the recording of that week's *American Top 40*, the producers, as Paton recalled, received "an emergency call from *Billboard*. They'd gotten the stats wrong: 'Shadow Dancing' was still number one and 'Baker Street' was stalled at number two." Naturally, this last-minute development irritated the show's staff, since the final segment of the countdown had to be redone. Moreover, the explanation from *Billboard* chart director Bill Wardlow for the abrupt about-face seemed suspicious.

By this point, as Paton explained in 2013, Andy "was a good friend of mine, and when I saw him a week or two later, I told him this story, thinking that he would enjoy it. His response? 'Oh yeah, when we got the advance chart numbers, we called Bill Wardlow and told him that if he dropped 'Shadow Dancing' from number one, I wouldn't perform at Billboard's Disco Conference in New York (Wardlow's pet project) later in the summer.'" Andy and his band did indeed perform at that event, which was televised later that year as a special titled *Billboard's Disco Party*.

Then again, "Baker Street" also stalled at number two on the *Record World* chart, where "Shadow Dancing" spent eight weeks at number one. Rafferty's single did reach number one on *Cash Box*, but only after "Shadow Dancing" had spent six weeks at number one. In fact, all three of Andy's number one hits reached the top on all three of the major trade publication charts. In addition to Andy's major success on the charts during 1977-78, he racked up three platinum records and four gold records during that time. Very few recording artists have ever gotten off to a better start. Hugh Gibb saw the danger in this, though, telling Paton in an interview in July 1978, "There's only one way you can go, isn't it? And that's down again."

As he racked up the number one hits, Andy found himself increasingly in demand as a guest on television shows. He performed on two ABC-TV specials that aired in May 1978, one starring Olivia Newton-John (a Gibb family friend who, she said in 2021, "most likely met Andy with . . . [his] brothers") and the other the Osmond Brothers. By this point, nationally syndicated gossip columnist Liz Smith had published reports of an alleged romance between Andy and Marie, although both Barbara Gibb and Marie's mother, Olive Osmond, insisted that the reports were exaggerated. Decades later, musician Kenny Hodges recounted an episode that revealed the Osmond family's attitude toward the possibility of a romance between Marie and Andy. Hodges, who was the percussionist in the Osmonds' band, was working at a recording session in Utah with the Osmond brothers around this time when the studio phone rang. Being nearest to the phone, Hodges picked it up. He was greeted by Andy, who was calling from an airplane, wanting to speak with Marie. "She wasn't in the studio," Hodges recalled, "but I remember Alan Osmond telling me to tell him she wasn't around. The Osmond brothers were good friends with Andy, but they did *not* want him dating their little sister. The Osmonds, being very Mormon, were wanting Marie to date only young Mormon men, and not people in showbiz. So I had to tell Andy she wasn't around. He was very nice and polite, but sad he couldn't reach her."

Hugh Gibb confirmed the Osmond family's reluctance to let Marie date Andy, telling a reporter in 1979, "Andy was invited on the show [*Donny & Marie*] to sing some romantic duets with Marie. They got on well together, so Andy invited her to an awards ceremony. Nothing romantic, in fact it was very public. Well, Olive had to consult the Mormon Church Elders. Can you believe it? They are lovely people, but oh dear." Olive's opposition to her daughter dating Andy only increased when she learned that he already had been married and had a child. Nevertheless, since Andy, accompanied by Tony Messina, was in Utah to tape an appearance on *Donny & Marie* during Thanksgiving week in 1978, the Osmonds invited them both to have Thanksgiving dinner with them. "I had never seen a spread like Olive put out," Tony remembered. "So much food." During the visit, Donny took Andy and Tony downstairs to play ping pong.

Despite the opposition of her family, Marie and Andy nevertheless dated, even while publicly denying it. "Andy was in love with Marie and marriage was discussed," Beri Gibb told a reporter in 1982. "But every time Andy and Marie went out, there was never a date alone. Sometimes it was Marie's unmarried brothers, sometimes her mother and father, but always there was a chaperone. Religion mattered a lot to Marie. She always said that she would marry someone who was a Mormon." Andy confirmed, in an interview in 1986, that the "religion thing" and their difficulty in ever finding time alone together had made them both realize that "nothing could ever come of it." He also admitted, "I wouldn't have been good for her then, anyway. I really was just too wild."

Nevertheless, the pair had a romantic relationship on some level. In 2019 Marie told a national television audience, on the CBS program *The Talk*, how she broke up with Andy. "He kept calling me, well we had known each other a couple of years, and were dating. One night he kept calling me and calling me. He was obviously"—here she paused and another one of the show's hosts said "not well," drawing a nod and a sad "no" from Marie, who then continued—"you know, I probably could have done it better, but I just said, 'We're done, we're done.' And we hung up. And I felt really bad, because it was something that I probably would have wanted to do in person, but it was just enough. It was breaking my heart to see what he was doing to himself."

Andy may have had a briefer romantic interlude with another famous singer in 1978. While taping *Olivia* that spring, he met the members of ABBA, who also co-starred in the hour-long special. In 2020 the Australian singer Daryl Braithwaite recalled that he and his manager, at Andy's invitation, visited him in Miami and stayed on his houseboat for a few weeks that year. "In that time with Andy we had a great time and then one day he said, 'There's someone going to come over and visit us on the boat.' He didn't tell me who, but then they showed up to the boat that afternoon, and it was Agnetha [Fältskog] from ABBA." Braithwaite was starstruck. At least one other person who was friends with Andy at that time suggested that he and Agnetha, whose marriage to her bandmate Björn Ulvaeus was ending, may have engaged in some clandestine encounters.

By the time the Olivia Newton-John and Osmond Brothers specials aired, Andy was about to launch his first major, headlining North American tour. (No one could have guessed that it would also be his last.) For this tour, the core of his studio band accompanied him: Tim Renwick and Joey Murcia on guitars, Harold Cowart on bass, and Ron "Tubby" Zeigler on drums. Jeff Lodin signed on as the keyboardist. Lodin actually had been hired to play keyboards on a Bee Gees' tour that was supposed to occur that year, on the recommendation of the unavailable Paul Harris, who had played on some of

Andy's recordings. When the Bee Gees' tour got pushed back to 1979, as they were still making the *Spirits Having Flown* album, RSO offered Lodin the job on Andy's tour instead.

Andy and the band rehearsed at the facilities of Maryland Sound, located in a small neighborhood on the edge of Baltimore's city limits known as Dickeyville. Lodin recalled that the hotel where Andy and the band stayed was surrounded by girls at night, all hoping to catch a glimpse of Andy. "He seemed unaffected by it all," Lodin said in 2021. Lodin and Andy were the same age, and they became friends. "One night he and I were talking about fame, and I commented that I wouldn't want to be 'him.' He didn't understand what I meant, but a few weeks later, he came back to me saying that he understood." Nevertheless, Lodin remembered, Andy "enjoyed seeing his face on the cover of *Tiger Beat* magazine."

The tour schedule called for Andy to perform in forty-four cities beginning with Richmond, Virginia, on May 28. Daryl Braithwaite's band, Sherbet, served as the opening act. Steve Morse covered the June 28 concert for the *Boston Globe*. What he experienced made such a strong impression on him that he still vividly remembered it ten years later when Andy died. "There have been many teen idols in the history of pop music, but none the object of more delirious worship than Andy Gibb," Morse wrote. "The evening was unforgettable. There were two sold-out shows, and about 98 percent of the 8,000-plus screaming fans were young girls. My chief memory was walking down a front aisle with a backstage pass pinned to my shirt—and being gang-tackled by three or four girls who leaped out of their seats, clawing me to the ground in quest of the pass." As for Andy's performance, Morse remembered that "Gibb ignited the crowd by taking his shirt off and strutting around to deafening applause. The blond, blue-eyed [actually, brown-eyed] younger brother of the Bee Gees exploited his good looks, but he also showed talent."

For Andy, the highlight of the tour unquestionably occurred at the Jai Alai Fronton in Miami on July 9. When Andy began singing "Words," Barry stepped out onto the stage singing along, and Maurice walked onstage and replaced Andy's piano player. Then when it was time for the encore, "Shadow

Dancing," as soon as the band began playing, all three Bee Gees joined Andy onstage and sang the choruses with him. Ken Hoffman of the *Fort Lauderdale News* reported that Barbara Gibb "sat on an offstage couch and cried," while Hugh Gibb declared, "This was the proudest moment of my life. It has been my ambition to see them together and now it's happened." Barry heaped praise upon his youngest brother, telling Hoffman, "I don't know where Andy got those moves, certainly not from me. That much I can tell you. What goes on in my brother's mind, I don't know. One thing, he's a great performer."

But while Andy, as his reaction made clear, was awestruck to have his brothers join him onstage, even to the point that at times he seemed unwilling to stand next to them (particularly Barry as they sang "Words"), he nevertheless insisted on being respected in his own right as a performer. His mother saw this firsthand. "We were in Dallas once, and as we were driving from the airport, he looked up . . . [and saw that] the arena had 'Andy Gibb' and, underneath it had 'younger brother of the Bee Gees,'" she recalled in 1997. "He went *crazy* . . . he got his personal assistant to go and get it taken down. Things like that would upset him." Nevertheless, friends such as Scott Paton and Peter Leinheiser would still recall, decades later, Andy proudly showing them a videotape of the Miami concert. Looking back, Paton would reflect that having the Bee Gees join him onstage that night "was probably the most important moment of his [Andy's] life."

The tour ended on a bit of a sour note with the cancellation of the last three scheduled shows because Andy had developed a "severe case of laryngitis." Throughout his career, Andy had a tendency to cancel performances for this claimed reason; sometimes, as his mother admitted in the 1997 VH-1 *Behind the Music* episode on Andy, it was an excuse that he used when the real reason was that he was abusing cocaine or was depressed or both. On the other hand, Andy was not physically strong, and he had a thin voice (especially before he began light opera training in 1981) that was prone to becoming hoarse or failing altogether. When Andy received some bad press for canceling the last three shows, he complained to a reporter, which was rare for him. "When I canceled the last three gigs on my forty-nine-gig tour, the press wrote things like 'Andy Gibb Cancels Second Leg of Tour,'" Andy told a reporter in November 1978. "It wasn't like that at all. My throat was extremely sore, nearly raw. It was giving out. I had to cancel those three dates or my doctor said my voice would go completely. But if I'd known the press was going to make me look like a prima donna, I would have done those last three dates. I'd have done forty-six others."

Joey Murcia later suggested why Andy's voice gave out. "We realized he wasn't sleeping," Murcia recalled in 2021. "Sometimes the next day when he would have to leave, you couldn't get the door open of his suite, so you'd have to call maintenance, and they'd have to take the fuckin' door off the hinge and wake him up because he was crashed so hard. He would stay up two or three days in a row sometimes. And anyone who sings will tell you, when you don't sleep, pretty soon you have no voice, and that's what happened."

Of course, Barry heard about all this. In an article published in the August 1978 issue of the rock magazine *Crawdaddy*, he bluntly expressed his concerns about Andy's lifestyle: "With the sudden success he's had, his head has been turned around. We're concerned for the boy. There's a lot of heavy drugs around, a lot of shady characters, and he's not always within the realms of the family." Yet Julie LaMagna, who was part of Andy's entourage on both his 1977 and 1978 tours, would later question how much the Bee Gees had tried to help Andy. "All the while Andy was on tour, the brothers were busy with their own life," she recalled. "They didn't have the time or knowledge to help Andy in any way other than music."

During a short promotional tour of Great Britain and Europe in March 1978, Andy fell asleep during a live radio interview and collapsed at a photo shoot. Andy discussed his collapse about two months later in a radio interview for *The Robert W. Morgan Special of the Week*, explaining that "for three weeks we would be going from like six in the morning until two in the morning. I wasn't eating all my meals, I was getting called away to all these meetings, not being able to finish my meals. I broke down, it certainly wasn't mental, it was a sort of physical collapse and we had to cut the tour a few weeks short and bring me home to Miami."

Andy did indeed work hard in 1978—as most pop stars do when they are at the height of their popularity—but a grueling schedule was not the only burden on his health. In fact, when Scott Paton, who was conducting the interview for Morgan, went to meet Andy in Los Angeles for that purpose, RSO publicist Ronnie Lippin told him that Andy was in the hospital. Andy, she told Paton, had done "a little too much coke, and he got a heart murmur." Lippin and the rest of Andy's handlers managed to keep the press from learning about his hospitalization (Paton was by now a friend who could be trusted), but as such episodes sent Andy to the hospital time and again in the years ahead and became more frightening, they would become fodder for the tabloids.

Paton also saw cause for concern when he managed to finagle a "work trip" to Honolulu to catch up with Andy and his entourage for Andy's sold-out concert at the Neal Blaisdell Center Arena on July 29, 1978. (The attendees included Olivia Newton-John and Karen Carpenter, who happened to be in Hawaii on vacation together, and they also visited with Andy in his hotel suite after the show.) Andy "had Tony [Messina] charter a boat for the band and [get] a caterer . . . we had to get up at dawn the next day to go deep sea fishing. This was *exciting*," Paton remembered. "We get out there and they're loading the food up and all the gear, the band's there, and we're holding up, 'Where's Andy? Where's Andy?' He never showed up. So the thing that he chartered, he didn't get to enjoy." Paton and Andy's band and crew had a great time while Andy, Paton lamented, "missed it." Tony, obligated to stay at the hotel with Andy after he couldn't get him out of bed, therefore had to miss it as well.

Joe Shane, who met Andy in 1977, oversaw his merchandising and fan club, and traveled with him on the *Shadow Dancing* tour as "sort of a bodyguard," saw what was going on too, and how it was affecting Andy. "When you get in a situation like that, you know, where guys are altering their reality all the time, they lose track of who they really are. Every night his best friend is the guy who's got the best cocaine tonight." Andy, of course, was far from the only famous young entertainer of the day to indulge in that drug, but, as his brother Robin later lamented, "he had an addictive personality" which led to him getting badly hooked.

Andy's spending habits, while less alarming than his cocaine abuse, also became reckless. He bought two boats, the first of which he named *My Marie* in honor of Marie Osmond, followed by a half-million dollar fifty-eight-foot Hatteras yacht, which he named *Shadow Dancer*. In a span of two years, he acquired a fleet's worth of cars, including a Pontiac Firebird, a Jaguar, a Ferrari, a Mercedes 450 SL, and a Porsche 924. Andy managed to blow the Jaguar's engine, so he bought another one. His friend Howard Albert, a renowned Miami record producer and engineer, recalled that shortly after Andy bought the Ferrari, his dog "chew[ed] half the bumper off!" "He blew millions," recalled Robert Stigwood after Andy died. "He got very paranoid. He couldn't fly on a public plane; he had to hire private planes." (Julie LaMagna concurred that Andy avoided commercial flights and airports because he was "paranoid of being attacked," although she added that she "didn't blame him," having witnessed some frightening incidents involving huge crowds of frenzied female fans.) Former RSO Records president Al Coury, who also spoke to the press after Andy's death, said of Andy's star treatment and lavish lifestyle, "You had to worry about him . . . because you knew someday the hits were going to stop."

As the end of 1978 approached, Andy should have been getting to work on his third album if he hoped to maintain his red-hot momentum. Of course, trying to maintain that momentum had to be a daunting task for the twenty-year-old superstar. As he told John Davidson in 1981, "It's definitely not an easy thing . . . the pressure [of] following up an album." When Andy talked to a reporter in November 1978 about his career plans, he didn't even mention his next album. Instead he excitedly discussed his plans for working with his brothers and making movies. Andy said that he would be going on the road with the Bee Gees in early 1979. "We're going to charter a 747 and go first class all the way," he told Richard Cuskelly. "My being with them won't be like a supporting act or anything. It'll be one big family show. Right now, the plans are for me to open for an hour, sharing a band with my brothers. Then the Bee Gees will come out for an hour of their music and then I'll return for the final half hour. I'm looking forward to the sheer pleasure of being on stage with the Bee Gees."

As would always be the case when Andy discussed plans to work with the Bee Gees, however, his hopes went unfulfilled. While he would indeed get to have "the sheer pleasure of being on stage" with his three brothers in 1979, his role would be far more limited than he had hoped. In fact, when a reporter asked Barry for a comment about the tour plans that Andy had mentioned, he "commented with a laugh, 'I think Andy's speculating a bit. I am going to be co-producing his album, but when we tour at the end of June, it's going to be the Bee Gees. Andy's not part of the tour.'" The journalist then concluded, "Maybe someone should tell Andy."

Andy closed out 1978 making television appearances. He appeared on *Donny & Marie* again; he and Marie sang the big 1977 hit by Dan Hill, "Sometimes When We Touch," together. The gossip columns continued to buzz with speculation about a romance between Andy and Marie, especially after Andy told a reporter, "I've found the right person and I really want to get married again." (Friends who knew Andy at this time that were interviewed for this book were unable to identify the woman in question, pointing out that sudden, hard crushes were the norm for him. He might have been referring to Marie.) An unnamed "close friend of Andy's" insisted to the reporter, however, that the couple had only "dated once or twice," and that Marie "was chaperoned and had to be in by 10 p.m." Andy subsequently told another reporter, "Sex turns me off." When the surprised reporter asked him to say that again, Andy "snickered" and said, "Sex turns me off when it's anonymous and cold. I don't believe in one-night stands. Really, just ask the girls I know." He told another reporter, "Girls are always running through my mind. They don't dare walk."

On a more serious note, though, in an interview in 1979 he said, "We [he and his brothers] are all marrying-people and I love children. I know I've never seen my little girl, but next time it is all going to be different. I want more kids because they change your whole life. They will give me a sense of responsibility and purpose. I won't be able to be selfish. I know it will happen one day. I just know."

After his return to the Osmonds' show, Andy appeared on shows hosted by two other stars with whom he would frequently appear: *The Merv Griffin Show* and *The Bob Hope All Star Christmas Special.* Andy appealed to a broader demographic than the average teen idol. Griffin and Hope would both be loyal to Andy in the years ahead, continuing to have him on their television programs after his star had faded—and, in Hope's case, even after Andy let him down badly in 1982 in what Andy called "the most embarrassing thing" among his many neglected professional commitments that year. Andy also guest starred on *George Burns' 100th Birthday Party*, which was taped in November 1978 and aired on CBS the following January when Burns turned eighty-three. (In stark contrast to the ill-fated Andy, though, who barely lived to the age of thirty, Burns actually made it to his one hundredth birthday, dying seven weeks later on March 9, 1996, just one day short of the eighth anniversary of Andy's death.) In the undoubtedly scripted inane banter between the two, which Andy's friend Kim Richards said Andy disliked because he thought it was disrespectful to Burns, Andy told his host, "I'd like to be your age. I'd like to be *old*." After the mild humor subsided, Andy lip synced "(Our Love) Don't Throw It All Away," which would become his fifth top ten hit before 1978 ended. Andy's fee for the appearance was $10,000 (equivalent to about $42,000 in 2021), which was paid to the Stigwood Group of Companies.

Andy achieved even more success in 1978 than he had the year before. At the end of the year, he won accolades from all three major record industry trade publications. *Billboard* named Andy the male artist of the year for his success on the singles and albums charts. He beat out the Bee Gees for the number one single of the year with "Shadow Dancing." The Bee Gees spent more weeks in the top ten that year than Andy (thirty-eight to thirty-five), but no one else even came close. (Olivia Newton-John came in third at twenty-four weeks.) *Cash Box* and *Record World* both named Andy as the male singles artist of the year. Andy and Billy Joel would tie for the annual People's

Choice Award for favorite male musical performer of 1978, which would be announced at the televised awards ceremony on March 7, 1979, two days after Andy's twenty-first birthday. Very few performers in pop music history have had a more successful year than Andy Gibb did in 1978.

It had been a remarkable year for the Bee Gees, too, but the facts that they had a lot more experience as performers, had achieved great popularity and then lost it before climbing back to the top of the charts, and were all roughly a decade older than Andy enabled them to keep their enormous success in greater perspective than he could. As Andy admitted in 1986, "It was quite a wonderful rollercoaster ride which we [he and his brothers] thought was going to go on forever—well I thought. They knew better."

Chapter FOUR

After Dark

"He was a great artist out of control, and his personality and emotions just couldn't deal with what was going on around him and the success that he had." Robin Gibb offered this assessment of his youngest brother's fate in 1997. He and his other two brothers had realized this while Andy was still alive, but despite their best efforts they could not rescue him from his inner demons.

Those demons, which had been slowly festering within Andy, reached a crisis point in 1979. Although only a handful of insiders could have possibly foreseen it, that year would be a turning point in the life and career of Andy Gibb, one that would lead him from dizzying heights of fame, adulation, and wealth to a shattered career, bankruptcy, and finally a premature death less than a decade later. His downfall, tragically, would be as spectacular as his ascent had been. As Tony Messina would later sadly reflect, "It all went downhill after the beginning of 1980," although he added that that wasn't entirely Andy's fault either. "A lot of people used him after 1980." Tony wouldn't witness that firsthand, though; after nine nearly non-stop years together, Andy fired him in early 1980.

The last year of the 1970s got off to a glittering start for Andy that certainly did not foreshadow the troubles that lay ahead. Andy participated alongside his brothers and other superstars such as Rod Stewart, ABBA, and Olivia Newton-John in a gala televised benefit concert in New York City, *The Music for UNICEF Concert: A Gift of Song*, which was taped on January 9 and broadcast globally the next day. Andy looked and sounded great performing "I Go for You," a self-composed song from the *Shadow Dancing* album, and a tender duet with Olivia, "Rest Your Love on Me," a Bee Gees song that was the B-side of their new single "Too Much Heaven." The original plan was for Andy and Olivia to each perform just one song (Olivia sang "The Key"), but, as Olivia recalled in 1981, "Someone on the production staff for UNICEF suggested we sing that song [together]."

The George Burns TV special aired later that month, and a few weeks after that Andy appeared on an Osmond family Valentine's special. But then Andy seemed to suddenly drop out of sight. By the spring, his fans were starting to wonder what was going on. A fan from Richmond, Virginia, wrote a letter to the syndicated "Pop Scene" newspaper column asking, "What has happened to Andy Gibb? Last year all I ever heard about was Andy Gibb and now there's no news." In her reply, published in May, columnist Barbara Lewis declared Andy to be "still very much alive and kicking." Lewis reported that Andy and Olivia had a "forthcoming single" with "Rest Your Love on Me" on one side and another duet on the other. "Andy's also working on a new album which is being produced by brother Barry," she added, "and there's also a lot of talk about Andy starting work on his first film later this year. Throw in plans for a tour, and it looks as though Andy will be around a lot in the next few months." While this information may have come from RSO's publicity department, a lot of it proved to be inaccurate.

Meanwhile, Andy was also getting press coverage for his non-professional activities. On his twenty-first birthday (March 5, 1979), the Gibb family threw a party for him at his rented house in Miami Beach; newspapers across the nation printed a photograph of his brothers presenting him with a large birthday cake. Andy made the news again, at least in Miami, in April when he went to the city's chic Jockey Club (where he often parked his yacht) when the Dave Brubeck Quartet performed at a $100-a-plate benefit and auction for the Florida Philharmonic Orchestra. Andy bought a two-year-old racehorse, which according to the *Miami Herald* was "said to be part of the famous Bold Ruler line," for $20,000; a female lion cub "the size of a fully-grown German shepherd" for $5,000; and two tickets for a balloon ride for $500. (His total expenditure at the auction, $25,500, would be the equivalent of a little over $95,000 in 2021.) Andy brought the lion cub (named Samantha) home that night to live on his boat. Once when Andy took the boat out to sea, the lion cub somehow fell overboard, and one of Andy's assistants, remembered Joey Murcia, "had to jump in and get it and it clawed the shit out of his chest. So anyway, the lion had to go." Andy donated her to the Miami Zoo. Andy named the racehorse Livvy's Choice, after Olivia Newton-John.

Andy loved boating and fishing, but he had the occasional mishap as the captain of his own ship. Joey Murcia recounted one such episode. "Andy decided he was going to sail his Hatteras yacht from Miami down to Key Largo, Florida, where I was living. He made it down there to a place called the Plantation Yacht Harbor, and he fuckin' walloped the dock, man. He had to pay for the whole dock. But he was very jovial about it . . . he just picked up the tab, no problem. He was just a kid looking to have fun, and he had a lot of money to do it with."

Beri was with Andy when a more frightening episode occurred off the Florida coast. They ran into a storm, and lightning struck the boat. "There were those blue sparks flying off the end of the radio antennae, hissing and cracking," she remembered in an interview in 1982. "Somebody had to go up there and unplug the radio. Of course, it was Andy. It was a very scary moment." Andy's love of boating and tendency for misadventure remained intact, though: Rick Lotempio, who became friends with Andy upon joining his band in 1985, and his family were among a small group of family and friends that Andy invited along when he rented a boat one Sunday for a trip from Redondo Beach, California, to Catalina Island. "Due to bad weather and high waves, the US Coast Guard advised us not to make the trip," Rick remembered. "Andy decided to move forward anyway with the voyage, and mostly everyone (except Andy) got severely seasick. Some guests had to fly back to L.A. by helicopter because they were too sick to boat back. What a day!"

Julie LaMagna also became a participant in one of Andy's daring adventures. In 1978, he bought a parasail. Julie recalled Allan LaMagna and herself, Bee Gees keyboardist Blue Weaver, and two members of Andy's band being with him the first time he used it. "We were down in Biscayne Bay," she said, "and we put the harness on Andy, stand him up on the beach, and Allan takes off [in the boat that was pulling the parasail]. And *boom*! In like flipping minus zero seconds, Andy's 300 feet in the air. And we didn't know anything about what we were doing, and you're not supposed to have nearly that much rope. And you could hear Andy up there screaming bloody murder, '*Get me down! Get me down!*' And oh my God, it was so funny. We finally get him down, and then he gets on the ground and he's like, 'Oh, mate, that's so much fun, you gotta do it, you gotta do it,' and all the guys in the band are going, 'Oh no, not me, not me.' And dumb ass me, I go, '*I'll* do it!'" Neither Allan nor Andy had learned much from Andy's flight, though, and Julie's went a bit worse. "I crashed and burned parasailing with Andy's parasail," she remembered, although she was unhurt. Andy was unfazed; in the mid-1980s, while performing in Las Vegas, he once took members of his band and entourage for hang gliding lessons and picked up the tab for all of them.

In May 1979, Andy finally returned to the recording studio for the first time in fifteen months, the longest he had gone without recording since his first sessions as an unsigned novice under Maurice's guidance in August 1973. His third album was overdue. RSO wanted Andy and Olivia Newton-John to record "Rest Your Love on Me" after they sang it during the UNICEF concert. As Olivia told a reporter in 1981, "Andy was doing a new album and asked me down to Miami to record it with him. I didn't have an album currently." Barry also gave them another song, "I Can't Help It."

The sessions got off to an inauspicious start. At first Andy didn't even show up, leaving Olivia to rehearse with Barry, who was producing the recordings with Albhy Galuten and Karl Richardson. When Andy finally arrived, it was clear that neither he nor his voice were in the best of shape. Galuten told music journalist Christian John Wikane in 2018 that "there was a lot of struggle getting a vocal out of Andy." Andy also recorded two self-composed songs in May 1979, "Back to the Wind" and "Warm," which would never be released. Galuten and Richardson probably produced those two recordings without Barry. On Andy's first two albums, the eldest brother Gibb only co-produced those songs which he had written or co-written. Barry couldn't stick around for the continuation of the sessions anyway; the Bee Gees had to begin preparing for their *Spirits Having Flown* tour (named after the album which would rank number two for the year in sales according to *Billboard*, surpassed only by Billy Joel's *52nd Street*).

Andy, as an unidentified friend told *People Weekly* in April 1980, "tried recording without Barry but he felt uncomfortable and had to wait." Furthermore, several of Andy's regular studio musicians—guitarist Joey Murcia, bassist Harold Cowart, keyboardist George Bitzer, and percussionist Joe Lala—were part of the Bee Gees' band on the tour. Most of all, though, Andy wanted to go on the tour with the Bee Gees. His brothers had nixed his plan to actually join them on the tour as an equal, but he was still happy, even eager, to tag along and join them onstage whenever he could. During some of the concerts Andy joined the Bee Gees onstage to sing the encore, "You Should Be Dancing," with them. A professional camera crew filmed one of these performances, at the Oakland–Alameda County Coliseum Arena on July 11, 1979, and it was included in *The Bee Gees Special*, which aired on NBC on November 21, 1979. As Bee Gees biographer David N. Meyer noted, "While Andy at moments seems self-conscious, mostly what he looks is overjoyed."

In interviews, Andy sometimes said he wished to be a Bee Gee and sometimes said he was glad that he had not joined his brothers' group. Barry knew better. To the writer of an early 1979 article that reported his desire to "crown Andy as the fourth Bee Gee," Barry declared, "I think Andy, in his heart of hearts, wants to be part of the four brothers instead of being the big male star, or whatever he is. He doesn't say it to me so much because he doesn't dare believe such a great thing will happen."

Of course, that "great thing" never did happen, even though Andy "really wanted it," recalled Tony Messina decades later. Former RSO president Bill

Oakes later suggested that Stigwood didn't want Andy joining the Bee Gees. "He was a teen idol," Oakes said. "There was talk about him becoming a Bee Gee. I think Robert saw he had a younger audience. It was smart to keep him on his own."

If Barry, Robin, and Maurice had wanted Andy to become the fourth Bee Gee, though, it is hard to imagine that Stigwood would or could have stopped them. Col Joye didn't think Stigwood ever had to try; in an interview in 2020, he said that "Andy was gonna be the fourth Bee Gee, and Barry said, 'No, that's silly, because you've got a talent, you've got a sound, you should be out on your own.'" In the spring of 1977, Barry told Scott Paton in an interview that making Andy the fourth Bee Gee "just wasn't thought of. And even for Andy at this period, he doesn't want to do anything like that. He wants to make it on his own name, and I think it would be harder to sort of join the Bee Gees and become a Bee Gee. I think it would be harder for his head. It might just screw him up." Robin said something similar about a year later, telling Merv Griffin, "I think it's important for him to do whatever he achieves, to achieve them in his own way, because . . . coming straight in with us . . . I don't think it would go through his head." Griffin then leaned toward Robin and jokingly suggested, "Tell me the truth, Robin, you don't want him in the group, do you?" Robin shook his head and laughingly said, "Absolutely not." Merv and Robin's exchange, even if it was cloaked in humor, would prove to be prophetic.

Once the *Spirits* tour ended in the Gibbs' adopted hometown of Miami on October 6, 1979, Barry and Andy returned to Criteria to get back to work on Andy's third album, *After Dark*. Barry was there more often though. "By that point," according to Galuten, "Andy was hard to work with. . . . He wouldn't show up, he wasn't there." Andy later admitted, in an interview in the autumn of 1985, that his cocaine problem had been the cause: "I started not turning up for recording sessions . . . leaving Barry to cover for me . . . on a couple of my albums you will hear Barry singing a line and you think it's me, but it was really him." (Andy was exaggerating or misremembering how many albums this had happened on; it didn't happen on *Flowing Rivers* and *Shadow Dancing*, even though Barry sang backing and harmony vocals on some songs on those albums.) Charlie Chalmers, whose trio Rhodes, Chalmers, and Rhodes also sang backing vocals on *After Dark*, recalled that "when Barry would have a session with Andy, or Andy was around, he made sure, he would tell the musicians, 'Don't bring anything around, any drugs.' He was just trying to protect Andy so much because he knew Andy had the weakness." Guitarist George Terry, who played on some tracks on the album, seldom even saw Andy in the studio. "The songs were done [recorded] with Barry," he said. Andy "only sang later on overdubs." Barry, said Chalmers, "would make Andy sing the lead exactly note for note the way he wanted it sung."

Despite Andy's unreliability, Barry and Galuten and Richardson kept the sessions proceeding steadily enough that, according to Andy, "I finished it [the album] just before Christmas." The three producers had another project to start in early 1980 with a superstar from whom they could expect a far better work ethic: Barbra Streisand. That album, *Guilty*, would be written by Barry with help from his brothers (one song on the album, "The Love Inside," had been written by all four brothers in 1978) and Albhy Galuten. Barry also wrote *After Dark*, with Andy as co-writer on two songs, Robin and Maurice on two others, and Galuten on one. Andy had written the bulk of his first two albums by himself, and only one song on the first and two on the second did not bear his name as either the writer or a co-writer.

In an interview shortly after the release of *After Dark*, Andy tried to explain the lack of self-composed songs to syndicated journalist Marilyn Beck, telling her, "I was going to put three of my own songs in the album, but I personally pulled them because he [Barry] was writing so wonderfully." But this explanation doesn't hold up under scrutiny. The album's first single, "Desire," was an unreleased Bee Gees recording from the *Spirits Having Flown* sessions with a new lead vocal overdubbed by Andy. Andy recorded the song during the initial *After Dark* sessions in May 1979, so he didn't withdraw any of his own songs to record it. He did indeed eventually withdraw at least the two self-composed songs that he recorded that month, but two songs that he recorded later in the year, "Falling in Love with You" (written by Barry and Galuten) and "Warm Ride" (written by the Bee Gees) both dated from 1977. "Warm Ride" had even cracked the top 40 as a single by the Detroit group Rare Earth in 1978. The Bee Gees had recorded Barry's "Rest Your Love on Me" in 1976. Apparently, Barry was digging deep into his songbook to fill out the album while Andy lacked the confidence to include any of his own songs. The two songs that he co-wrote on the album, "One Love" and "Someone I Ain't," are reminiscent of some of his self-composed ballads from his first two albums, and the wistful lyrics and mood of the latter would become even more poignant after his premature death.

RSO released "Desire" in January 1980. *Billboard* featured the record as one of its "Top Single Picks" in its January 26 issue, calling it "a breathy falsetto ballad with a semi-reggae beat." "All five of the singer's previous singles have gone top 10 and gold," the review noted, "and this one enters [the Hot 100] at a lofty 44." "Desire" would extend Andy's top ten streak to six, reaching number four, but it didn't quite reach the million mark in sales. *After Dark* came out at the beginning of February. *Record World* featured it on the cover of its February 16 issue as one of four "Hits of the Week," along with albums by Chuck Mangione, John Denver, and David Sanborn. "Gibb's breathless vocals," the brief review noted, "have matured somewhat but the energy in the higher ranges remains." The review also favorably commented on the duets with Olivia Newton-John and "vocal assists from the Bee Gees throughout," even though Robin and Maurice did not sing on the album with the exception of "Desire."

As Andy was about to return from what *Billboard* deemed his "yearlong absence from the marketplace"—although actually it had been more like fifteen months—he had a meeting with a familiar face and a new face from Australia during one of his frequent visits to Los Angeles. In January 1980 Andy's ex-wife, Kim, arrived there for matters relating to family business, and she brought Peta. She hadn't heard from Andy since she had left him about two-and-a-half years earlier. She called RSO Records, which was located on Sunset Boulevard in West Hollywood, and, putting on an American accent so as to conceal her identity, asked if Andy was in town. Upon being told that he was, she revealed her identity and said that she was in town with their daughter, whose second birthday (January 25) was the next day. At that point, the receptionist at RSO referred her to Andy's lawyers, who she said told her, "Andy doesn't want to see you."

The lawyers, Kim recalled, suspected that she was looking for money. Once she convinced them that all she wanted was for Andy to meet his daughter, they told her they would let him know. Kim stayed in her hotel room awaiting her ex-husband's call. When it came, Andy greeted her with "Hello Kim, how much money do you want?" Kim would recall that when she told him that she merely wanted him to meet his daughter, he replied, "I don't know if I can cope with that." Nevertheless, he told Kim to meet him at his suite at the Beverly Hilton Hotel. Kim later said that she was shocked by Andy's appearance. "He was clearly not well."

Nevertheless, Andy told a reporter for *People* magazine that his meeting with Kim and Peta "went real well," and Kim remembered that "he was gentle with Peta and bought her a bracelet engraved with the words 'All my love, A.G.'" In fact, Kim was happy enough with the meeting that she wanted to see Andy again before she had to leave Los Angeles, but it wasn't to be. "I didn't know it then," she said after his death, "but that was the last time I would ever see Andy alive. The next day I called the hotel, but he had gone." Andy said in an interview not long after the meeting that he wanted to see his daughter again, but his only subsequent contact with her and Kim would be via telephone. "I could tell it haunted Andy . . . splitting from Kim and especially not being a real father to Peta," observed Scott Paton.

Yet rather than take any responsibility, Andy blamed Robert Stigwood. "Robert didn't want me to be married," Andy told Paton. "He said, 'It will hamper your career.'" Bassist Jerry Manfredi, who toured with Andy in 1977, indeed remembered that Andy "was told in no uncertain terms that he couldn't be married and be a pop star and a teenage idol." Stigwood, according to Manfredi, said to Andy, "Do you want to have a record career or do you want to have a baby with your wife and stay in Australia?"

Shortly after the visit from Kim and Peta, Andy made a brief trip to Great Britain and Europe to promote *After Dark*. In 2008, Andy's personal assistant Scott Sands recalled a highlight of the trip that the public did not get to see or hear. "We were in Munich, Germany, and we met Freddie Mercury. We're in the studio one night and Freddie Mercury couldn't hit a high note, and he told Andy, 'Get out there! That's your family's forte, the high notes.' So Andy went and sang with Queen backtracks and it just sounded so incredible."

Upon Andy's return to the United States—in time for his twenty-second birthday party at Le Dome in Hollywood—he was supposed to be embarking on a fifty-two-date tour of the United States and Canada in support of *After Dark*. The teen magazines of the day (most notably *16* and *Tiger Beat),* which capitalized upon and at the same time bolstered the popularity of teen idols, dutifully reported the tour to their faithful readers. "Andy's planning a huge America-wide tour!" proclaimed one article. "As you read this, it's already started, and it's gonna continue all summer long!"

Rhodes, Chalmers, and Rhodes, who had sung backing vocals on most of the songs on the album, signed on to be both Andy's backup singers on the tour and, under the name RCR, his opening act as well. RCR had signed with the Florida-based label Radio Records and had a new album of their own out, *Scandal*, and a single of the same name that was starting to get airplay. RCR had produced the album with Ron and Howard Albert and Blue Weaver. Barry, who had been hearing *Scandal* while the trio was recording it at Criteria in between session work for Andy and others, "was really digging it," remembered Charlie Chalmers, and it was his idea that RCR open for Andy in addition to backing him in concerts.

But the *After Dark* tour never happened. According to Chalmers, "Ten days before the tour, Andy—who knows the whole story, but anyway—Andy canceled." RSO told promoters that Andy was sick. After Andy died, a south Florida music journalist wrote that the cancellation had occurred because Andy had "needed to be hospitalized for cocaine-use complications," an explanation that did not appear in press reports in 1980. Despite the best efforts of everyone in the RSO and Gibb camps to conceal it, however, Andy's drug problem was becoming known within the record industry—as Andy and his handlers were about to find out.

The last-minute cancelation of the tour was unfortunate for RCR; the trio's single entered the Hot 100 around the time the tour would have been getting underway and stalled at number ninety-four. The cancelation caused problems for Andy too. In fact, Chalmers said that it marked "the end of his [Andy's] career" because "none of the promoters would ever book Andy again after that." Moreover, without a tour to support the album, RSO released only one more single from it: "I Can't Help It," one of the duets with Olivia Newton-John. Olivia, according to *People*, "reportedly complained" that her two duets with Andy "were stale by the time the record was finally released." When she and Andy sang the new single together on the ABC-TV special *Olivia Newton-John: Hollywood Nights*, which aired on April 14, 1980, only a portion of their duet even aired. The single peaked at number twelve on the Hot 100—still a hit by most standards, but it was the first Andy Gibb single to miss the top ten.

Andy wanted the title track from *After Dark* to be released as the album's third single. He performed (or lip synced) the song more frequently in U.S. television appearances than "Desire," but RSO refused. The album peaked at number twenty-one on the *Billboard* chart, only two notches lower than *Flowing Rivers* had, but it had a far shorter stay on the chart (fifteen weeks) and only achieved gold record status (signifying 500,000 copies sold) rather than the platinum (million-selling) status that each of his first two albums had. A tour would most likely have resulted in the release of "After Dark" as a single and certainly a longer stay on the charts and higher sales for the album.

Then *People* magazine dropped something of a bombshell on Andy's image. Andy and Olivia made the cover of the April 21, 1980 issue, for an article that was mistitled "The Bee Gee & Sandy." (The title was also misleading; the article was primarily about Andy, although he did dismiss rumors about a romance between himself and Olivia by saying, "I'd like the rumors to be true, but it takes two to tango.") *People* was hardly known for publishing exposés, but the author of the article, Fred Bernstein, was out for blood.

In considering the reason for the longer-than-expected period between the release of Andy's second and third albums, he wrote, "One industry insider close to the Gibbs claims that Andy's drug use—purportedly a mix of cocaine and Quaaludes—distracted him from work." This was not an inaccurate charge, but it was hardly the type of revelation that one would have expected to read in *People* in 1980.

Bernstein also reported that Andy's video cassette collection included porno films and that Andy carried "two semiautomatic machine guns, a .357 magnum [a gift from the Osmonds], and a riot gun to protect the three-stateroom, three-head cruiser [his Hatteras yacht] from modern-day Caribbean pirates" while cruising the Bahamas. The brass at RSO were appalled and furious; Bernstein wrote in 1998 that "Mr. Gibb's publicist [Ronnie Lippin] tried to get me fired, and said she wouldn't allow her other clients to cooperate with *People*."

RSO executives were also frustrated with Andy, though, even if they viewed him sympathetically, as did most people who knew him. Freddie Gershon, president of the Robert Stigwood Group, would comment just after Andy's death that "Andy grew older, but he didn't grow up. He froze in time at about age seventeen." But Gershon also remembered Andy as "too sensitive, too delicate." Stigwood was by now well aware of Andy's substance abuse and tried to help the only way he could. "So you try to protect them, you try to protect their finances, so they can't have access to so much money [that] they can just throw it away," Stigwood explained sadly twenty years after Andy's death. "You're trying to help them, you then become the enemy and you lose that sympathy that you shared." Stigwood also played a role in arranging at least two attempted interventions (to no avail) to get Andy into a rehabilitation program.

Some of Andy's friends, however, would later suggest that Stigwood hadn't been all that good for him. Tony Messina would reflect that Stigwood made "some really, really bad mistakes" in managing Andy. Julie LaMagna felt that "Stiggy was all in it for himself. He was a money man." Julie saw that Andy's parents didn't help much either, though. "Barbara and Hughie were in for the ride," she observed. Allan told her how during one of the attempted interventions, as he and others were trying to convince Andy to board a Lear jet and fly off to a treatment clinic, Barbara told her youngest son, "You do what you want." Andy then said, "No, I'm not going," thus scuttling the effort to help him. "Mum and Dad," Barry recalled in 2009, "were in denial that there was any real problem."

Amidst the bad publicity and turmoil, Andy had to be aware that sales of *After Dark* and its singles didn't match his previous successes. He always paid attention to how his records fared on the charts, even mentioning the chart peaks of his records (albeit incorrectly, sometimes) in concerts and interviews years after the records had been released. Moreover, he knew that his first two albums had been certified platinum and that every single off those albums was at least certified gold. How concerned he was about the decline, which to some extent was inevitable after he started off with three consecutive number one singles, is difficult to discern, though. He didn't mention his slipping (although certainly still more than respectable) sales in interviews at that time.

Andy now seemed more interested in making movies; he told Bernstein that he would be starring in the sequel to *Grease*, then tentatively titled *Son of Grease*, which was slated to be co-produced by Stigwood starting in the summer of 1980. Recent press reports had stated that Andy would star alongside Olivia Newton-John in the upcoming film *Xanadu*. Andy also told Bernstein that he was considering releasing a *Greatest Hits* album—an odd move for someone who had only released three albums and, even with sagging sales, was still selling records in significant quantities. Andy already seemed to have lost interest (or self-confidence) in writing songs before recording *After Dark*; while recording that album, he seemed to lose interest in making records, as well as in touring after the album came out. He had told reporter Marilyn Beck before his own tour was canceled that he would be joining the Bee Gees for some of their concerts later that year, but the Bee Gees ended up not touring either in 1980—in fact, their next tour would be in 1989, the year after Andy died.

Surprisingly, an uncredited writer for *16 Magazine*, which was even less likely than *People* to engage in critical coverage of its celebrity subjects, offered an incisive bit of analysis of this problem in 1981: "Wasn't that [releasing a *Greatest Hits* album] a strange move (one most performers save for well into their careers) for a hot singer to make, when his following of fans would just gobble up *anything* new he'd record?" The article then offered an answer to the posed question: "In fact, at this stage in his career, Andy hadn't made a single record by himself, and he began to take the criticism that he just couldn't make it without his brother [Barry] to heart. The result was that he stopped doing what he loved doing most and started looking for another way out." Some of Andy's public statements around this time suggested that this explanation bore at least some truth, one instance being when he told John Davidson in January 1981 that he felt he owed his string of hits chiefly to Barry. At roughly the same time Andy told a writer, "I feel I've done very little. I know I've been very lucky, and wouldn't have gotten as far as I have so quickly if it hadn't been for my family." Jeff Witjas, Andy's agent from 1983 to 1985, realized, as did others, that "Andy did have an insecurity. I think he may have felt that he was in the shadow of his brothers, and maybe specifically Barry, though he loved Barry very much."

Despite being unwilling or unable to tour in support of *After Dark*, Andy made a plethora of television appearances to promote the album. In February, he made a guest appearance on Dinah Shore's daytime talk and variety show; other guests on the episode were Carol Burnett and Shore's former longtime boyfriend Burt Reynolds. In March, Andy hosted an episode of *The Midnight Special*, on which he lip synced "Desire," "After Dark," and "Falling in Love with You." Later that month he took part in the CBS-TV special *Celebrity Challenge of the Sexes*; he fell and broke his ankle running through an obstacle course (he returned to the taping on a pair of crutches), resulting in the newspaper headline "Andy Gibb wounded in sex battle." The show aired in April, as did the Olivia Newton-John special. In May he appeared on an episode of *The Merv Griffin Show* on which he encountered an obnoxious Chevy Chase. Andy also made a more significant television appearance that month on *Bob*

Hope's All-Star Comedy Birthday Party at the Air Force Academy: A USO Salute on NBC. Andy lip synced "After Dark," appeared in some comedy skits, and he also met twenty-year old figure skating star Tai Babilonia, who was another one of the guests on the show.

Andy asked Tai out, and they began dating. "I knew it wasn't serious, but it was fun . . . and it was fun to be around someone so popular at that time. I mean, teen idol and . . . just the chaos and the girls," she recalled in 2014. "I would sit back and . . . watch and learn how he handled himself and he was great. He was very, very courteous and loved his fans." Tai found Andy to be "such a sweet person . . . almost too sweet for the world he was in at that time 'cause it kinda gobbled him up in a way." She was taken aback at the publicity machine around him. "They would have you married and then you would be dumping him, and then you're married again and then he wants you back 'so bad' and it's like who is feeding all this stuff to these outlets? 'Cause I didn't have a publicist . . . at that time but he sure did." She said that "his world . . . was crazy, fast paced" and filled with "'yes' people." But Andy, she said in 2021, "was always a gentleman." The romance between Andy and Tai didn't last long, but they remained friends even though they eventually drifted apart.

Around the beginning of the summer of 1980, Andy returned to the recording studio with Barry, Albhy Galuten, Karl Richardson, and most of his regular session musicians. (The studio was not Criteria though; instead, Andy used the Bee Gees' own new Miami Beach studio, Middle Ear.) Andy wanted to record some new material for his *Greatest Hits* album. He had just written two songs. One of them, "Time Is Time," was more of a rock and roll song than most of the songs he had written or that Barry had written for him, and, amidst a growing anti-disco backlash, it seemed to bode well for his prospects in the new decade. The other, "Me (Without You)," was a dramatic ballad. When Andy finally started playing concerts again in 1983, the song would become a staple of his repertoire and one of his biggest crowd pleasers.

Andy wrote both songs in Los Angeles, and he had high hopes for them. "People think here's just a good-looking guy. There's more music to me," he told *Washington Post* reporter Carla Hall in July before a concert at the Kennedy Center, where he and Irene Cara each performed for Olympic athletes.[4] "I'd like to see some adult response to me." He described "Time Is Time" to Hall as "less soft and lush, more assertive, more upbeat" than his previous singles. When he played "Time Is Time" for Barry in Miami Beach, Barry "altered one little thing in the song and for that reason you will see A. and B. Gibb [listed as songwriters], but it is mostly my record," Andy told an interviewer in 1981. Of "Me (Without You)," Andy said that "it took me about 2 weeks to write that song." "A lot of people that have heard it think it is one of the . . . prettiest I have ever written," he added, "but then again I am very critical, I don't know."

Andy wanted these two songs to be his next singles, but he also recorded two more songs, both of which dated back to the 1960s. Somewhat surprisingly, given his desire to establish his own identity, he recorded an old Bee Gees song, "Morning of My Life." Barry wrote this song in 1965, while he was still in his late teens. The Bee Gees recorded the song in 1966 but did not release it until they re-recorded it four years later. Andy made a video for the song, which may have been solely for a television special that was produced in 1981 titled *Grandpa, Will You Run With Me?* That special, which didn't air until April 1983 (on NBC), would be the only release that Andy's video ever saw. RSO never released his recording of the song.

Andy also recorded the classic Gerry Goffin/Carole King composition "Will You Love Me Tomorrow" as a duet with Pat Arnold. An American soul singer from Los Angeles, Arnold had come to England in 1966 on tour as one of Ike and Tina Turner's Ikettes. After the tour, she quit the act to pursue a solo career. Later in the decade she signed with the Robert Stigwood Organisation and recorded some songs written and produced by Barry Gibb. Most of those songs wouldn't be released until 2017, but Barry reestablished contact with her in Los Angeles after her daughter Debbie died in a car accident in 1977, and he invited her to the premiere of *Sgt. Pepper's Lonely Heart Club Band* during the summer of the following year. Barry then suggested

---

4 The United States boycotted the 1980 Summer Olympics, which were held in Moscow, in response to the Soviet invasion and occupation of Afghanistan.

that she move to Miami so that they could resume making their unfinished album from almost a decade earlier.

By the time she did, however, Barry was busy working with other artists, including Andy and Barbra Streisand. She was still in Miami in mid-1980, though, so Barry asked her to record the duet with Andy, whom she remembered fondly from the late 1960s. While she and Barry had rehearsed songs at his and his future wife Linda's house in London's Eaton Square, "Andy would be out in the square playing football [soccer] with my son and my daughter," Arnold recalled in 2019. "He was a little boy." Of their duet, she said, "What a beautiful version of that song." The duet would be released on *Andy Gibb's Greatest Hits*, along with "Time Is Time" and "(Me) Without You," in November 1980.

The short recording project of coming up with some new tracks for the *Greatest Hits* album seemed to mark a return to form for Andy. He had written two good songs and had the self-confidence to record them for release as singles (even though Barry ended up listed as co-writer on one of them). Moreover, his voice, which at times sounds thin and wispy on *After Dark*, sounds strong on these recordings. On the album version of "Time Is Time," which has a cold ending unlike the faded single version, it seems apparent that Andy was singing live with the band, in contrast to *After Dark* where Barry was singing guide vocals while the band recorded the basic tracks. After his disappointing effort on his last album, Andy had pulled himself together for these sessions. But while Andy may have appeared to have rededicated himself to writing and recording, it turned out to be a last gasp before he abandoned his recording career altogether.

Andy had planned on embarking on a film career that summer by beginning work on the sequel to *Grease*. At the beginning of June, newspapers across the nation reported, "Superstar Andy Gibb will star in 'Son of Grease," a sequel to the box-office hit movie, 'Grease,' and stars of the original version—John Travolta and Olivia Newton-John—will make cameo appearances." But by the end of the summer, the newspaper reports had changed drastically: "Andy Gibb secretly made a screen test for the 'Grease' sequel, and one Paramount exec says, 'We all were less than thrilled.' That's probably why the sequel plans have been shelved temporarily." In 2015, Maxwell Caulfield, who ultimately played the male lead in *Grease 2* (1982), repeated this story. "It was Andy Gibb's part to lose," Caulfield recalled. "He obviously looked like a million bucks and sang like a dream but then they realized he had no screen presence or couldn't act."

But according to Bill Oakes, the executive producer of *Grease 2*, the rumors, press reports, and Andy's own hopes regarding the film were all ill-founded. Andy was never given a screen test for that or any other movie that RSO was involved in making. "Robert [Stigwood] talked about finding a movie for Andy," Oakes recalled, but that was as far as it ever went. The difficulties that Andy had had in completing his third album, and the cancellation of the tour, probably didn't inspire confidence in the likelihood of a smooth production were he to be cast in a film. Moreover, as Oakes pointed out, Stigwood had learned from the *Sgt. Pepper's* movie that pop music stars don't necessarily make the best film stars.

Once his plans for the *Grease* sequel fell through, Andy returned to making frequent television appearances, even though he wouldn't have a new record to promote until November. He appeared on two new syndicated programs that would soon play, for different reasons, important roles in his life: *The John Davidson Show*, which was intended as competition for the Merv Griffin and Mike Douglas shows on which Andy continued to be a frequent guest, and *Solid Gold*, a show that combined the concept of the 1950s *Your Hit Parade* weekly countdown of top pop hits with the presentation of a Las Vegas revue (most notably the "Solid Gold Dancers," who became stars of the show themselves). During Andy's first appearance on Davidson's show, in July 1980, Ringo Starr and Barbara Bach appeared as well. Ringo, whose behavior was, to put it charitably, erratic, told Andy to say hello to his old drinking buddy Maurice and took a Polaroid selfie with him, and then proceeded to vex Davidson so much in the interview that followed that the normally genial host stormed off the set.

RSO initially planned on releasing "Me (Without You)" as the first of the two new singles from the *Greatest Hits* album but decided at the last minute to release "Time Is Time" instead. Andy sang or lip synced the song on several programs, including another appearance on *Solid Gold*, and two new NBC series, *Barbara Mandrell and the Mandrell Sisters* (on which Andy and Barbara also sang a duet) and Marie Osmond's series sans Donny, simply titled *Marie*. Marie and Andy also sang a duet, "Suddenly," which Olivia Newton-John and Cliff Richard had recorded for the soundtrack of the *Xanadu* film for which Andy had been considered (some said even chosen at one point) as a cast member. (Michael Beck, who was cast in that role instead, would be referred to in at least one review of the film as an "Andy Gibb look-a-like.") Only seven episodes of *Marie* were made, however, and after airing four during December 1980 and January 1981, NBC waited until September 1981 to air the remaining three. The episode that featured Andy was the last one, and by the time it aired, "Time Is Time" as well as the *Greatest Hits* album had long since entered and departed the *Billboard* charts.

Making television appearances now required considerably less traveling; in the fall of 1980, Andy moved from Miami to the west coast. He rented a house, which previously had been rented by his friend Robert Redford, in the Malibu Colony. (Andy frequently hit the slopes at Redford's Sundance Mountain Resort in Utah, where the Osmonds also spent a lot of time.) Andy's new neighbors included Larry Hagman, Neil Diamond, and Barbra Streisand, whose *Guilty* album, which included two hit duets with Barry, spent two weeks at number one that fall. The front and back cover photos of *Andy Gibb's Greatest Hits*, which was released in November, were taken near Streisand's rented house.

Andy was not far from family when he moved to Malibu. Earlier in the year, Hugh, Barbara, and Beri had moved into a house in Woodland Hills (about twenty miles away) which Barry bought for them for the then considerable sum of $300,000. Still, Barry was not pleased to see his youngest brother move away from his watchful eye. Andy would later admit that what he saw as Barry's stifling oversight had played a role in his decision to leave

Miami. Barry had become increasingly alarmed over his youngest brother's drug abuse. "Barry told him, 'Look, we heard you're doing some bad things. It's gonna stop, or I'm not going to write you any more hit songs,'" recalled Joey Murcia. The two brothers argued in the recording studio, to the point that Barry lost his temper with Andy on one occasion and, according to one friend of Andy's, struck him in the face.

Andy discussed his decision to move to the west coast during an interview in June 1986. "We had a Gibb compound [in Miami Beach]," he told Kenny Hodges. "Thirty people with Gibb aides . . . I had to get out because I was a party boy then, and everything I did . . . if I did something today that was not good, say, Barry would know by tomorrow morning. Even if it was nowhere near anybody that was with me, and I was alone in a room [and] did something bad or got into drugs . . . just if I did anything, he would know about it." "I don't know how, it's frightening but he's got this . . . I don't know if he's got . . . Mafia watching me or what," Andy said laughingly. "We call it the 'Gibb Mafia' . . . and I got out because everything I did in Miami . . . everybody that lived there knew exactly . . . even if I dated a girl . . . that I'd never dated before . . . all those thirty people would know the next day every detail, and that really used to make me mad."

Andy was correct about Barry keeping close tabs on him and trying to be, as he told Hodges, "the big protector of the family." Barry told an interviewer in 1989 that he had tried to stop Andy from using drugs when Andy lived in Miami Beach. "We even got together with Robert Stigwood to try and kidnap him early on [to stage an intervention, in early 1979]," Barry recalled. "But he was living on a boat and we couldn't get him." As for Andy's move to California in 1980, Barry explained it quite succinctly: "Once he realized that everyone in Miami was trying to stop him from doing it [drugs], then he moved to L.A."

Chapter FIVE

Me (without you)

"I always wanted to be a Bee Gee very badly. And I think today I'd give up what I have now for that." Andy Gibb made this admission on national television, to *Good Morning America*'s Joan Lunden, at the beginning of February 1981. Yet four months later he told a reporter for *People* magazine, "I love my brothers dearly but I knew I had to be independent." The contradiction suggests that perhaps Barry's assessment of Andy's motivation for his move from the east coast to the west was accurate, or that perhaps Andy, having twice been rebuffed or thwarted in his efforts to tour with the Bee Gees, realized that there was little likelihood of his dream coming true. In fact, once Andy moved away from Miami Beach, his brothers would have almost no involvement in his career until 1987, by which time Andy had returned to his brothers' adopted hometown with that career in shambles.

Initially, Andy didn't seem to be taking on any new types of career activities after arriving in Malibu. He appeared on a Dean Martin Christmas special on NBC, singing (or perhaps lip syncing) "Time Is Time," doing a comedy-and-song skit with Martin, and joining Mel Tillis and Erik Estrada for a rendition of Rupert Holmes' number one hit from the previous winter, "Escape (The Piña Colada Song)." Andy also continued to make the rounds on the talk/variety shows. As his friend Kim Richards noted, "They [talk show hosts] liked him. He was an easy interview and he was pleasant, and he was a nice combination of shy but willing to talk openly."

Andy had practically become a semi-regular guest on one of those shows, *The John Davidson Show*, since its premiere during the middle of 1980. He returned to the show on January 6, 1981, to promote his *Greatest Hits* album. He lip synced "Time Is Time" and "Me (Without You)" and then sat down for an interview. Initially, Davidson asked Andy about his *Greatest Hits* album and his career more generally, but then, to Andy's surprise, he mentioned the actress Victoria Principal. A researcher on Davidson's staff had come across a recent *People* magazine article in which Andy was quoted as saying that seeing Victoria was the "one reason" he watched the hit CBS-TV program *Dallas*, in which she portrayed the character Pamela Ewing. Victoria had read this article, too, and she wrote Andy a thank-you note but hadn't mailed it. As fate would have it, while Andy was making his appearance on Davidson's show, Victoria was at the studio next door, where she would be making an appearance that evening on *The Tonight Show*. "Davidson staffers," as an article in *Us Weekly* reported, "made plans to sneak Principal onto their show to surprise Gibb." She did indeed surprise him, giving him a kiss on the neck and handing him the unmailed letter which had still been in her purse. Andy, noted the *Us Weekly* article, "flipped, blushed and managed to stammer a few words. Principal was charmed, and the two hit it off immediately."

Davidson's spokesman Paul Nichols told *People Weekly* writer David Gritten that Andy "was acting like a sixteen-year-old" when he met Victoria on the show, but as Gritten noted, "That did not prevent the Bee Gee baby brother—who has squired such beauties as Marie Osmond, Olivia Newton-John and Susan George—from acquiring her phone number." Two days later, Andy called Victoria. When she told him she was in bed with the flu, he made her chicken soup, and left that and some roses on her doorstep. They talked on the phone for a long time that night and for each of the following two days, by which time she was well enough that Andy came to see her. "They immediately knew they were in love," wrote the veteran Hollywood journalist Jane Ardmore in December 1981, "though Victoria didn't want to admit it." "Andy and I," Victoria told Ardmore, "had to face a fear factor. I, because my marriage [to actor Christopher Skinner] had broken up—my divorce becomes final this month—and Andy, because of his broken marriage. We were doubly fearful that once we were seen together the media would destroy our privacy." "It frightened me to love him," she added, "so I hid it from myself. I responded as I felt, but I didn't admit it." For his part, Andy told Ardmore, "Before I met Victoria, I didn't date at all. I'd been out here a year [actually, only a few months] and hardly ever came out of my house except to visit my parents in Woodland Hills. I just lived in my little place at Malibu, looked at the sea through open windows, and came into town to work."

"I was head over heels in love," Andy later said. "I wanted to spend my life with this woman. Nobody else existed." For the next fourteen months Andy more or less lived in Principal's Hollywood Hills home, although he kept his rented beach house in Malibu (and would spend more time there alone as the relationship became increasingly rocky). Initially the pair kept their relationship under wraps, but when they started appearing together in public, the affair received an immense amount of media coverage. Following a benefit gala at Ford's Theater in Washington, D.C., in March, where Victoria served as an emcee and Andy sang two songs, the *Washington Post* published an article that began "Victoria Principal and Andy Gibb. An item. Pam Ewing leaves Bobby so she can go 'Shadow Dancing' at Ford's Theatre with the youngest Brother Gibb?" The relationship also carried a whiff of scandal for many observers, since Victoria was still not legally divorced and was at least eight years older than Andy. Some media sources claimed that she was older than that; *Us Weekly* reported that she was thirty-six. Andy would tell guest host Joan Rivers on *The Tonight Show* in December 1983 that Victoria had been thirty-three when he met her, which would have made her ten years older than him.

When the relationship began, Victoria and Andy both seemed defensive about the age gap. Victoria's soon-to-be ex-husband was only about one year older than Andy, and she told reporter Carla Hall (with, Hall noted, a smile), "I date two younger men, and suddenly I like younger men. I like what I like at the time. You know when you meet someone and they're spontaneous? That's the way Andy is. I didn't check his I.D." Andy, meanwhile, told another reporter, "I'm tired of being a teen love object. I'm twenty-three going on forty-five. I've had a lot of adventures and I've already traveled to most countries of the world. Sometimes I feel old because I've never mixed with kids my own age. I've always been around older people and been accepted as an adult equal. My feelings and my outlook on life are adult because I've had so many adult experiences."

Indeed, many of the people that Andy was closest to were older than him. His siblings were his seniors by from about eight to thirteen years. Tony Messina, who was close to Andy throughout the 1970s, was also about thirteen years older than him. And as *Us Weekly* noted, "Gibb has a well-known penchant for older women," pointing to his relationships with Susan George and Olivia Newton-John, even though both Andy and Olivia always described their relationship as a close friendship. Ann Jillian, who along with her husband, Andy Murcia (Joey's brother), became friends with Andy and his parents, agreed that "he apparently felt very comfortable calling people who were not his age at all . . . [but] much older."

At the same time that Andy's relationship with Victoria was blossoming, his career seemed to be stagnating. "Time Is Time" had peaked at number fifteen on the Hot 100 and spent seventeen weeks on the chart. It would register at number 100 on *Billboard*'s annual chart of the top 100 hits of the year (1981). By most recording artist's standards, this would be considered a hit, but not by Andy's. To him, the single "didn't do so hot," he told a reporter. His next single, "Me (Without You)," released at the end of February 1981, just scraped the very bottom of the top forty. *Andy Gibb's Greatest Hits* reached only number forty-six on the *Billboard* chart, and it failed to sell the 500,000 copies required for a gold record, although the recentness and very strong sales of Andy's past hits may have hindered the album's success, as many of his fans probably had a good deal of its contents in their collections already. Still, the downward trend was all too apparent, and it had to bother Andy, particularly since the two singles represented an attempt to break away from relying on Barry to write or co-write his hits (even though Barry had ended up with a co-writing credit on "Time Is Time"). By December 1982, when

Joan Lunden asked Andy on *Good Morning America* why he hadn't released a record in a year, he replied, after pointing out that it had been more than a year, "I kind of lost interest for a while."

Joey Murcia later suggested a reason why Andy may have "lost interest" in making records. "When the record company heard that song ["Time Is Time"], they said 'We're not doing any more Andy Gibb-written songs, we want Barry's songs again.' The songs, he [Andy] realized, were just not quite up to par with what Barry was doing for him. And he became very depressed," Murcia recalled, sadly positing that this depression exacerbated Andy's drug abuse.

Nevertheless, Andy returned to the recording studio in 1981, not to record songs written by anyone named Gibb, but rather to record a classic "oldie" with yet another duet partner: Victoria Principal. Victoria had no experience as a singer, but she was openly very ambitious in her career goals. Jeff Witjas, who met and became friends with Andy in 1981 and later became his agent, suspected that Victoria was "[riding] on Andy's coattails because she wanted a recording contract. She wanted to record a song."

If this was indeed the case, however, Andy didn't require much coaxing. John Davidson asked Andy and Victoria to appear on a television special that he was hosting, which would air on CBS on May 26, 1981, the *Fourth Annual National Collegiate Cheerleading Championships*. "We were asked to do a duet," Andy told Associated Press music reporter Mary Campbell later that year, "with the cheerleading kids around us. I decided I was going to go in a studio and do a prerecord for this. Victoria was nervous so I picked a simple song for her and we went in a studio. I did harmonies to her singing. We lip synced to it. Everybody loved the results." The song was "All I Have to Do Is Dream," written by Boudleaux Bryant, originally recorded by the Everly Brothers in 1958. The Bee Gees had counted the Everly Brothers among their biggest early influences. In February 2021, Barry Gibb told Al Roker on NBC's *Today Show*, "Andy and/or Maurice loved the Everly Brothers. . . . Maurice and I were the Everly Brothers more often than not . . . we would sit up late at night and sing Everly Brothers songs . . . and I did that with Andy as well."

The studio in which Andy and Victoria made the "prerecord" was apparently the Bee Gees' Middle Ear. During the first week of April, newspapers across the United States published a United Press International photo of Andy and Victoria with headphones around their necks and the caption, "Recording star Andy Gibb and actress Victoria Principal, who plays Pamela on the TV series 'Dallas,' record a duet for an upcoming TV talk [*sic*] show in a Miami studio. The couple has been dating for several months." In March, a fan had photographed the happy couple on their way into Middle Ear.

After the broadcast of the cheerleading special, Andy told Campbell, "I decided we should go into a studio and record it properly. She has a very pretty voice but won't admit it. She doesn't think she can sing. I think she has a gorgeous voice; it's very, very sweet. We recorded two songs. The other one we banked to use in maybe a future time. It's 'Will You Still Love Me Tomorrow?,' the [Gerry Goffin and] Carole King song," which was an odd choice since Andy had recorded that song one year earlier with Pat Arnold and released it on his *Greatest Hits* album.

RSO Records' New York-based senior vice president, Bob Edson, arranged for Michael Barbiero to co-produce "All I Have to Do Is Dream" with Andy. Barbiero was an up-and-coming producer who was then best known for having remixed a number of R&B and dance hits, including the Jacksons' "Blame It on the Boogie," and his wife worked in RSO's publicity department. The first session for the record took place at Manhattan's Mediasound Studios, but only the instrumental tracks were completed there. Andy arrived first and didn't want to start recording vocals without Victoria. When she arrived and entered the control room, Barbiero recalled, she "stripped off her sweatshirt," revealing a sleeveless white t-shirt that looked like an undershirt. The drummer, veteran session performer Allan Schwartzberg, was so taken aback that he stopped playing, which caused the rest of the band to stop as well.

"Andy went *crazy*," Barbiero remembered more than forty years later. "He didn't have a sense of humor about it. He said, 'Put that sweatshirt back on! Can't you see you're wrecking the entire session?'" Victoria complied but was visibly embarrassed. "Because of that outburst," Barbiero observed, "the tension between them was really, really difficult to deal with from a production standpoint. So we agreed . . . that we would do the vocals at another date." Barbiero had to fly to Los Angeles with the master tape for that session, which went smoothly. Andy and Victoria sang together throughout most of "All I Have to Do Is Dream," with Andy taking a couple of solos.

RSO released the single in late July 1981. *Cash Box* picked it as one of four "Hits Out of the Box" in its August 8 issue, along with singles by Kim Carnes, REO Speedwagon, and Quincy Jones featuring James Ingram. Andy and Victoria sang or lip synced the single on several television programs, including *Solid Gold* and an episode of Phil Donahue's talk show in which the genial host seemed enthralled by the couple, telling them, "Boy, you'd better be having fun, because if you're not, nobody is!"

Despite *Cash Box*'s faith in the single's prospects and the promotional television appearances, it failed to crack the top forty, reaching only number fifty-nine on the *Cash Box* Top 100 Singles chart. It fared just a little better on the *Billboard* Hot 100, where it peaked at number fifty-one, and it was the least successful single Andy had ever released. Andy, of course, was well aware that the record had not been much of a hit (although it at least reached number twenty-five on the *Billboard* Adult Contemporary chart and number thirty-nine on the Canadian trade magazine *RPM*'s pop singles chart). After the record had fallen off the charts, Andy told Mary Campbell that "it didn't do very well. It was my first production effort and her first chance on record."

Oddly, Andy and Victoria did not make a video for the record, even though MTV made its debut on August 1, 1981. Andy had made videos for "I Just Want to Be Your Everything" and "Shadow Dancing." Of course, with RSO Records now losing money, Stigwood and other label executives may have not wanted to pay for making a video, especially when there was no new Andy Gibb album to sell.

Many years later, long after Andy's death, Principal told an interviewer, "Warner Brothers offered me an album deal [after the duet with Andy was released] and I declined because I knew that I was not a great singer." Principal also said that "Andy and I were deeply in love and really enjoyed the project together." But Bill Oakes expressed what was probably the prevailing sentiment at RSO about the project: "I thought, 'If Al Coury can't get Andy a hit, no one can.'" When the single had finished its climb up the charts, *Billboard* referred to it and a current Debbie Harry solo single as commercial "disappointments," noting that there could be "little cheering in the RSO camp" over the chart placing (and sales) of the Andy/Victoria duet. The *Billboard* column added that this was "the first time Gibb hasn't been produced by brother Barry, Karl Richardson and Albhy Galuten. It also marks the first time he hasn't reached the top 40. Draw your own conclusions." For Andy, who was insecure about his own contributions to his success as a recording artist and who, like his brothers, followed *Billboard* whenever he had a record out, the comment had to sting.

Aside from the two duets with Victoria, Andy got involved in one other recording project in 1981—in fact, while "All I Have to Do Is Dream" often has been listed in Andy Gibb discographies as his last single, he appeared on one more duet of sorts. At some point Andy had met Cheryl Lynn Flor, a former model from San Diego who made disco-pop records, without much success, under the name "Flower" during the late 1970s and early '80s. In 1981, she recorded her last album, a self-titled release that came out in 1982 on the small Los Angeles-based label Montage Records. Sessions for the album took place in Montreal and Los Angeles. The L.A. sessions were held at Jennifudy Studios, a small studio in North Hollywood, later known as Entourage Studios until it closed in 2015. Andy contributed to the album's single, "Here Inside," by arranging and recording what were referred to on the label of the single as "background vocals," but in reality, although Andy can scarcely be heard in the first minute, his voice is prominent enough after that point that the record almost qualifies as a duet.

"Here Inside" was released in 1982 in the United States, Canada, and some European countries, but it did not become a hit and in fact was so obscure that many of Andy's friends never knew about the record. Scott Paton recalled, four decades later, that "Andy made a passing reference to it during a discussion about his 'next album' in which he was going to be 'more involved in the creative process.' When he mentioned 'Flower,' I asked, 'Fleur?!,' maybe only 10 percent serious." (Paton was referring to Fleur Thiemeyer, a fashion designer who was an intimate friend of Andy's.) When Andy explained that "Flower" was actually a woman named Cheryl Lyn, Paton thought that he meant the R&B/disco singer Cheryl Lynn, who had a major hit in the winter of 1978-79 with "Got to Be Real." Andy "clarified that it was someone else," Paton recalled. Andy's friend Michael Miller, who worked with him on *Solid Gold*, said in 2021 that he could "remember him talking about" the record with Flower but "never heard it." Paton, who worked in radio, never saw or heard the record, either, probably in part because it was released by a small record company that lacked promotional clout.

"Here Inside" would be the last single ever released with Andy Gibb's name on the label. The Bee Gees wrote a song in 1981 called "Heart (Stop Beating in Time)" and intended to give it to Andy to record, but when it became clear that he wasn't interested, they gave it to Leo Sayer. Sayer's version reached number twenty-two on the British charts in 1982 but missed the American charts.

By the time RSO released Andy and Victoria's single, Andy finally had started to take advantage of some of the new career opportunities that he ostensibly had moved to L.A. to pursue. In early February 1981, Broadway producer Joseph Papp and director Wilford Leach saw Andy's appearance on *Good Morning America* and invited him to see their Broadway musical *The Pirates of Penzance*. This fast-paced Gilbert and Sullivan operetta was just over a century old, having premiered in both England and New York in 1879. Papp and the New York Shakespeare Festival freshened the operetta just enough to make it more appealing to modern audiences, and Wilford cast

Linda Ronstadt and Rex Smith in the starring roles of Mabel and Frederic. The production opened in July 1980 at Central Park's open-air Delacorte Theatre, and it became enormously popular. In January 1981 Papp and Leach took *Pirates* to Broadway, with Ronstadt and Smith still onboard, and reaped not only outstanding ticket sales but numerous Tony Awards as well. Papp and Leach then made plans to put together a second production which would tour theaters in major cities, starting with Los Angeles. Therein lay the motive for Papp and Leach's invitation to Andy to see the Broadway production. Andy was "enthralled" by the show, according to an article in *People*, and told Leach, "I'd love to be involved in something like this." "Good," Leach replied. "When can you start?"

Andy agreed to accept the role, with an opening date of June 10 at L.A.'s Ahmanson Theatre. When he started rehearsing, he soon realized that he was going to need formal voice training to sing the demanding arias of *Pirates* on a stage without a microphone in front of him. "My voice was so worn out," he told *People*, "that when I went to blast, it came out like a croak. It scared the life out of me." Papp arranged for Andy to spend three weeks training with a renowned New York voice coach, Marge Rivingston, who had helped many a star of Papp's productions train for the demands of singing in theater. In 1982 Andy said that training for *Pirates* had made him realize that he was basically a "weak pop singer." He added that Rivingston "is like my second mother—she's my security blanket." Working with Rivingston, he said, extended his range by six notes.

Papp and Leach found their West Coast Fredric before they found their Mabel. Some newspaper reports said that Papp was offering the role to Marie Osmond, while other reports said that he had offered her the role in the Broadway production after Linda Ronstadt started missing shows. While Andy undoubtedly would have welcomed starring alongside Marie, he publicly suggested that Pat Benatar and Nicolette Larson would each be a good fit. Papp and Leach ended up hiring Pam Dawber, who at the time was starring alongside Robin Williams in the ABC-TV series *Mork & Mindy*. Andy did not complain, and in fact he and Pam became very close.

Andy credited Victoria with giving him the confidence to step into the new role. "I was ruining my own career before I met this woman," he told *People* in June 1981. Victoria, he said, helped coach him for his stage debut, and "was the best acting coach I could have had." *Los Angeles Times* reviewer Dan Sullivan, who had panned the Broadway production, raved about the L.A. version, writing that it "blows you out of the water."

At first, Andy seemed delighted with the new turn that his career had taken. According to *People*, he "loved the glitter of opening night." "But after three weeks," RSO publicist Ronnie Lippin later recalled, "he called me and seemed lonesome. He wanted every night to be opening night." That he would seem lonesome makes one wonder about the state of his relationship with Victoria at the time, especially since she reportedly attended twenty-six performances of *Pirates*. According to the celebrity gossip tabloids, which covered Andy and Victoria on a regular basis, Andy was pressuring her to marry him but she was resisting. Furthermore, her marriage to Christopher Skinner wouldn't legally end until later in the year. Nevertheless, the *National Enquirer* reported that Victoria did promise to marry Andy as soon as possible while she was at his bedside at the Cedars-Sinai Medical Center in Los Angeles on the night of Tuesday, July 7, 1981, where she had rushed him from her house when he suddenly became ill with severe stomach pains—a frightening and also foreboding occurrence that foreshadowed his sudden death less than seven years later.

Andy left the hospital after four days and returned to the stage the following week, and when Brad Lachman, the producer of *Solid Gold*, caught one of his performances, he decided to offer Andy a job as the show's co-host. "What I liked about him was that he was a very charming, vulnerable, and charismatic performer," Lachman would tell a reporter for *People* following Andy's death. The executive producer of *Solid Gold*, Bob Banner, received a good word about Andy from Andy Murcia, whom Banner knew from when Ann Jillian had appeared on a TV special that he had produced.

Andy replaced Dionne Warwick, amidst press reports that Banner and officials at Paramount Studios, the show's distributor, had "made the switch in a bid to add a 'more contemporary' flavor to the program and to increase the number of young-adult viewers." Banner signed Andy for forty-six episodes at a salary of $10,000 each (equivalent to $30,000 in 2021 dollars), which was $2,000 less per episode than what Warwick had made. (But if one Gibb brother indirectly damaged Warwick's career and income, the other three made up for it one year later by giving her their song "Heartbreaker," which became her first top ten hit in over three years. The Bee Gees rode out the anti-disco backlash by writing hits for other recording artists, but Andy did not have that outlet, which was at least in part why he turned to theater and television.)

One reason why Banner paid Andy less than he had paid Warwick, most likely, was that the producers had decided that he would have a regular female co-host, while Warwick had not had a regular co-host. They wanted Tanya Tucker alongside Andy. "Tucker, however, wanted her income and billing to be equal to those of Gibb," wrote journalist Gary Deeb, "a reasonable request that the 'Solid Gold' bosses somehow refused to grant. Too bad for us." Ironically, Andy and Tanya would become romantically involved, briefly, one year later and would remain friends for the rest of his life.

After failing to reach terms with Tucker, the producers "auditioned five or six women with me," Andy told Mary Campbell, "to see how we looked together. Marilyn McCoo got it. I think it was Marilyn I worked best with right away. We clicked." Marilyn agreed, telling *Jet* magazine in early 1982 that "we have a nice working relationship. It's easy to interact with him." Marilyn had been a vocalist in the 5th Dimension, whose run of hits from 1967 to 1973 included two that reached number one on the Hot 100, "Aquarius/Let the Sunshine In" and "Wedding Bell Blues," in 1969. She and her husband, Billy Davis, Jr., who had also been in the group, also hit number one in 1976 with their duet "You Don't Have to Be a Star (To Be in My Show)."

Andy's relationship with Victoria seemed to be generating more publicity, however, than his career activities. In Australia, his ex-wife Kim told a reporter that "Andy will never marry again. Although we're thousands of miles apart, I know Andy better than anyone else. I know why he won't marry, but I can't say. But I can tell you he's not serious about Victoria. He just doesn't know what he wants to do." To Kim, Victoria was just another in the procession of Andy's celebrity girlfriends, although clearly she was wrong. "I don't get upset by these things anymore," she said. "I'll know when he's ready to marry again—if ever." In fact, Andy would later lament in interviews how close he and Victoria had come to getting married and how he believed that doing so would have saved their relationship.

By this time, Peta was three-and-a-half years old, but Andy had had no contact with her since their meeting on her second birthday. She would see him on television, though. "I remember mum calling me into a room once, pointing at *Solid Gold* on the TV and saying, 'That's your dad,'" she recalled in 2017. "It was so difficult for me to reconcile that this guy in gold pants was anything to do with me or my life, or the guy who called me from time to time. It was pretty confusing actually."

Andy began working on *Solid Gold* in late August 1981. The first episode hosted by him and Marilyn aired during the weekend of September 12-13, with the date and time varying from market to market since the show was syndicated. Andy sang "(Love Is) Thicker than Water," and he and guest Olivia Newton-John sang "Rest Your Love on Me." (Olivia was on the show to perform her new single, "Physical.") In subsequent episodes, Andy would sing "Shadow Dancing" and "(Our Love) Don't Throw It All Away." He and Marilyn would sing "I Just Want to Be Your Everything" as a duet, in a lower key than the record (sans falsetto), and Victoria Principal joined Andy on one episode to sing "All I Have to Do Is Dream." "We rehearsed that in the dressing room," recalled *Solid Gold* musical director Michael Miller, "and they were just as happy as could be. And they sang really well together." "She was there often," Miller added, "at a lot of the tapings."

Since Andy sang at least one song per episode, either by himself or as a duet, he also sang hits by other recording artists, as did Marilyn, and sometimes Andy and Marilyn duetted on current hits, such as "Endless Love" and "Through the Years." Andy also sometimes duetted, as did Marilyn, with guests on their hits. For example, he sang "All I Ever Need Is You" with Dottie

West, who had recorded that song with Kenny Rogers, and "Best Thing That Ever Happened to Me" with Gladys Knight. Andy, Miller observed, "could sing with anybody and it wouldn't sound out of place. Whereas a lot of singers trying to do duets, they just don't blend, but he had one of those voices that does."

In addition to performing the duet with Victoria, a personal highlight of *Solid Gold* for Andy came in November when he got to proudly introduce a recorded clip of the Bee Gees performing their new single "Living Eyes." Robin and Maurice visited Andy on the set once; Maurice brought his son Adam, who was five years old at the time, and Andy introduced to him to his co-star, the puppeteer Wayland Flowers, who let Adam "meet" the puppet Madame. Michael Miller could still remember that day forty years later. "We had a lot of fun backstage!" More generally, Miller recalled, "Andy and I always had a lot of fun together backstage, whether during rehearsals in his dressing room, or during breaks when we'd talk about anything and everything. We were only two years apart in age, so we shared a lot of the same interests and, therefore, had a lot to yak about. Plus, he really liked my endless jokes!"

For about three weeks, Andy was working on both *The Pirates of Penzance* and *Solid Gold*. This meant that during those weeks there were days that he had to be on the set of *Solid Gold* from 11 a.m. to 7 p.m. and then be onstage at the Ahmanson Theatre at 8 o'clock. "I was really exhausted," he told Mary Campbell. It was an impressive display of work ethic, and the assertion on the 1997 VH-1 *Behind the Music* episode on Andy that the *Pirates* production left him behind when it moved on to San Francisco because he was unreliable was false. Andy could not go with the production to San Francisco because of his role on *Solid Gold*. He threw a party for the cast as the L.A. production came to a close, but within days newspapers were reporting that his co-star Barry Bostwick, "a real pro who boasts a Tony Award for his work in the theater, is scathing about the legit efforts of Andy Gibb and Pam Dawber" and "thinks they should stay in TV where they belong." (Yet Bostwick would co-star with Andy again in another *Pirates* production a year later.) Another syndicated column reported "dark mutterings from Andy Gibb's 'Pirates of Penzance' co-stars in L.A.," who were "still tsk tsking about his 'indifference, unprofessional attitude and lack of enthusiasm.'" But Andy's castmate Wally Kurth, who was just a few months younger than him, would remember him forty years later as "surprisingly shy and unassuming. He was a good Frederic."

Despite Andy's indefatigable efforts during his first few weeks on *Solid Gold*, he soon started missing rehearsals and tapings. Marilyn McCoo recalled, years after his death, that Brad Lachman and the show's writers would have to prepare two versions of each episode: one for Andy and one in case Andy didn't show up. "At times," revealed a 1985 newspaper article about *Solid Gold*, "Lachman simply grabbed a guest and begged him to be co-host." Lachman was quoted in that article as saying, "He [Andy] was going through a lot of emotional problems with his involvement with Victoria Principal." "If something wasn't going well between them," Lachman told *People* just after Andy died, "he was devastated." Unfortunately, this was the case all too frequently; as Andy later admitted, "We split up several times before the final split-up." Lachman was sympathetic, though; he had liked Andy. "He really meant well," Lachman remembered. "He wasn't being difficult. He was going through problems he couldn't deal with. He wanted everyone to love him. He had so much going for him, and he just couldn't believe it."

The "problems" with Victoria also exacerbated Andy's reliance on cocaine, which he had seemingly gotten under control for a time. Michael Miller said that whenever Andy was at the KTLA-TV studio for rehearsals and tapings, he "was always fully together, with a twinkle in his eye, ready to work and happy to do whatever was needed." Nevertheless, Hugh Gibb, who was normally fairly passive with his grown sons but could sometimes be gruff, confronted Andy one day while visiting him in his dressing room on the set of *Solid Gold*. "I said to him, 'What are you taking this rubbish [cocaine] for?'" Hugh told Mary Murphy when she interviewed him and Barbara for *Entertainment Tonight* one year after Andy's death. Andy replied, "It's the only way I can handle her."

Andy's friends had their doubts about the relationship. "I didn't think that relationship would ever last," Jeff Witjas recalled four decades later. "He was a boy, she was a woman." Joey Murcia would look back on the Andy-Victoria romance by saying that she wasn't "good for what was wrong with him . . . and I don't want to go any further into it." In an interview for *Entertainment Tonight* in 1989, Barry Gibb admitted that "Andy's troubles were going on long before he met Victoria," but nevertheless many of Andy's friends as well as his family would view the relationship as a turning point—for the worse—in his life. Among his family, only Maurice would dissent from this point of view. "I think his relationship with Victoria Principal was absolutely beautiful. It was everything he dreamed of," Maurice said in the VH-1 *Behind the Music* episode. "And that's the only important thing here. It's not what I think or what anybody else thinks. Andy thought the world of her."

When the veteran Hollywood scribe Jane Ardmore profiled Andy and Victoria's relationship in late 1981, Victoria admitted or at least implied that Andy wanted to marry her, but, she told Ardmore, "I need time, and Andy understands that." Andy seemed to agree. "Nothing's going to change the relationship we have," he insisted. But Ardmore, who had seen it all in Hollywood, seemed to have her doubts. "These two do and say all the right things," she wrote. "But Hollywood romances often *sound* like they're forever. Then days later, the love birds sue each other for palimony and go their separate ways. Some say the Principal-Gibb match is just too good to be true. Perhaps their future could be summed up in the title of their next record: 'Will You Still Love Me Tomorrow?'" Ardmore's speculation would soon prove to be accurate, other than the fact that the "next record" was never released.

As it became clear that that record would not be released, Andy began to express renewed interest in—as well as concern over—his recording career. "I need a hit record out badly at the moment," he told Mary Campbell in December 1981. "I've got to get back in the studio and do it again. The trouble is my time schedule is so busy. . . . I may have to try to cut an album the days I'm not taping the TV show. I may just have a shot at it. I may do a couple of singles instead. But I really should do something. It has been long enough already." Campbell then asked Andy if his brothers couldn't write another hit single for him. "Yes," he replied, "but I'd like to get to writing my own songs. It's very important to me. I've got about eight new songs I've written. I'd like to do as many of mine as possible."

As 1982 began, he told journalist Ron Cowan that he no longer dreamed of becoming the fourth Bee Gee. "I'm very happy with what I'm doing on my own," Andy said. "I've grown up a lot." "Gibb, in what he calls a 'role reversal,'" wrote Cowan, "is no longer pursuing his brothers' advice and direction. Interviewed recently by phone, he said he is out to make his own career." Andy told Cowan that he wanted to get back to recording and touring. "I don't think I'll be that keen to do another [TV] show right away," he suggested, also indicating that he might not stay on *Solid Gold* after finishing his 46-episode contract. He told Cowan that he wanted to shed "his 'younger brother of the Bee Gees' reputation." "I don't think I gave them [his fans] the Andy Gibb that is Andy Gibb," he said. He told Cowan that he was determined to get his recording career back on track on his own. "I've had my teenybopper breakthrough albums, but I haven't had my serious breakthrough yet," Andy insisted.

Almost two full years after the release of his last all-new album, though, Andy was nervous. "I've been terrified the last two years," he admitted. "I don't know what to expect. It's very touchy for me." Andy told Cowan that he hoped to start recording his next album in February, adding that the record would surprise his fans. "It's certainly not going to be anything people expect," he declared. In mid-February, he confirmed to another reporter that he'd be returning to the recording studio that month. "It's been a long time since I've done something, and I'm going to come back strong," he vowed.

Recording an album without the involvement of the Bee Gees seemed particularly important to Andy. "I don't want to be a clone of my brothers," he told yet another interviewer around this time. "My sound is similar to theirs—that's not easy to escape. Now I intend to do it my way. I must do it for my own piece of mind." He even told RSO's Associate Director of Artists and Repertoire (A&R), Jan "Cash" Landy, to be on the lookout for good songs for him to record. Even though neither of Andy's two 1981 releases—"Me (Without You)" and the duet with Victoria—had been big hits, he still had a large fan base. In January 1982, an annual Gallup Youth Survey poll of American teenagers' favorite male and female singers had Andy ranked as the eighth most popular male vocalist, down only two notches from the previous poll.

By then, however, his relationship with Victoria was becoming increasingly rocky, and, as Brad Lachman already had discovered, for Andy the relationship took precedence over his career and professional commitments. The timing was ironic, as newspapers were reporting that Andy had "counted out sixty thousand dollars [about $170,000 in 2021 dollars] for a super deluxe Porsche—Victoria Principal's Valentine gift." Andy's friend Pam Rossi, who was one of the *Solid Gold* dancers, recalled that he surprised Victoria with the car when she visited the show's set late one night. "I think it was red, and he was so excited . . . but unfortunately, which was weird . . . she didn't really like the color, so he made the guy from the auto place, like at two in the morning, open up and exchange the color of the car." Pam was "flabbergasted" at how "picky" Victoria was. But Pam knew that Andy was "*so* in love" with Victoria. "She was his world."

Unfortunately, that world was about to implode. On March 11, just six days after Andy's twenty-fourth birthday, New York *Daily News* gossip columnist Liz Smith reported that "it's all over between Andy Gibb and Victoria Principal. He has moved back to his own house in Malibu. She'll keep the Porsche he gave her and he'll keep the speedboat she gave him." (He ended up selling it not long after the split though.) Andy's plans for reentering the recording studio apparently fell by the wayside.

On March 18, Marilyn Beck's syndicated Hollywood gossip column reported, "Talk about taking the breakup of a romance hard! Andy Gibb is so shook up about his split from 'Dallas" Victoria Principal, he not only didn't show up for his scheduled appearance on Monday night's 'American Movie Awards,' he has informed producers of his 'Solid Gold' series not to expect him for shooting the balance of the week." Andy was to have sung the Christopher Cross hit "Arthur's Theme (Best That You Can Do)" on the movie awards show; his absence proved to be a lucky break for his last-minute replacement, a little-known singer-actor named Brad Maule. The performance thrust Maule into the spotlight, and in 1984 he began a role on the popular soap opera *General Hospital* that he would hold for twenty-two years.

On the very day that Beck's column ran, however, Andy and Victoria reunited and attended another awards show, the *People's Choice Awards* on CBS. While there, Andy saw Bob Hope. Andy had been on two previous Hope TV specials and was scheduled to appear on another that was to be taped over the coming weekend (starting in two days). Hope had Andy slated to be in three skits and, with no new single to perform, sing, ironically at this point, "(Our Love) Don't Throw It All Away." Hope apparently had heard about Andy's recent no-shows, but Andy, as Beck wrote in her March 25th column, "assured Hope he would definitely be on hand for [the] taping of Bob's special."

But Andy and Victoria started arguing, albeit quietly, at the awards show. Afterwards, as Andy later told a journalist, "Victoria and I went to pick up some Indian curry and went back to her house. We were fighting in the car and when we got back to the house we just started ranting and screaming and pushing and shoving. In the end, it got a little physical. I stormed out and drove back to my house at Malibu Beach. That was the last time I saw Victoria." Andy didn't show up for the Hope special, and when Hope phoned him and tried to coax him into doing the show, Andy, who later admitted that he was "spaced out on cocaine" at the time, apologized and hung up on him. Hope managed to bring in Pat Boone as a last-minute replacement, but Boone at that time certainly wouldn't have drawn young viewers like Andy would have. Andy would later repeatedly and publicly express embarrassment and regret for having brushed aside his obligation to Hope; eventually Hope forgave him and let him appear on television specials in 1984 and 1986.

Andy also left Brad Lachman and *Solid Gold* stranded. "I just fell apart," he later admitted, "and didn't care about anything. I started to do cocaine around the clock—about $1,000 a day. I stayed awake for two weeks locked in my bedroom. The producers kept calling up, sending cars for me, but I refused to go. . . . I really think the major reason I fell from stardom was my affair with Victoria." Lachman finally had no choice but to fire Andy. While Andy's claim to have been spending about $1,000 per day on cocaine may have been one of the exaggerations that he was prone to making, if it was true then he was using about six grams per day, an enormous amount that would cause a fatal overdose for most people and which certainly would have damaged his heart.

As Andy spiraled into a dark, desperate depression that damaged his health and his career, his contract with RSO expired in March 1982. Robert Stigwood did not offer to renew it. Relations between Stigwood and the Gibbs had become strained when the Bee Gees sued him and RSO in October 1980, which led to an almost immediate countersuit from Stigwood. The suits were settled out of court in 1981, but some bitterness lingered, and Andy had barely recorded since 1980 anyway. Furthermore, Stigwood was about to leave the record business; RSO Records, which had made him a fortune during the mid-to-late 1970s, was by now losing millions. Stigwood already had begun downsizing the label's operations and staff considerably and would shut it down by the end of 1983. Nevertheless, he would recall in the VH-1 *Behind the Music* episode that "[it] absolutely broke my heart" to drop Andy. Looking back almost four decades later, former RSO president Bill Oakes said that dropping Andy must indeed have been difficult for Stigwood, who thought of all the RSO artists—especially the Gibbs, the lawsuit notwithstanding—"like family." But by then, as Oakes pointed out, Andy himself was costing the label more money than he was bringing in.

Suddenly Andy no longer had a television contract, a recording contract, a song publishing contract, or a manager, although his personal manager and friend Marc Hulett, who was only two years older than him, had in essence been serving that role already for the past two years and would officially begin doing so after the break with RSO. Not that Andy was ready to start working again anyway. He remained entirely out of the public eye—although certainly not out of the gossip columns and tabloids—for the next four months.

"I wanted to commit suicide," Andy later admitted. His family suspected as much. The Bee Gees' personal manager, Dick Ashby, told a reporter, "The family called to make sure he was okay. Barry Gibb's wife [Linda, with whom Andy was close] spoke to him . . . and he sounded very calm." Journalist Michele Willens, whose father owned the Malibu beach house Andy was living in, would later recall that her family heard a rumor that Andy had "tried to commit suicide in the house when [Victoria] broke up with him." Andy spent three days at a hospital in Santa Barbara, where he was registered under the pseudonym "Roy Lipton," being treated for what his father called "a nervous breakdown." After that, seventeen-year-old Beri, with whom Andy had spent much of his childhood, moved into the beach house to try to help him recover. She told a reporter why she thought the relationship had failed: "The trouble there was that Victoria has too much ambition and doesn't have the time to put into a relationship." Andy's mother later said that she had known the relationship would not end well for her youngest son. "He was obsessed with her," Barbara told Australian journalist Sharon Krum in 2004, "but she didn't treat him well."

A syndicated newspaper column in August 1982 quoted an unnamed "source close to both" Andy and Victoria as saying, "He was much more dependent on her than she wanted him to be, and than she was on him. I think she loved him but not as much as he loved her. I think he took the whole thing much more seriously than she did. Actually, I think he got to be a pain in the neck . . ." The same column also reported that shortly before Andy and Victoria split, they were spotted in a New York restaurant, and when he extended a hand toward hers, she slapped it and snapped, "Don't do that."

Victoria was quoted in *People* in January 1983 as saying, "Our breakup was preceded and precipitated by Andy's use of drugs. I did everything I could to help him. But then I told him he would have to choose between me and his problem." In the context of the article, it is difficult to tell if this was a fresh quotation or a statement that she had made months earlier.

In the fall of 1985, Andy suggested a different version of events when Canadian radio interviewer Bob Durant asked him about Victoria. Andy told

Durant that Victoria had "had a drug problem when I met her, she was an alcoholic, and [had] a coke problem and I was off it, and we got back onto it together . . . and just because of sexual things and other things we got back onto it together . . . and that got me heavily back into it . . . and then we stopped . . . when we really fell in love we agreed to stop everything, because we didn't like each other on drugs . . . of course . . . and at the very end of it all, after about fifteen months or something, we just started arguing. I don't think we were meant to be. . . . . she is a 'siren on the rocks.' She is a very seductive woman . . . very few men can resist her. But I will say that yeah, she took me basically back to it . . . but I wish her all the best."

In 1986 Barry Gibb wrote a song with George Bitzer, who had played keyboards for the Bee Gees and Andy, and Randy Jackson, later of *American Idol* fame. Barry recorded the song for an intended solo album, but his label, MCA Records, declined to release the album. The song, "The Savage Is Loose," can be heard today online, though. Its lyrics mention "the woman in Dallas [or *Dallas*?]" and describe her as having a runny nose.

A few (although not most) of Andy's friends, however, said they believed that Victoria was very much in love with him. As the first anniversary of Andy's passing approached, *Entertainment Tonight* aired a segment looking back at his life and death. It included an interview with Hugh and Barbara, and short snippets of Beri, Tanya Tucker, and Victoria talking about him. "What I know," Victoria said, "is that I tried everything that I was capable of, and that I think any human being would be capable of, in an effort to rescue someone that you love very much. And there came a point in time when I had to face the fact that I could go on trying to rescue Andy and sacrifice my own life, or I had to stand apart and hope that he would be able to help himself."

Chapter SIX

Any Dream Will Do

"I have been to hell and back, I suppose, literally. I had a very, very bad nervous breakdown. . . . I did quite a lot of cocaine, which I no longer do. . . . I had everything I wanted and I just blew it all up." Andy Gibb made this confession to Joan Lunden before a national television audience on *Good Morning America* on July 23, 1982, four months after his final split from Victoria Principal. He also disclosed that he had been seeing his psychiatrist (and Malibu neighbor), James Grould, every day, and said that Grould "literally saved my life."

It was a remarkably bold and brave television appearance, especially given how the tabloids and gossip columns had been sensationalizing Andy's problems ever since the end of his relationship with Victoria. (Andy admitted, though, in 1983, that notwithstanding the tendency of tabloids like the *National Enquirer* to "overexaggerate," their reports were "not that far off, either.") Andy looked extremely uncomfortable at several points in the interview and on the verge of tears at other points. "For about twelve months" after the breakup with Victoria, Barbara Gibb would recall in 1997, "he was devastated. We had a bad time with him, and he'd cry for hours and hours."

Marc Hulett had decided that Andy should do the *Good Morning America* interview, not only to announce his return to work but also to explain for himself why he had failed to fulfill his obligations to, among others, the producers of *Solid Gold* and Bob Hope, and to assure his fans and future employers that he was now back on track. To broach the idea with Andy, however,

Hulett turned to Andy's publicist at Rogers & Cowan, George Dassinger. As Dassinger recalled more than three decades later, "[Andy's] manager calls me one day, his friend—often that's the case [that stars have friends as managers] . . . some of them are professionals and some of them are inadequate authorities. Andy's manager was a friend, and he was a pretty good manager, actually. And he calls me up and says, 'You know, Andy's got a cocaine problem.' And I said, 'Mmm hmm, no kidding.' And he said, 'I need for you to do me a favor.' And I went, 'What?' And he said, 'I want you to call him up and convince him to go on *Good Morning America* and talk about his cocaine addiction.' And I went, *'What?* Why is Andy going to listen to me?' And he goes, 'George, he's been with you several times, believe me, if you call him . . .' I said, 'You're his friend for years, how come you don't do it?' 'He won't listen to me . . . call him!' And I go, 'Marc, [sighs] . . . I don't know, I feel awkward about this.' He said, 'I'm *begging* you, please call him.'"

"So," Dassinger continued, "I call up Andy, and Andy says, 'Do you realize what you're asking me to do? You're asking me to bare my soul, the thing that I keep the most secret, even my brothers don't know how bad my problem is.' And I go, 'Yeah, Andy, I do. I fully do. I couldn't do this. *I* couldn't go on *Good Morning America* and talk about a *drug problem* that I have. I couldn't do that!' He said—and there's a pregnant pause and I'm going, 'Uh, this could go one way or another'—and he said, 'Okay, but I'll only do it on one condition, one condition only.' And I said, 'What's that?' And he said, 'You have to go with me.' I said, 'Of course. Absolutely.' And I hung up the phone and I'm sitting there thinking, 'Oh my God! I can't believe what I just did. I know it's gonna help him. But this is gonna be a really weird day, and this is stuff I had no idea that I would ever be put into those positions.'"

After, indeed, baring his soul to Joan Lunden and a national television audience, Andy concluded the six-minute interview by discussing his plans to get back to work. He had just accepted an offer to once again play the role of Frederic in *The Pirates of Penzance*, this time for two weeks at the Royal Alexandra Theater in Toronto in August. He told Lunden that his was the only major role to be cast in the production at that point, but subsequently his Los Angeles co-star Barry Bostwick signed on as well. Despite the press reports from the previous fall that claimed that Bostwick had been unhappy with Andy's efforts, in April 1982 Bostwick told a reporter that he thought it had been a good idea to cast Andy in the role. "It brings in a younger audience," he explained. "I think it's a way to tap an untapped audience. And it was good for us as well as for the audience; it's ultimately modernizing the theatrical experience. Gilbert and Sullivan always provided popular entertainment, and I think by reinterpreting the show we brought it back to the people of today."

At the time of Andy's appearance on *Good Morning America*, the Broadway production of *Pirates* was still running, albeit by then with Maureen McGovern and Patrick Cassidy in the starring roles that had been held by Linda Ronstadt and Rex Smith. Andy stayed in Manhattan for just over a week and went to see *Pirates*, and he also attended several parties: a birthday party for McGovern, a party that some friends threw for him at the famed disco Studio 54, and, just before he left for Toronto, another party held for him at another well-known Big Apple disco of the day, Xenon. At McGovern's birthday party, Andy hugged actress Donna Pescow while posing for a photo and, according to *People Weekly*, said "Wait till Victoria sees this." In fact, as tabloids noted, Principal was in Manhattan at the time herself, picking up a "Woman of the Year" Award at the Waldorf Astoria, but she left town more quickly than Andy did, and he was apparently unaware that she was even there.

Before Andy went to Toronto, he met a woman with whom, briefly, he would be linked romantically by the tabloids and gossip columns: Tanya Tucker, the country music star who might have become his *Solid Gold* co-star in 1981 had the producers been willing to meet her demands for equal pay and billing with him. In her autobiography, *Nickel Dreams: My Life* (1997), Tucker recalled meeting Andy one night at Cafe Central on the Upper West Side. The book includes a photograph that captured the moment, although Tucker isn't in it herself. A few feet away from a smiling Andy, though, is a beaming Barbara Gibb, who, with Victoria out of her youngest son's life, resumed her practice of frequently traveling with him. Tanya remembered Andy as "handsome" with "particularly striking" eyes, which she described as "so open, trusting, and friendly."

Tanya, who was coming out of a recent high-profile romance of her own (with Glen Campbell), was interested in Andy, and Andy told Scott Paton that he was interested in Tucker too. On Monday, August 2, 1982, the New York *Daily News* reported that "you should have seen Tanya and Andy cooing it up at Xenon" at a late-night Saturday party, and that Tanya had "placed a call to the disco to make sure Gibb really was there" before she came. "The moment she arrived, she sat on Gibb's lap and hardly left the laddie alone. They were still going strong after 3:15 a.m., when we called it a night. This was the second time in less than a week," the gossipy report continued, "that Gibb and Tucker have displayed their affections in public. Now, he's telling pals that he will begin looking for a pad here in the Big Apple just as soon as he finishes his two-week Toronto gig. (So he can be close to Tanya when she comes to town?)"

Eighteen days later, the *Daily News* published another item involving the pair, noting that Tucker "recently . . . has been linked with [Chris] Atkins, Andy Gibb and boxer Gerry Cooney. 'Nothing serious with any of them,' she said while puffing on a Kool and sipping a Pepsi." Tucker said that she had also met tennis stars Bjorn Borg, John McEnroe, and Ilie Nastase and that she would be participating in a charity tennis tournament in Forest Hills. "They're *all* nice guys." She went on to say that while she already had a 2,000-acre ranch near Nashville and another home in Las Vegas, she was thinking of getting an apartment in Manhattan too. "I'd like one right next to Andy Gibb," she declared. "He's *real* nice."

But as Tucker recalled in her autobiography, she soon realized that a romance with Andy was not to be. "Andy," she wrote, "was one of the most fragile men I've ever met, very sad and hurting so much over his breakup with Victoria Principal." "Andy was such a gentle, fragile soul," she reiterated, and while she tried to convince him that he needed to get over it and move on, she could see that it was hopeless. She also saw that he was still using cocaine, contrary to what he had told Joan Lunden, and regretfully admitted that she obtained a gram for him on the night they met. The romance turned into a friendship, and while their paths would soon diverge, they remained friends for the rest of his life. Their last conversation, on the phone, occurred just a few months before Andy died.

Andy also appeared in public with another famous female singer during his brief stay in Manhattan. Karen Carpenter was there undergoing treatment for anorexia nervosa. She and Andy had become friends after being introduced by their mutual friend Olivia Newton-John in Honolulu in 1978. Andy knew that Karen was staying at the Regency Hotel and called her. They went to see *The Pirates of Penzance* together and, according to a gossip column, they "seemed to enjoy it . . . interrupting their hand-holding only to applaud." In an interview in 1979, Barbara Gibb had mentioned the actress Olivia Hussey and Karen as friends who "look after" Andy. By the summer of 1982, both of the famous young singers were probably feeling lonely; Karen had recently ended a brief, turbulent relationship of her own with a man whom she had married in 1980.

Andy arrived in Toronto one week before *The Pirates of Penzance* began its two-week run on August 9. Producer Jan McArt had further plans for the production. She had worked out a deal with Lorimar Productions, producer of the hit series *Dallas, Knots Landing*, and *Falcon Crest*, to film *Pirates* at the Royal Alexandra for broadcast on the Entertainment Channel, a pay-cable network (which soon folded but merged into the Arts & Entertainment [A&E] Network). But McArt's production ran into some controversy; the Joseph Papp/New York Shakespeare Festival production of *Pirates* was still touring. Since *Pirates* was in the public domain, anyone was free to put on a production of it, but the New York Shakespeare Festival, as the *Miami Herald* explained in 1982, retained "control [over] the rights to its distinctive version" of the operetta. Accordingly, the company sent "observers to monitor other productions for blatant appropriation of its concepts." McArt's production, which in casting Andy, Barry Bostwick, and Caroline Peyton, featured three stars from Papp's 1981 Los Angeles production (Peyton had seen some stage time as Pam Dawber's understudy), drew the scrutiny of these observers. McArt stood her ground, telling the *Herald*, "The New York Shakespeare Festival said I was using its stars. I don't think the Festival had engaged them for a lifetime contract."

The controversy apparently scared off the Entertainment Channel, however. The network, under what McArt called "heavy pressure" from the Festival, canceled its plans to broadcast her production. Plans for the cast and crew to take their show to Montreal's Expo Theater for one week following the Toronto run also fell through due to what the promoter said were "technical difficulties," which a reporter suggested were "regulations that would have required the unneeded services of too many people on the technical staff." Andy later complained of "a very, very cheap production budget" during the Toronto run of *Pirates*, and said that he and Barry Bostwick had threatened to leave the show twice. Andy also recalled getting "a lot of bad press for my throat because I was coughing up blood every night between shows. I had a terrible, terribly bad infection." He said that a bad PA system only added to the stress on his throat, and recalled that on some nights he was getting catcalls from the audience. "It wasn't a very pleasant experience."

For all the questionable press reports from the previous year that stated that Bostwick had not been pleased with Andy as his *Pirates* co-star, Lenard Allen, who became one of Andy's backup singers in 1984, clearly saw that the two castmates had become friends. Allen met Bostwick after a performance that Andy gave at a cancer fundraising gala in Beverly Hills, where other luminaries such as Kenny Rogers and Lionel Richie were present. Bostwick "had brought a whole bunch of food [for a party after the show] . . . and just wanted to spend time with Andy. Barry had nothing but terrific things to say about Andy and working with him."

The scrapping of the cable television deal for *Pirates* would have been a pecuniary blow to Andy, who admitted to Joan Lunden that his lost income and expensive cocaine habit had caused "a financial crisis," but another opportunity came along immediately. The Showtime cable network made a deal with two production companies to broadcast a taped production of *Something's*

Afoot, a musical comedy that spoofed Agatha Christie-type murder mysteries. After several weeks of rehearsals, the show was taped over the course of two days, October 4 and 5, at Toronto's Elgin Theater before a live audience. Aside from Andy, who had to get a short haircut since the play was set in 1930s England, the cast also featured another big-name star, Jean Stapleton of *All in the Family* fame. Showtime first aired *Something's Afoot* in December 1982 and ran it repeatedly until as late as April 1984.

Andy's contract called for him to be paid $25,000 (about $70,000 in 2021 dollars) in three equal installments. On January 7, 1983, however, he filed a $150,000 lawsuit in U.S. District Court in New York against Manhattan-based American Video Productions, Inc., and its president, Ellis Eisenstein, in which he charged that the company had not paid him. Andy sought not only the $25,000 fee, but also $100,000 for deceit and fraud and another $25,000 for punitive damages.

During his two-month stay in Toronto, Andy became reacquainted with musician Bob Segarini. A native of California, in 1974 Segarini co-founded a band in Montreal called The Dudes. The band signed with Columbia Records and released its debut album, *We're No Angels*, in 1975. After the album's release, the band set off on a three-week Canadian tour as the opening act for the Bee Gees, who were on the road in support of their career-reviving *Main Course* album. Segarini recalled in 2012 that for the Bee Gees, the tour "was a family affair," as they brought along their wives and Hugh and Andy. The Dudes didn't see Maurice and Robin much offstage, but they spent time with Barry, Andy, and Blue Weaver. Hugh and Andy left the tour before it ended, and Hugh thanked Segarini "for being so nice to Andy."

When Andy came to Toronto in August 1982, Segarini received a phone call from John Frankenheimer, Andy's lawyer at Los Angeles-based Loeb & Loeb. Frankenheimer and Segarini had been friends since attending school together, and Frankenheimer had managed one of Segarini's earlier bands. Frankenheimer told Segarini that he would be coming to Toronto "to take care of some business" for a client and invited him to join them for dinner. Segarini agreed without being told who the client was. When Segarini arrived at Barberian's, a well-known steakhouse in downtown Toronto, he discovered that the client was Andy.

Segarini would see *The Pirates of Penzance* several times at the Royal Alexandra Theater. Sometimes, after leaving the theater, Andy would come to Segarini's house on Armadale Avenue, about half a dozen miles away, "with a bottle of Jack Daniels and a baggie of pot. He would occasionally ask me to find some cocaine," Segarini remembered, "which in those days was not a problem." Segarini found that Andy "was still the nice kid I had met years earlier on the Bee Gees tour, but he was going through a very difficult time in his life." Andy "needed to talk," and, as he had with Tanya Tucker, he talked to Segarini mostly about his heartbreak over the end of his relationship with Victoria Principal.

When Andy started rehearsals for *Something's Afoot*, he began dating another cast member, Lenore Zann, an attractive actress and singer who was about a year-and-a-half younger than him. Andy had been hired and joined rehearsals after the rest of the cast had already begun rehearsing. Lenore, who was born in Australia and lived there until she was eight years old, would identify with him as a fellow Aussie. "When Andy showed up at the rehearsal that first time," she recalled in 2021, "I just remember him bounding into the room with this energy that reminded me of a young kangaroo, very eager and pleasant and big brown eyes and, just, big smile, lots of energy, really positive, very warm. And the entire cast . . . we just fell in love with him. He was very sweet and kind of vulnerable, really. He had a vulnerability about him. And we all felt very, I think, protective of him."

"We became very close very quickly," Lenore remembered. She and Andy started going out almost every night to parties and other events in Toronto. "He felt comfortable with me. He trusted me. I felt the same way about him." "Because I was Australian," she added, "I also knew all the Bee Gees songs. I kind of grew up on them." When she and Andy went to parties, there would often be a piano in the room. "Andy and I would gravitate to the piano, and he'd start playing, usually, Bee Gees songs. He would sing and I would sing with him and we'd do harmonies. We really had fun."

Lenore also got a glimpse into Andy's relationship with his brothers, although she never met them nor Hugh and Barbara either. "It was clear he was very proud of his brothers," Lenore said. "He was proud of their music and loved their music." But when she and Andy were alone in private, he admitted to her that "it had been extremely painful for him growing up in the shadow of his brothers and the fact that he always wanted to be a Bee Gee. He wanted to be a fourth Bee Gee, but he was told by his brothers, 'Well, we don't really need you, we already *are* the Bee Gees. We don't need another one.'" It seemed to Lenore that "no matter how much money he made or how famous he got on his own, it was never enough" for Andy. "And it would never be enough. Because his ultimate dream was to be a Bee Gee like his brothers, which he never could be. . . . He always was in the shadow of his brothers, and he would never be good enough, in his own mind. He would never be good enough."

Lenore could see that Andy was troubled. Despite the lawsuit that he later filed, Lenore remembered him (as well as Jean Stapleton) being paid in American cash, and nearly four decades later she could still recall riding in the back seat of a limousine with Andy while he counted a wad of it. As he did, he said to her, "I was making a million dollars a week off 'Shadow Dancing' [a sizable exaggeration] when I was your age." "He didn't say it in a cruel way," Lenore said, "but it was a little bit of a put-down. But I remember looking at him . . . and seeing the lines and the crow's feet kind of around his eyes and in his forehead, like from worry and anxiety and, to be honest, from doing drugs and not looking after himself. And I remember thinking at that time and at that age, I didn't say it out loud, but I thought to myself, 'Well, I'd rather be who I am, where I am, right now than be you.' And I remember thinking, 'This guy could be dead by the time he's thirty.' That's a clear recollection."

In fact, when Andy had to get a routine checkup by a doctor for insurance purposes as a condition of being hired for *Something's Afoot*, he told Lenore that he was "worried, because he said he had a heart problem. Already, he knew, and he said he knew also that a lot of it had to do with doing coke. And he was very worried about whether or not he would pass that [medical] inspection." Andy also admitted something else to Lenore that contributed to his palpable anxiety. "He told me," she recalled, "that he was still broken hearted about Victoria Principal, that he really had loved Victoria . . . he was really broken up about that."

Lenore knew that her relationship with Andy would be short-lived. "It felt like we were meant to meet at that time, and then we were meant to go on our own ways again," she reflected. "I could see in Andy then that he was hell-bent for self-destruction, and . . . I didn't want to be part of that." She did attempt to reach him once in the spring of 1983 when work took her to Los Angeles; she called Marc Hulett, whom she also had gotten to know in Toronto, but Andy was either away or unavailable at the time. Lenore, who became a Member of Parliament in Canada in 2019, never saw Andy again after he left Toronto upon the completion of *Something's Afoot.*

While working in that musical, Andy accepted an offer to play the title role in another one, *Joseph and the Amazing Technicolor Dreamcoat*. The contract called for him to debut at the Forrest Theater in Philadelphia in late October, where the show would run for four weeks, with eight performances per week, before moving on to the Royale Theater on Broadway at the beginning of December. There, too, Andy would be required to perform eight shows a week, for five months. Andy had discussed the possibility of taking the role with the director of *Something's Afoot*, Tony Tanner, who would also be the director of this production of *Joseph*. Earlier in the year, Susan George had seen the opening of *Joseph* in Los Angeles, and at a party afterwards she suggested to the show's lyricist, Tim Rice, and its composer, Andrew Lloyd Webber, that Andy would be ideal for the role.

Susan wasn't the only close acquaintance who supported Andy as a prospect for *Joseph*. Robert Stigwood owned a majority share of the rights to the musical. Andy's former personal manager, James Dayley, who was still working for RSO at the time, recalled that Stigwood helped "get Andy in for an audition on that and helped him get that job, just kind of to help him out, because he had been part of the [RSO] family, so to speak." After Andy auditioned for producer Zev Buffman, Buffman offered him the job. Tony

Tanner, Andy recalled, had expressed skepticism to him at first about his suitability for the role, but he changed his mind as he worked more with Andy in *Something's Afoot*.

It would be demanding. Andy would have only five days of rehearsals before taking the stage. But he told journalist Robert Baxter that this was the comeback vehicle that he had been looking for. While still in Toronto working in *Something's Afoot*, Andy listened to a tape of the *Joseph* soundtrack at night. By the time he got to Philadelphia, he was bounding with enthusiasm, making much the same impression there that Lenore Zann recalled him having made in Toronto. Before the opening, Andy "excitedly" told Baxter how "after every preview performance, the audience has given us a standing ovation." Andy wasn't the only Gibb who was feeling good about his new opportunity. "When he started rehearsals his brothers were jumping up and down with excitement," Buffman told *People* after Andy died. "His mom and dad came from England [more likely, California]. He was always talking about it as a new start."

But even a starring role on Broadway couldn't make Andy's demons disappear. In his interview with Baxter, he spent a good deal of time discussing his breakup with Victoria Principal and what he described as the "dark and desperate" time that had followed. He repeated essentially some of the same things he had told Joan Lunden three months earlier, while making some additional comments about Principal. "Victoria," he told Baxter, "has this image. She has the reputation for being a man-a-year woman. She'll sue me for saying this [she didn't], and I don't mean it nastily. She's a very strong socializing girl. I've never been that way. Romantically, I'm very vulnerable." "It hurt me to see she could survive without me," he added. "She's called me twice since we broke up. I never had the courage to call her. She's a very strong lady."

By the time *Joseph and the Amazing Technicolor Dreamcoat* was about to leave Philadelphia and move on to Broadway, the producers realized that Andy's troubles were approaching a crisis point. One of them phoned actor Doug Voet, who had played Joseph in off-Broadway productions on and off since 1979. "We think you're going to have to go to Philadelphia because Andy's on coke again," Voet later recalled being told. Andy, who had been reliable while working in Toronto, rallied once he reached New York. The Macy's Thanksgiving Day Parade included a *Joseph* float, and Andy, in full costume, sang the show's refrain, "Any Dream Will Do." At the end of his performance, Bryant Gumbel, one of the hosts of the NBC-TV broadcast, commented, "That's good stuff, Andy Gibb . . . terrific stuff." Days later, though, Andy missed a dress rehearsal at the Royale Theater.

Nevertheless, opening night, on Wednesday, December 1, 1982, proved to be a smashing success: a standing-room only sellout, accompanied by plenty of press coverage and the presence of Barry and Maurice in the audience, which caused a brief delay while they signed autographs for fans. (Hugh and Barbara were there, too, and Robin saw the show and visited backstage with Andy about a week later.) Critics gave Andy's performance what an Associated Press report characterized as "generally favorable notices." One of those critics, Bruce Pollock, wrote that Andy "projected a warmly unassuming affability that was as surprising as it was captivating." Even more importantly to Andy, he won the approval of Barry. "Barry was so proud and impressed with my performance," Andy told Pollock, "that he was itching to get me back in the [recording] studio."

Signs of trouble appeared instantly though. As reported in a tabloid, "Rude Andy Gibb didn't speak to a soul as he plowed through a crowd of guests gathered to honor him at the opening of his Broadway play . . . and he disappeared into a private back room for the entire evening. His 'honored' guests were insulted by the snub." Andy didn't show up at the theater either of the next two nights. He then got back on track, but about three weeks later, "Christmas morning, I got a telephone call," Doug Voet remembered in an interview eight months after Andy's death. "Andy had disappeared and no one could find him."

Andy showed up for work the next day; he was photographed backstage putting Joseph's dreamcoat onto Henry Kissinger, as newspaper readers all over the country would see over the next couple of days. But on January 4,

1983, New York *Daily News* gossip columnist Liz Smith reported that "Andy Gibb has been out of 'Joseph and the Amazing Technicolor Dreamcoat' since Dec. 27. (Better get your act together, honeyboy!) But audiences don't seem to mind or ask for their money back. And they give his understudy, Doug Voet, a standing ovation nightly."

After a week of absences, Zev Buffman warned Andy that he was about to be fired. "He promised me he wouldn't miss another," Buffman later told *People*. "He said, 'If I do, you won't even have to call me, I'll be gone.'" Andy returned to work that day, January 5. Pollock reported that Andy "had been suffering from a bit of laryngitis for a few days before I interviewed him in mid-December," and he contacted Marc Hulett to try to get the inside scoop. Hulett told the reporter that Andy had been sick with "a severe bout with the flu." "Nothing more, nothing less," Hulett insisted. "Andy's had a tough year, and now everybody's quick to jump at every rumor. But we're on through May, and maybe longer."

On January 12, however, Andy failed to show up at the Royale for a matinee show. He and Barbara, who had been in Manhattan with him at the time, "flew immediately to L.A.," according to *People*, which reported that "Andy is now resting at his Malibu home." Buffman was sympathetic but resolute. "When Andy was at the theater, he was a joy. But he wasn't there enough. It wasn't fair to the audience," Buffman told *People*, adding, "Of the five Josephs we've had so far, Andy was definitely the best actor." Notwithstanding the strong audience approval that Voet received, Buffman resolved to find another well-known star to replace Andy; soon he hired David Cassidy.

As *People* reported, Andy's *Joseph* castmates were "mostly sympathetic" when he departed. "I hear he spent most of his time in his hotel room in front of the TV," one anonymous cast member told the magazine's scribe. "I guess he was frightened and insecure. That's what happens when you're the baby brother of the Bee Gees." Andy's twenty-one-year-old co-star, Sharon Brown, told the New York *Daily News* a couple of months later, "I liked Andy Gibb, and we got along very well. But too much was made of his missing performances. A lot of people miss performances on Broadway. Andy had a lot of things on his mind, not only Victoria Principal." Given that Andy had missed a dozen performances in six weeks, Sharon's assessment was sympathetic indeed.

Another cast member, Jessica Molaskey, who was also twenty-one, seemed a bit less sympathetic in speaking to a reporter a few days before Andy's departure: "You know how everyone sometimes fantasizes about closing the door and shutting out the world? Well, Andy does that. He lives out his fantasies. Sometimes he stays shut up like that for several days." She was right. Barbara Gibb recalled the abrupt end to Andy's brief run on Broadway in the VH-1 *Behind the Music* episode in 1997. "He used to say it was because of his throat, but of course it wasn't. And they . . . bought that for a while. And then they realized what *was* happening." With a pained expression on her face, she then added, "And we couldn't get him out of bed . . . his door would be locked and he wouldn't come out." For nearly three years, Andy would blame his failure to last more than two-and-a-half months (including his time in Philadelphia) in *Joseph* on not only throat problems but also a lack of discipline. In the fall of 1985, though, he admitted to interviewer Bob Durant, "my past history . . . has shown what the drug [cocaine] has done to me. I lost a lot of work through it. I lost *Solid Gold.* I lost *Joseph* on Broadway."

At the time, though, Andy's spokesman, Michael Sterling, denied press speculation that cocaine use may have been responsible for his unreliability on Broadway. "He has gotten control of that," Sterling insisted. "The summer of 1982 was the conclusion of that problem." Sterling, who was a master at issuing carefully worded statements in Andy's behalf during the early-to-mid-1980s, did not actually say, however, that Andy was not using cocaine at all. Buffman wouldn't speculate on whether cocaine abuse had contributed to Andy's chronic absenteeism, but in March 1983, he remarked to a reporter, "I told Andy Gibb, 'You may be a very sick boy, with throat problems and chest problems and so on, but you may also be staying up too late and running around.' I tried to stress the fact that he had to stay in training and protect his voice."

Two months later, Buffman appeared on the program *2 On the Town* on WCBS-TV (New York City's Channel 2). "I think new stars who come from other fields of entertainment than Broadway simply do not fully comprehend the tradition that the show must go on," he said. "If someone will get sick on three different occasions within a period of eight weeks, you would have a problem and you made a mistake, or the star made a mistake and cannot handle the task of being on Broadway eight times a week. That is basically what happened to Andy Gibb." After Andy died, Buffman remembered that he had seemed "physically frail," adding, "When I called his agent and asked if we could hire him, his agent thought it was the greatest news possible, but when Andy first arrived, he was a wreck. He was just getting over Victoria . . . he was still just trying to get his act together."

While starring in *Joseph*, Andy received scripts for another Broadway show and another cable TV special for his consideration, and he expressed hope that he would soon get an opportunity to make his film debut. His early exit from Broadway came as a dashing blow to those opportunities. Furthermore, days before his departure, a newspaper report noted that despite his unreliability, Andy had received "good notices from the critics" and that "his name is salable enough that now there's talk of another tour with Gibb as Joseph." Obviously, that didn't happen. Andy's career in theater ended when he left Broadway; he told interviewer Kenny Hodges in June 1986 that he was involved in talks to potentially return to the Great White Way later that year, but it wasn't to be.

The ignominious conclusion of what had been a promising stage career also resurrected much of the bad press that Andy had received during the spring and summer of 1982, as newspaper and magazine articles speculated not only about whether he was still abusing cocaine but also if he was still suffering from depression over the breakup with Victoria Principal. Andy had been a regular subject of the tabloids and gossip columns almost since his initial success in 1977, but increasingly they were treating him as an object of pity and perhaps with a tinge of contempt as well. Andy admitted to Joan Lunden on *Good Morning America* in August 1983 that he "was very depressed when the thing came down with *Joseph*," and he kept a low profile for the next several months.

This wasn't necessarily by choice. Although Andy had spoken of his desire to get back into the recording studio—with many of his own self-composed songs—while doing interviews for *Joseph*, he had no recording contract, and the decline of his record sales during 1980-81 and, especially, his reputation for cocaine abuse and unreliability meant that record companies weren't knocking on his door. Film and, of course, theater offers were out of the question. Even opportunities to appear in television specials, which in previous years had come in abundance for Andy, had dried up after his no-show on the Bob Hope special and the *American Movie Awards* in March 1982, except for an appearance in which he lip synced "An Everlasting Love" on the modeling competition *Face of the '80s*, which aired in first-run syndication in August 1982. In April 1983, NBC finally broadcasted *Grandpa, Will You Run with Me?*, which featured Andy's video for his unreleased recording of "Morning of My Life," two years after the special had been recorded.

Otherwise, Andy was relegated to making guest appearances in the spring of 1983 on two inconsequential NBC game shows, *Fantasy*, hosted by Peter Marshall and Leslie Uggams, and *The New Battlestars*, hosted by Alex Trebek, who went on to much greater success the following year when he began hosting *Jeopardy!* Trebek gave his celebrity guests the opportunity to tout their new or forthcoming projects, but when he got to Andy, Andy told him that he had nothing in the works, prompting Trebek to reply, "Well, you're always welcome here." Trebek also told Andy how much he had enjoyed seeing him perform in *The Pirates of Penzance*. Andy, who was always glad to donate his time and talent for good causes, continued doing that during this period of limited activity, appearing on April 17, 1983, at the Aladdin Hotel in Las Vegas for the Nevada Special Olympics.

Around this time, Andy phoned his ex-wife and daughter, who hadn't heard from him since their meeting in Los Angeles on Peta's second birthday in January 1980. Kim described the phone call in an interview after Andy's death, saying that "it was clear he'd woken up to the fact he had a daughter.

Peta was five years old and Andy, who had developed an American accent by then, wanted to know all about her." He asked Kim to send him photographs of Peta. "We talked for five hours about our families and he asked me why I hadn't married again. When I asked him the same question he said, 'Because my girls keep leaving me like you did.'"

Bored and making far less money than he was accustomed to, Andy began taking steps to get his career—which he now had sabotaged severely twice in less than one year—back on track. He requested that the William Morris Agency, with which he had been signed since 1977, assign Jeff Witjas as his new agent. Andy had met Witjas while co-hosting *Solid Gold.* At that time, Witjas represented Marilyn McCoo and therefore had visited the show's set frequently.

Witjas eagerly took Andy on as a client. "I got to know Andy very well [from *Solid Gold*], and I adored him," he recalled in 2008. "He was very charismatic, very talented. And when I set my mind that I wanted to represent him, that's all I focused on, was, 'How could I represent Andy Gibb?' Because he was that charismatic." Witjas felt that Andy's versatile singing ability and exceptional stage presence would make him a natural for the showrooms of the Las Vegas and Atlantic City casinos. Andy had received offers going "many years back," as he told Joan Lunden, to perform on the casino circuit. At this point, it was probably the most viable option that he had and, as Witjas recalled, it was a lucrative one too, paying Andy $100,000 (about $275,000 in 2021 dollars) for fourteen shows in a week, although he would have to pay a number of salaries and commissions out of that money.

Witjas quickly followed through with his plans. He had no difficulty getting Andy booked; when he told the agents who acquired performers for the casinos that Andy was available, "They were all over it right away," he recalled. "We got offers right away." On May 25, 1983, the *Philadelphia Daily News* reported that "pop singer Andy Gibb substitutes for Dolly Parton August 22 to 28 at Resorts International Hotel-Casino [in Atlantic City]. Parton's had a recent history of canceled appearances—for reasons ranging from health to threats to fears for her personal security. Gibb himself, the youngest brother of the Bee Gees, is no stranger to the replacement syndrome."

Andy also decided that he needed a new manager to help him resuscitate his career. Witjas recommended his friend Marc Gurvitz, a young manager (only about two years older than Andy) at Bash, Neufeld, & Bernard (BNB), a well-established Beverly Hills artist management firm whose clients included Natalie Cole, the Carpenters, Helen Reddy, Herb Alpert, Sergio Mendes, Andy Williams, and the O'Jays. (Karen Carpenter tragically and suddenly died on February 4, 1983; she and Andy had seen each other one last time just before her passing.) Initially, a more senior figure in the BNB hierarchy, Michael Gardner, also played a role in the firm's efforts to relaunch Andy's career. Marc Hulett remained onboard as Andy's personal manager for a while before going to work for Barry Manilow in that capacity with a recommendation from Andy. As of this writing, Hulett is still working for Manilow.

Andy had not had a band since 1980, and with the engagement in Atlantic City looming ahead, he would need to assemble one quickly. It would have to be a new one; most of the members of the "Andy Gibb Hit Orchestra" were still working on records being produced by Barry Gibb, Karl Richardson, and Albhy Galuten, such as the platinum-selling number one hit "Islands in the Stream" by Kenny Rogers and the aforementioned Dolly Parton, which would enter the *Billboard* Hot 100 during the same week that Andy made his Atlantic City debut. Gardner, Gurvitz, Hulett, Witjas, and Dan Wohleen, who became Andy's road and production manager, all assisted in putting together a group of musicians and backup singers for him. Gurvitz called his friend Joey Carbone, a versatile musician, songwriter, and record producer, who for many years was the musical director of the syndicated television series *Star Search*. Carbone recruited guitarist Rick Robbins, who had just completed a tour with Ray Parker Jr., and bassist Bryan Garofalo, whose recent credits included working with Glenn Frey, Kim Carnes, and the band America. Bill Purse, who had worked with Andy and the Bee Gees as a horn arranger and player, joined the band as the keyboardist, and John Eidsvoog became the band's synthesizer player and conductor, perhaps, figured Carbone in 2021, on the recommendation of Purse.

The band's drummer, at least until early 1984, would be an old friend of Andy's. Marc Hulett called Dennis Bryon, who had known Andy since joining the Bee Gees' band in 1973 and had played on Andy's hit "Desire," which had begun as a Bee Gees track. Hulett, recalled Bryon in his memoir, "told me Andy wanted me to be his drummer."[5] "He was forming a new band in L.A. and wanted Jenny [Bryon's wife] and me to move into his house in the Los Angeles [Hollywood] hills," which Andy had just recently moved into himself. "Andy loved Jenny, and Marc thought the presence of the two of us at the house might be a positive, sobering influence. I told Marc yes." Upon his and Jenny's arrival at Andy's house, Dennis found that Andy "looked great; he was happy, sober, and full of energy." He and Andy began playing tennis every day, sometimes even twice a day.

Andy wanted a trio of backup singers. Dan Wohleen made a phone call to Jim Photoglo, who had recently had a pair of top forty hits of his own with "We Were Meant to Be Lovers" (1980) and "Fool in Love with You" (1981). Wohleen had been Photoglo's road manager, and Mike Gardner was his manager. They "brought up my name when the search for background singers began," Photoglo recalled in 2021. "Andy knew my name from hearing me on the radio. And that was that." Another male vocalist, an aspiring singer-songwriter from Minnesota named Chris Emerson, who was already a friend of Andy's, also joined the trio. Andy landed Emerson an appearance on one of the episodes of *Fantasy* that he guest-starred in, in which Emerson sang a self-composed song. Initially, Bill Purse's wife, Teri DeSario, agreed to round out the trio. She had had a million-selling hit single in the winter of 1979-80 with her fellow Miamian K.C. (Harry Wayne Casey), a duet version of the 1965 Barbara

5 In his memoir, which was published in 2015, Bryon writes that Hulett called him in 1985, but he clearly has the year wrong. On the next page, he reminisces about appearing with Andy on the NBC-TV sitcom *Gimme a Break!* The episode in which Andy and his band appeared, titled "The Groupie," first aired on September 29, 1983.

Mason hit "Yes, I'm Ready." She had a Gibb connection, too: her 1978 debut single ("Ain't Nothing Gonna Keep Me from You") had been written expressly for her by Barry. At the last minute, though, she withdrew from the position with Andy and was replaced by Petsye Powell, whose long list of credits as a backup vocalist included Olivia Newton-John's album *Totally Hot* (1978).

Before Andy made his Atlantic City debut, Jeff Witjas booked him at the Turn of the Century nightclub in Denver for four nights (July 28-31, 1983) as a way of "trying out his show." (Jeff would recall with a chuckle that when he made a little suggestion to Andy about how he might improve part of the show, Andy gave him a slightly indignant reply: "You just be an agent, don't be a critic.") To generate publicity for the shows, Andy did an interview with G. (Gary) Brown of the *Denver Post*. Andy's publicist, Michael Sterling, told Brown, "The real news is that Andy is doing a nightclub tour instead of rock concerts. Please don't ask him about Victoria." Of course, Brown couldn't resist, and Andy once again had to explain how he had suffered "what doctors call a nervous breakdown" following the split. "I'm just too sensitive—I always have been," Andy admitted, a candid self-assessment with which many who knew him agreed.

When Brown got around to asking about the upcoming shows, Andy seemed a bit self-conscious and unsure of himself. "It's been so long since I made a record," he said, "and I can't get into the studio to make one until later this year. It's impossible to do a regular concert tour without an album out, so I'm doing 'Vegas-ized Andy' instead." Andy also told Brown that he was embarking on this new endeavor without any assistance from his brothers. "They are simply the most special, talented people I've ever known. But they haven't had anything to do with my new act," he insisted. "I don't want that right now. When I had those hit records, I basically became an extension of the Bee Gees by dint of their writing and production, their whole sound. I want to do this by myself." The act would include a Bee Gees medley, however, as well as a tribute to the Mills Brothers, who had influenced the Bee Gees as well as Andy.

"I'll be quite honest—I'm scared," Andy told Brown. "After what's happened to me in the last few years, I'm afraid I've got an inferiority complex. I don't know what to expect—I know the show is good, and I know the band is killer, but I don't know what my old following will think. I'm coming off of a few years of bad press, so people probably don't know if I'm really together or not. I guess that part will be up to me."

Andy proved to be a hit with audiences at the Turn of the Century. "They adored him," Witjas recalled. But Jeff soon realized that Andy had a hard time seeing that. "Sometimes I'd say, 'Andy, look in the mirror. You've got everything—good looks, talent. Women love you.' Men liked him too. But when he looked in the mirror, you always had the feeling he didn't see anything."

Chapter SEVEN

Andy's Song

"I feel the need to grow and branch out, to reach more people. Before I leave this earth, in fact before I'm thirty, I want to try everything in show business. I want to be a complete entertainer." Andy Gibb made these remarks to UPI Hollywood reporter Vernon Scott in August 1983 as he prepared to make his casino showroom debut, first in Atlantic City and then for a week at the MGM Grand in Las Vegas starting on September 1. Andy was still nervous despite how well his new show had gone over with audiences in Denver. "I'm concerned about my reception. No matter how big you are or what you've accomplished, you have to prove yourself all over again in Vegas."

He need not have worried. *Entertainment Tonight* showed a clip of adoring female fans crowding around the stage while he sang "(Love Is) Thicker than Water" during his first show in Atlantic City. His Las Vegas debut didn't get that kind of television coverage, but probably more gratifyingly for Andy, it received a quite favorable review from Ira Sternberg in *Billboard*'s "Talent in Action" column.

"Andy Gibb," the review began, "despite a recent history of bouts with lost love and lost shows, still projected strong charm, enthusiasm and youthfulness at his show here." Sternberg noted that after opening with "I Just Want to Be Your Everything" and "After Dark," Andy "wisely" performed a Bee Gees medley of "How Deep Is Your Love?," "How Can You Mend a Broken Heart?," "Massachusetts," and "Words" as a way of reaching the older fans who may not have been as familiar with his own hits. (Ironically, though, Andy had told an interviewer in June 1983 that while he had sung Bee Gees hits in his live performances early in his career, before he came to the United States, "after a while, I realized that I am not the Bee Gees, I don't want to spend my whole life singing Bee Gee hits. And of course, now I don't.") Sternberg also reported that "for those in the audience who may be older than even original Bee Gees fans," Andy performed a medley of Vaughn Monroe and Mills Brothers songs, including "There! I've Said It Again" and "Up a Lazy River," the latter of which Andy and his backup singers performed while doing a dance routine. The song with which Andy received the strongest audience response, though, was his own "Me (Without You)." Sternberg was impressed. He thought that Andy's voice was "strong" and that he "presented a solid show, one he can build on for future expansion as he becomes more relaxed with himself."

Indeed, Andy had found a new outlet for performing. Jeff Witjas quickly booked him for a return to Las Vegas (this time at the Riviera, where his opening act was his BNB roster-mate Natalie Cole) and at Caesar's Tahoe. Over the next three-and-a-half years, Andy would perform frequently in Las Vegas, Lake Tahoe, Atlantic City, and at the Sparks Nugget just outside of Reno. "He did love to perform to live audiences," Barbara Gibb later recalled. "He liked the response, especially in Vegas where he used to get standing ovations after every show, you know. He loved that." Witjas also began booking Andy at state fairs and in nightclubs in large cities.

Andy went over well wherever he performed. "He had a *huge* fan base," observed guitarist Rick Robbins. "Those women just loved him." Yet Witjas saw that Andy's insecurities were never far from the surface. He often attended Andy's shows. "I would stand behind the wings," he recalled in 2008, "and I'd look out at the audience and see how they were reacting, because after the show we would discuss the reactions of the audience. But as soon as this [one] particular show was over, Andy came back and said, 'I gave a terrible performance.' I said, 'Why? I watched everybody.' He said, 'Did you see that young girl in the second row? She was practically falling asleep.' I said, 'Andy, there may have been a thousand people in the audience.

Why are you focused on this one person?' He was, in some ways, a perfectionist. He wanted the entire audience to react." Andy admitted as much to April Sandefer, a journalist for the *Reno Gazette-Journal*, in September 1985, telling her that there were some nights when he'd come off the stage "screaming mad" because he didn't feel his show went as well as he wanted. But, he conceded, "Nobody's ever agreed with me yet. Mom doesn't ever notice anything wrong, and she sees every show. Maybe she's just being nice."

At the same time that Andy launched his nightclub act, he also began making frequent television appearances again. As well as doing interviews for *Good Morning America* and, over the course of two nights, *Entertainment Tonight* to promote his shows in Atlantic City and Las Vegas, he also appeared on the season premieres of *Solid Gold* and the NBC sitcom *Gimme A Break!*, on the annual Jerry Lewis MDA Labor Day telethon, on Alan Thicke's short-lived late-night talk show *Thicke of the Night*, and on several shows produced and/or hosted by Dick Clark. Although Andy and Clark weren't friends in the sense of socializing with each other, the two got along well and Andy made many appearances on Clark's numerous series and specials.

Clark featured Andy as the star of an episode of his syndicated series *Salute!* The series spotlighted a different performer each week, singing a couple of his or her hits alone as well as duets with guests. The episode featuring Andy, which first aired in November 1983, was undoubtedly a memorable experience for him. Clark conducted a short taped interview with Barry and Maurice for the program, in which he asked them about their earliest recollections of seeing Andy perform in front of an audience. "We went to see him at a little hotel in the Isle of Man where he was probably doing his first professional shows," Barry said, "and we all got a very big surprise. You could see that there was definitely a gift inside Andy as a performer, and an incredible will to reach an audience, to get to an audience, be it vocally or verbally." The camera then cut to Andy breaking into a big smile. As the interview came to an end, Maurice said, "We'd just like to say hang in there, keep in touch, and have a great night. We both love you very much, and Robin sends his love."

Barry quickly added, "And give us a call." The clear impression was that neither Barry nor Maurice had heard much from Andy lately.

The show also featured Andy singing duets with Lisa Hartman, Frankie Valli, Leslie Uggams, Pam Dawber, and Ann Jillian, as well as a brief Mills Brothers medley with Donald and Herbie Mills. The two surviving Mills Brothers were friends of the Gibb family. Andy probably invited them to appear on the show, and he invited Dawber and Jillian as well. Ann and her husband, Andy Murcia, were friends with Hugh and Barbara as well as Andy. "Ann and I," Murcia recalled in 2021, "became friends with Hugh and Barbara Gibb back in 1982, when Joey [Murcia] brought Andy to our home [in the San Fernando Valley] that we had just purchased. Andy and Joey were visiting in our guest house and asked if they could invite his parents over. We had Ann's mom and dad here back then, and we all had a great time. Most of our furniture had not arrived yet, so we only had Ann's grand piano and some sound equipment in our living room. Hugh and Barb loved to ballroom dance, and dance they did in our mostly empty living room. Andy and Ann sang songs around the piano. We also had another singer pal visiting us from Canada, Dawn Aitken, and so with these three fine singers, it was a glorious musical filled day that went into evening for us all."

While that Dick Clark show probably ranked as the most significant of Andy's television appearances in 1983, returning to *Solid Gold* for the season four premiere as the guest co-host one year and a half after he had dropped off the show, and working again with host Marilyn McCoo and friends such as Pam Rossi and Michael Miller, was a highlight for him as well. Andy and Marilyn sang "Every Breath You Take," which had recently been a number one hit for the Police, and Andy received an ecstatic reaction from the many young women in the audience when he walked off the stage and through the seating area while he sang "I Just Want to Be Your Everything." "I was in the booth with the producer of the show," remembered Miller, "and we were smiling at how good he sounded and how well he looked. And I know that that performance meant a lot to him." Andy taped the performance just before his first week performing in Las Vegas, and he flew Miller in to see his show.

For Andy's band members, however, the most memorable television appearance during the fall of 1983 would be the episode of *Gimme A Break!* in which they, along with Andy, played themselves. Rick Robbins and Dennis Bryon both still fondly recalled the experience decades later. For Andy the highlight of the show, aside from singing a powerful duet with Nell Carter of "Up Where We Belong," came in meeting the show's pretty blonde cast member Kari Michaelsen, who was about three-and-a-half years younger than him. They began dating, which the tabloids reported despite Andy's attempt to keep his personal life private after his affair with Victoria Principal. For their first date, he picked Kari up and took her to Hugh and Barbara's house in Woodland Hills, where, she recalled, they all watched a movie together. Some of Andy's friends from that period would later suggest, however, after hearing her discuss her relationship with him in documentaries in 2008 and 2020, that she exaggerated its seriousness and longevity. Her credibility was hardly bolstered when an Andy Gibb fan revealed online that the photo of the couple that Reelz had used in the 2020 documentary, which looked like a close pose between them, was actually a photoshop creation made from a photo of Andy with Victoria Principal and another of Kari with another man. Kari posted the photo herself on social media a number of times.

As Andy continued to perform in casinos and nightclubs and make television appearances, he had an extended run-in with the acid-tongued comedienne Joan Rivers that briefly sent him into a tailspin. On December 2, 1983, Andy performed on *The Tonight Show*, on one of the many evenings at that time when Rivers was substituting for regular host Johnny Carson. (When Rivers later tried, unsuccessfully, to take on Carson with her own late-night show on the fledgling Fox network without telling him first, he stopped speaking to her and never had her on *The Tonight Show* again.) Andy sang "Me (Without You)" and received thunderous applause from the audience. But when he sat down for an interview with Rivers, she noted that it was a "really sad, tragic song" and then asked him, "Do you ever sing it while you watch *Dallas*?" That set the tone for almost the entire interview, in which

Rivers harangued Andy incessantly about his relationship and breakup with Victoria Principal.

Andy seemed to take the interview with good humor, but unfortunately for him, his encounter with Rivers didn't end when he left the television studio that night. As Rivers noted when she introduced Andy before he sang, he would be traveling to Montreal to make an appearance over the weekend at the Palais des Congrès de Montreal, or as Rivers put it, the "palace de congress," for a televised charity telethon. Undoubtedly to Andy's chagrin, when he boarded his American Airlines flight from Los Angeles to Montreal, he discovered that Rivers was on the flight, too, as she was scheduled to perform four sold-out shows at the O'Keefe Center in Toronto. When Andy arrived he told CFCF-TV's Peter King, who was in charge of hospitality for the telethon performers, that Rivers had "continued the insults on the plane." According to Montreal *Gazette* reporter Thomas Schnurmacher, Andy was so upset that "he locked himself in his room" at the Ritz-Carlton and "refused to speak to anyone. He [also] refused to attend any rehearsals."

Andy almost missed the telethon altogether. "It took King," according to Schnurmacher, "a full forty minutes and a can of Dry Look hairspray to convince Gibb to put in an appearance, which he did at the very tail end of the show." Ironically, noted Rick Robbins, Rivers was "a friend of the [Gibb] family." Rick's wife Cathi even recalled having a photograph of Joan with Hugh and Barbara.

The sour experience with Rivers notwithstanding, Andy made good progress in rebuilding his career under the direction of Marc Gurvitz and Jeff Witjas during the latter half of 1983. But he failed to take that next step to complete his comeback. In interviews, Andy kept talking about making a new album; he told veteran UPI Hollywood reporter Vernon Scott in August 1983 that he would be recording it in the fall, and that it would include from eight to ten songs that he had written by himself. "My new album will be the first time I've gotten away from the Bee Gee sound," he told Scott. "I'm trying to create a sound that I alone will be responsible for. At my age and with my past success I can afford to take the risk." For all the times he mentioned it in interviews, though, Andy never made the album.

Part of the reason for that, at least in the short run, may have been that he stayed busier throughout the remainder of 1983 with live performances and television appearances than he had anticipated. He told another reporter in August 1983 that the album would "probably be out in the new year. First I'll finish this little tour in about four weeks' time, and then I'll go into production for the record." But he continued performing in casinos and nightclubs, and on television, almost until Christmas.

Andy also suggested another obstacle to his return to the recording studio when he appeared toward the end of the year (from a Los Angeles television studio) on *The Mike Walsh Show*, an Australian talk/variety program. When Walsh asked Andy if he would have a record coming out soon, Andy replied, "Well, I've got about eight new songs finished [written] for my new album, and I'm looking for a record company right now to record it on, but hopefully I can have it released some time about spring or summer next year." Jim Photoglo recalled "some talk about him being included on the *Scarface* movie soundtrack, but that didn't happen." In fact, *Minneapolis Star and Tribune* reporter Jon Bream, in a review of one of Andy's concerts at the Carlton Celebrity Dinner Theater in Bloomington in November 1983, wrote that Andy had "last week . . . recorded his first single in three years [actually, it would have been closer to two]—the theme song to Al Pacino's new film, *Scarface*, with record producer Giorgio Moroder of *Flashdance* fame. Now there's talk of an album with Moroder for early next year."

Bream didn't mention who had told him that Andy had recorded with Moroder, but it hadn't happened and never would. Andy's band members encouraged him to get back into the recording studio. "I remember sitting at his house with [bassist] Bryan Garofalo and a couple of other people," recalled Rick Robbins, "and we were prompting him to write, to get him to write songs. 'Hey, here's an idea, here's an idea,'" but "he never really got . . . motivated to commit to doing it." Jeff Witjas concurred that Andy "didn't have the drive. He just didn't have the drive for his career." "He just couldn't believe in himself at all," Witjas sadly reflected. "He never ever had confidence."

Robbins knew that it was a lost opportunity. "He should have made a record right then and there." James Dayley felt the same way and told Andy so. "I remember at that point . . . I talked to Andy about this. I said, 'Andy, what are you doing in Vegas? I mean, Michael Jackson [a friend of all the Gibb brothers] has got the biggest selling album of all time right now, you should be out there doing that, writing new music, creating new stuff.'" Jim Photoglo thought that Andy "was always interested in getting back in the studio" during this period, but he just never followed through. In late 1985, while telling a journalist of his plans to have a new album out in 1986, Andy said that "my head wasn't ready" for making records after his breakup with Victoria Principal.

Press reports also had Andy set to finally make his film debut, a goal that he had mentioned repeatedly since his initial burst of success in 1977. In September 1983, the Toronto *Globe and Mail* reported that "Andy Gibb may be able to draw on personal experience when he makes his screen debut in a film called *Rock and Roll Nightmare*. He will star as a rock singer whose life turns into a morass of drugs, drink and depression after waning popularity and a fall from the top of the charts." The article went on to note how Andy's own career had gone "downhill" following his breakup with Victoria Principal the previous year, and reported that Principal's *Dallas* co-star Charlene Tilton, a friend of Andy's, would co-star in the movie as the girlfriend of Andy's character. The movie never got made, though; a 1987 film of the same name, which was a direct-to-video release, was apparently not the film that was being planned in 1983.

In 1984, while Andy continued to perform in Atlantic City and Las Vegas (including a starring role that spring in a live stage revue of *Solid Gold* at the Riviera, for which Brad Lachman reunited him with Marilyn McCoo), he also decided to take his act abroad. Except for some television appearances, Andy had not performed outside the United States and Canada since a brief return to Australia in January 1977. Jeff Witjas booked Andy to perform at the Viña del Mar Festival in Chile. This six-day festival featured a long list of performers, and Andy and Sheena Easton would both be headliners on the last two days, February 12-13, 1984. Andy received the prestigious Silver Torch award, which was only given to selected performers at the festival, during his last show, and he was clearly overcome with emotion upon the presentation of the award, which was greeted with much enthusiasm from the audience of some 35,000.

After the shows in Chile, Andy and his entourage then headed to South Africa for a brief engagement at the Sun City resort and casino. Many American and British stars performed at Sun City during this era, but doing so was controversial given that apartheid still existed in South Africa. (It finally ended in stages during the early-to-mid-1990s.) In fact, later that year, Andy would be placed on a United Nations "blacklist" of entertainers who had performed there, along with 387 others including Ray Charles, Elton John, and Dolly Parton. In an interview in 1985 Andy seemed a bit defensive about having performed there, saying that he wouldn't do it again because of the "touchy" situation, but that he had only gone so that his fans there could see him perform. Members of his band and entourage remembered that they stayed there for about two-and-a-half weeks and that it was mostly a vacation filled with safaris and golf. Jim Photoglo recalled that on one of the safaris, "Andy got out of the vehicle and was a little too close to a rhino that we were photographing. The road manager [Dan Wohleen] was nervous that Andy was in danger, and yelled, 'Andy, get back in the guitar.' I don't know why we thought that was so funny, but at the time it was hilarious."

While Andy was performing in Sun City, so were the Landers Sisters (Audrey and Judy). While they were best known as television actresses in the United States—Audrey was a castmate of Victoria Principal's on *Dallas*—they also recorded and toured, with more success internationally than at home. Andy began dating Judy, who would sometimes be at his shows in Las Vegas upon their return to the States. In February, gossip columns and tabloids had linked Andy romantically with Pam Dawber, who also sometimes was at his Las Vegas shows, and two months later they had him paired with eighteen-year-old tennis star Andrea Temesvari. Temesvari, who later said that the reports of a romance between herself and Andy were the creation of overzealous writers, attended his performance at an IBM sales meeting at Orlando's Buena Vista Palace on April 25, 1984. That show proved to be a memorable one for Andy as well as his band members, for Maurice was in attendance and, as Rick Robbins remembered, joined them onstage and "played some bass and piano with us . . . and just sharing the family a little bit was also an honor." Robbins also recalled another occasion when a famous musician sat in on piano and played with Andy and the band: Liberace, at the Riviera in Las Vegas.

At the beginning of July 1984, Andy, his band members and crew, and Marc Gurvitz all headed back to South America, this time for about a week and a half of concerts in Argentina, Brazil, and Chile. Andy wasn't necessarily in the best frame of mind at the time. Joey Carbone, who filled in for Bill Purse on electric piano on the tour, remembered sitting next to Andy on a flight, and Andy started talking to him about Victoria Principal, "how heartbroken he was about the breakup and how much he missed her, and he got very teary-eyed as he was telling me that story." Andy gave a press conference upon the arrival of his and his entourage's flight to Santiago from Miami, which had followed a flight from Los Angeles, but after they arrived in Buenos Aires later that afternoon, a weary Andy irritated the promoter, Javier Capallo, by refusing to attend a planned press conference and dinner.

From there, things got worse. When the tour moved on to Brazil, the flight was frighteningly turbulent. "We really thought we were going to go down," Carbone remembered. "We were freaking out, and Andy was pretty upset." By the time the plane landed safely, "You could almost see Andy's handprint in the armrest," Carbone recalled with a chuckle. Still more trouble lay ahead in Chile. When they arrived, the promoter (not Capallo, but rather a man who apparently belonged to the Chilean Mafia) told them that they had to give him their passports. Some of the band members objected, but Gurvitz prevailed upon them to do so. Then the promoter tried to get Andy and the band to agree to add an unscheduled show, a performance for a television program in the Chilean coastal city of Iquique (more than one thousand miles away) two days after the last scheduled show in Santiago. When they declined, the promoter refused to return their passports, and implied that if they refused to play the additional gig, drugs might be found in their luggage at the airport. At this point, Andy "was literally in tears, I mean, he was so freaked out he was shaking," Carbone remembered. Gurvitz and Bryan Garafolo went to the US Embassy, which happened to be across the street from the hotel where the band was staying, but they were told that their problem sounded like a contractual matter and no real help was offered.

Carbone had to leave for California to return to work on *Star Search*, as did the three backup singers (Lenard Allen, Eric Butler, and Chris Emerson) for another gig. Gurvitz managed to negotiate the return of those four men to the United States, but not for Andy or anyone else. Andy phoned his parents, and Barbara Gibb called US Defense Secretary Caspar Weinberger, with whom she and Hugh were friends. Andy and the band (minus Carbone and the backup singers) still played the television show in Iquique, but two representatives from the US Embassy showed up. When Andy and his entourage returned to Santiago for a day and a half before flying back to the United States, Andy stayed at the home of the US Marine Detachment Commander at the US Embassy. Andy and his entourage received a Marine escort to the airport, where agents of the US Drug Enforcement Administration saw them to their airplane. The Marine Detachment Commander, Adam Marshall, said that the Bee Gees phoned him and thanked him for helping Andy.

It may have been a coincidence, but Andy seemed to go into a downward spiral upon returning from the difficult South American tour. Then again, problems had become apparent in the months leading up to that ordeal. When Dennis Bryon joined Andy's band in mid-1983, and he and his wife Jenny moved into Andy's house, Dennis thought that Andy was doing well and "living a clean and sober life." But by the time of the Viña del Mar Festival in February 1984, Dennis was out of the band—fired, he revealed in his memoir, after trying to confront Andy, in a well-meaning way rooted in more than a decade of friendship, about his increasingly reclusive behavior and rising consumption of vodka and cocaine. (Rick Robbins recruited his friend Richard "Moon" Calhoun, with whom he had performed before, to replace Bryon.) Dennis also recalled that twice in one month, Andy had himself taken to an emergency room for chest pains which he believed were symptoms of a heart attack. Being hospitalized with chest pains, stomach pains, and an erratic heartbeat was nothing new for Andy by this point, but these episodes were becoming more frequent. In June 1984, about two weeks before Andy left for South America, gossip columnist Susan Stewart, in a story on his apparently budding romance with Judy Landers, mentioned "wild rumors that he has a heart problem—*aside* from the broken heart he suffered at the hands of Victoria Principal."

Andy's problems certainly escalated, though, upon returning from South America. By late July, he admitted to an interviewer, his romance with Landers was "up in the air." (A Canadian magazine article on the Landers Sisters would later report, as translated from French, "He [Andy] has always had drug problems and he did not seem to want to quit, so she has had to let him go with a flood of tears.") Up to this point, Andy had been reliable in turning up for concerts and television appearances since he had begun working with Marc Gurvitz and Jeff Witjas, but that was about to change. In early August, he skipped two scheduled interviews on Philadelphia television stations to promote an engagement at Caesars Hotel and Casino in Atlantic City. Then on August 17, he failed to even arrive in Bossier City, Louisiana, where he was scheduled for four concerts in two nights at the LeBossier Hotel Celebrity Theater. Andy's band and crew had already flown there from New York City, but after they arrived, Bud Horowitz, who was Andy's lighting technician, received a phone call from road manager Dan Wohleen telling him not to set up the stage "because Andy wouldn't come out of his [hotel] room" in New York.

On Saturday, August 18, newspapers across the nation published a UPI story: "Pop singer collapses, cancels part of tour." According to the article, which cited Andy's longtime spokesman Michael Sterling, Andy had been "found unconscious Friday afternoon in his New York City hotel room by a member of his band." Yet the same article also reported that "seventeen members of Gibb's band arrived at the Shreveport, La., airport Friday but returned Saturday to New York." Sterling's statement may have been one of his numerous attempts during the early-to-mid-1980s at public relations damage control for Andy, who Sterling said had "collapsed from exhaustion." In 2021, Bud Horowitz was reading this UPI article online while being interviewed over the phone by the author, and when he read that Andy had been found unconscious in his room, he said, "I don't know if that's true or not."

From this point on, Andy once again became the unreliable performer that he had been on *Solid Gold* and Broadway. Jeff Witjas recalled an instance in Lake Tahoe where Andy didn't want to come out of his hotel room to perform. Marc Gurvitz called hotel security to break open the door. "He eventually got out," Witjas said, "and he performed. But to go through all that, and if the hotel entertainment division sees that, they're not going to hire the act back again." "Whenever he was depressed on tour," Gurvitz told *People* magazine just after Andy's death, "he wanted to cancel the engagement."

Not surprisingly, remembered Witjas, "all the excitement [surrounding Andy's comeback] started dissipating a bit because Andy started showing he wasn't really capable of doing all that, and he needed, you know, a watchdog at all times." Even though Hugh and Barbara were still at most of Andy's casino engagements, Witjas (like Julie LaMagna years earlier) thought that they "didn't really help. His parents did not help. I don't know, either he didn't listen to them, or something, but they just weren't, they went along to enjoy the time. They had no influence on him." Barbara later recalled feeling helpless as Andy ordered his staff to get cocaine for him before he took the stage, which happened often. "He would threaten them [that] he wasn't going to go on stage if they didn't get him some. And of course, everybody would be running around flustered trying to find some. I don't know where they got it from, but somebody always managed to get it for him."

Andy resumed performing one week after missing the Bossier City engagements (for which, according to the venue's manager, 800 tickets had been sold in advance) with two concerts at a state fair in Salem, Oregon, on

Friday, August 24, where he drove himself from Los Angeles in his black Porsche. "It's a long drive, believe me," he told a reporter. "I blew out two tires and a fan belt, but I still got here this morning." The first show drew an audience of about 2,000, "many of them young," according to the local newspaper. On September 1, Andy and a cast of *Solid Gold* dancers brought the stage show that he had successfully done earlier in the year in Las Vegas to Miami's James L. Knight Center for a benefit show for the American Diabetes Foundation, where Maurice once again joined Andy onstage, this time accompanied by his eight-year-old son, Adam. Andy returned to Miami in December for the first of many annual Barry Gibb Love and Hope Festivals, which combined a celebrity tennis tournament and charity ball for the benefit of Miami's Diabetes Research Institute. Andy would participate in all of these that were held during his lifetime. At the end of December, Andy took part in another charity tennis event in Miami Beach, along with, among other celebrities, Barry and the tennis great Arthur Ashe.

Andy also continued to make guest appearances on television, including two episodes of the NBC-TV sitcom *Punky Brewster*, whose two young stars, Soleil Moon Frye and Cherie Johnson, have often spoken of him in glowing terms in the decades since. "We were so in love with him. I still love him so much," Frye said in 2021 while she and Johnson were being interviewed for the *Punky Brewster* reboot. She fondly recalled him giving her a black glittery jacket that he often wore on television. "He wrapped it around me, and it was just so beautiful. He was just so kind, and that has always stuck on me—the kindness of what you create and how you interact with people. You know, it does leave a lasting effect. And I think it's just a testament to who he was."

Andy's two appearances on *Punky Brewster* originally aired on November 25, 1984, and January 20, 1985, respectively. According to James Cox, who was the show's associate director at the time, Andy's second episode proved a bit challenging. Andy called at the last minute and said that he wanted to postpone his appearance; he was visiting his ailing friend Peter Lawford, the British actor and one-time brother-in-law of President Kennedy. Cox knew that Andy's excuse was a true one. Lawford, after many years of alcohol and drug abuse, had been in and out of the hospital, and he died on Christmas Eve, 1984, at the Cedars-Sinai Medical Center in Los Angeles at the age of sixty-one. Months earlier, Andy and Lawford had been hospitalized there at the same time. Andy had called Lenard Allen and asked him to come visit him at the hospital. While Allen was there, Andy introduced him to Lawford, who was just a couple of rooms away, and the former movie star asked Allen if he could bring him some cocaine.

The producer of *Punky Brewster* told Andy it was too late to reschedule his appearance, so he came, accompanied by his parents, whom Cox remembered as "the nicest people in the world." Cox knew that Andy "was having drug problems" at the time, and he recalled that Andy's acoustic guitar, which he'd brought along to play while singing "I Can't Help It" in the episode, "was out of tune and he couldn't tune it." "It was hard," Cox said of the taping, "but we got through it." Despite the difficulties of working with Andy on that episode, Cox would remember him fondly, lamenting that "he died way too young."

Earlier in December 1984, Andy had appeared on *The Don Harron Show*, a Canadian talk show. Harron immediately brought up the subject of Victoria Principal, compelling Andy to again confess to having suffered a nervous breakdown at the end of the relationship. ("She can do that to people," Andy said, adding with a laugh, "and has.") With that apparently inevitable topic out of the way, Andy went on to tell Harron that he was making plans to return to weekly television and had signed up to make a movie (tentatively titled *Satan and Eve*) in which he would star as Adam, alongside Vanessa Williams as Eve, Orson Welles as God, and Malcolm McDowell as Satan. Terence Young, director of three James Bond films in the 1960s, was to serve as director. Later press reports said that Ben Gazzara would play Satan and that Maurice Gibb would be responsible for the soundtrack. That the movie never got made could not be blamed on Andy; first the production, according to a newspaper report, "ran into dire financial straits," and then Welles died in October 1985.

But the unspecified television series that Andy had mentioned never materialized either, just like his plans to make an album with producer Richard Perry, which he discussed in interviews in the summer of 1984, never came to fruition. (For all his success, Perry would have been an ironic choice for Andy, since his attempt at producing the Bee Gees in 1976 had been quickly aborted by Barry, Robin, and Maurice when he seemed unimpressed with their new songs, including "You Should Be Dancing.") Andy had become better at publicizing his plans in interviews than at actually following through. "I would actually see him self-sabotage at times," said Rick Robbins. "I remember he was called in for a TV show or movie or something, and I recall that it was a big part, and we had spoken to him, 'Oh man, are you ready to go and do your thing?' And he didn't show . . . the opportunity was unbelievable, and he just didn't show." Robbins was still puzzled at the memory decades later. "I don't know . . ."

Those around Andy could see that something was wrong. He began performing less and became reclusive. Jeff Witjas, who had played tennis in college at Bowling Green State University and subsequently taught tennis and ran a tennis club, played with Andy frequently after becoming his agent. But one day, out of the blue, Witjas recalled, Andy "gave me his tennis stuff. For some reason, he gave it to me. He didn't want to play anymore. He gave me his racquet and all that. I kept it as, you know, just because it was Andy, but . . ." Witjas thought that Andy seemed lonely and depressed. "I felt bad," Witjas said. "Obviously, he was suffering in his own way."

By the beginning of 1985, Andy's problems had reached a crisis point. His emergency room visits for chest and stomach pains were becoming more frequent, although his mother began to doubt if they were really necessary. She suspected that "he wanted some kind of drug or something, 'cause if you're in pain they give you a shot of Demerol or something and you go to sleep," she said in the 1997 VH-1 *Behind the Music* episode on Andy. "And I think that's what he was [after], he never said he was, but . . . I got to a point where, when I'd take him into the hospital and he said he had a pain, of not believing him. He was crying wolf again." But Dr. William Shell, a Beverly

Hills cardiologist who began treating Andy for heart inflammation in early 1985, said in an interview for the VH-1 program that Andy's pains were undoubtedly real. "These weren't heart attacks in a lay sense, [but] they were heart attacks in the sense that he destroyed small amounts of heart muscle."

Ironically, as Andy's career and health were both deteriorating, Barry Gibb told syndicated columnist Marilyn Beck in January 1985 that all four Gibb brothers would be going into the studio and making an album together during the year ahead. "It'll mark the first time," Beck wrote, "youngest brother Andy has joined his three siblings—The Bee Gees—on wax. Barry also says the Brothers Gibb (as they now refer to themselves) expect to go out as a quartet on a worldwide concert trek, 'but that won't be till next year.'" This would have been a dream come true for Andy. "He *always* talked about Barry and he always wished he could be a Bee Gee," remembered Cathi Robbins.

But it soon became clear that Andy needed help before he could make any further career plans. By now, Hugh and Barbara were pleading with him to enter the Betty Ford Center in Rancho Mirage, California, for treatment for his cocaine addiction. Peter Lawford, despite an unsuccessful stay at the clinic himself one year before his death, had also urged Andy during their last visit to check himself in. Andy did not seem enthusiastic about the idea. "Weeks of family conferences were required before he would commit himself to the full regimen," *People* reported after Andy's death. "Even then, publicist Michael Sterling says that he had to put Andy on the phone with Elizabeth Taylor before he was finally convinced."

Dire warnings from doctors may also have helped Andy make the decision. According to what seems to have been a mostly accurate article in the *National Enquirer*, published in April 1985 under the headline, "Docs Warn Andy: Quit Booze & Drugs or Die," Andy had been diagnosed with pericarditis, an inflammation of the heart lining. An "unnamed source" close to Andy said, "When the condition flares up, it leaves him breathless and clutching his chest in agony. Andy has been hospitalized 14 times in 15 months for treatment of his heart condition." The source also disclosed Andy's ongoing battle with "deep depression" and said that "Andy's parents blame many of his setbacks on his disastrous affair with Victoria Principal." According to Cathi Robbins, who got to know Barbara Gibb well during the couple of years that her husband was in Andy's band, this was true. Barbara, Cathi recalled, "told me personally that she blamed Victoria for a lot of this. She really felt she took advantage of him . . . she said Andy had problems before, but after Victoria, Andy's problems got much worse."

Andy entered the Betty Ford Center on March 21, 1985, sixteen days after his twenty-seventh birthday. He didn't want his parents taking him, so he had Marc Gurvitz drive him there instead. Andy insisted that they make the trip in his Porsche, and even though her romance with Andy was on-and-off by this point, Judy Landers came along for moral support (which must have made for a crowded ride in the Porsche). Andy would spend six weeks at the clinic, and two weeks after he arrived, newspapers across the country reported, "Pop star Andy Gibb, the younger brother of the famed Bee Gees, has entered a rehabilitation center to overcome a cocaine habit." Michael Sterling issued a statement: "Andy is making extraordinary progress at the center, has become ardently involved in its program and will continue an additional maintenance program upon the completion of his counseling."

Not everyone who visited Andy during his stay at the Betty Ford Center was convinced, though, that his rehabilitation attempt would be successful. "I never got the feeling," Jeff Witjas recalled, "that he was under strict supervision . . . not that he was drinking or taking drugs but . . . he had a lot of freedom there . . . it wasn't like you're really going to rehabilitate." Rick and Cathi Robbins visited Andy too. "He was struggling with his addictions," Rick observed, "and he seemed to find some healing there, but it had gotten to the point where he had just gotten confused and didn't really know kind of where he was going." Rick and Cathi both thought that Andy seemed lonely, and that one of the things that tormented him was his lack of a relationship with Peta. "He felt bad about it," Cathi said. "He felt real bad about it." Jeff Witjas agreed. "He talked about his daughter a little bit," Witjas remembered. "It probably tortured him in a certain way."

Jeff thought that Andy's insecurities were "the catalyst" for his drug and alcohol problems. Barry Gibb said much the same thing not long after Andy died. "To me," Barry told a *Washington Post* reporter in the summer of 1989, "Andy's problems were not drugs and booze; to me they were a massive insecurity, psychological problems compounded by the drink and cocaine. Maybe they also caused it, but at the end of the day you were dealing with a person who was tremendously insecure and had no confidence in himself at all, yet had a lot of talent and needed to use it. He seemed to have lost the will or desire to use it."

Nevertheless, when Andy entered the Betty Ford Center, his family, as Maurice Gibb remembered, felt optimistic and relieved. Maurice had had his own battle with alcoholism, for which he had been treated at a clinic in Santa Barbara, California, in 1980. After that, he had gently tried to get Andy to confront his own addictions, telling him that his health and career depended upon doing so, but to no avail. "We all did what we could to help Andy," Maurice said, "but I had to accept that all I could do was plant the seed for his recovery. When he finally went into the Betty Ford clinic, we thought, 'Thank God.'"

While he was at the Betty Ford Center, Andy wrote lyrics for a song in which he expressed his loneliness. He never recorded the song, or even wrote any music for it; it would be copyrighted under the title "Andy's Song." It was essentially a poem, and in fact Barry read it at Andy's funeral. In it, Andy seemed ambivalent or uncertain about his career, which, he lamented, had kept him on the road so much and made it hard for him to form a lasting relationship. Yet, he also reflected upon how hard he had worked to become a successful performer, a "dream achieved" that he couldn't just abandon.[6]

James Dayley heard the poem as soon as Andy wrote it. James was still working for Robert Stigwood but was by then living in New York City, and he was stunned to get a phone call at 3 o'clock in the morning from Andy, who he knew was at the clinic. Dayley feared that Andy must have left if he

6 The lyrics to "Andy's Song" can be found online at https://www.angelfire.com/music5/archives/andygibb.html.

were able to make a phone call, but Andy explained that in fact he had had his counselor dial Dayley's number. Andy wanted Dayley to hear his poem, which Dayley found to be moving. Given how the poem discusses Andy's hope that his fans remember him after the spotlight dims and the show ends, Dayley couldn't help but be struck when he heard it again at Andy's funeral. "When that final curtain closed on his mausoleum, it hit me," Dayley remembered in 2021, "that it was his final closing. I get chills even now thinking of it."

Chapter EIGHT

Don't Throw It All Away

"It's still very hard. It's one day at a time, and . . . you're never cured." Andy Gibb had just completed his six-week stay at the Betty Ford Clinic and earned his medallion for completing the rehabilitation program, and now, once again, he was back on television, this time on a syndicated talk show called *Lifetime*, discussing his latest attempt to get back on his feet and resume his career. In some ways, this appearance, in which he spoke with Tiiu Leek, was reminiscent of the one he had made on *Good Morning America* nearly three years earlier, although this time he was on a program with a smaller audience. But he was now being more honest about the ongoing nature of his cocaine addiction. One thing had not changed in three years though: he still seemed to be afflicted with pain over his breakup with Victoria Principal. Leek brought it up, but once she did, Andy's heartbreak came pouring out yet again. "What hurt me" after the split, he told Leek, "was that she didn't seem to go through any pain at all. And I felt a bit strange being the man feeling the pain and the weakness. And it really was hell for me, it really was."

Andy also discussed his plans to get his career back on track. He told Leek that he would be performing in a Royal Command Performance ("Australia Salutes the UK") for Princess Anne in London in three weeks and then finally, after an absence of about four years, would return to a recording studio with Barry as his producer. Andy seemed eager to get back to making records, telling Leek, "I can't wait to start. It's been a long time."

The London concert apparently didn't happen, but those who had been working with Andy for the past two years shared his eagerness to finally revive his recording career. Barry would not be available to work with Andy right way, since he, Karl Richardson, and Albhy Galuten were producing *Eaten Alive*, a Gibb-written Diana Ross album (including two songs co-written by Andy) which, according to Andy, would be followed by a Barry Gibb solo album. In the meantime, Marc Gurvitz asked Joey Carbone if he would be willing to try writing some songs with Andy, to try to "get his creative juices going" before his planned return to the studio. Joey, who would remember Andy as a "sweet, sweet guy," gladly agreed.

The three men met for lunch at Sushi-Ko, a Japanese restaurant in Bel Air. Joey could still recall the occasion some three dozen years later. "We sit down . . . and the waitress comes over, and Andy orders a beer. Marc Gurvitz looks at him with this incredulous look and says, 'Andy, what the fuck are you doing, man, you just got out of rehab!' And Andy was like, 'Oh it's alright mate, it's alright, just one beer, mate.' And Marc is looking at me like, 'Oh boy,' you know . . ." Nevertheless, they ate and discussed Andy's recording plans, but Andy "kept on getting up and going to the bathroom . . . every ten or fifteen minutes . . . and Marc couldn't believe it. And we never got together after that."

For Gurvitz, it was apparently the last straw. He had been managing Andy for two years, during which time he had tirelessly labored to make sure that Andy was where he was supposed to be when he was supposed to be. The longer that he had been with Andy, though, the harder, and more exasperating, that had become. In one instance, he had been with Andy in New York, where Andy was booked for multiple performances at the famed Westbury Music Fair as well as some other nearby shows, and Andy simply disappeared for two days, missing his first scheduled concert. Not long after the lunch meeting with Andy and Joey, Gurvitz stepped down as Andy's manager. Mike Gardner, who had been involved in the efforts to revitalize Andy's career when Andy had signed with Bash, Neufeld, & Bernard in 1983, replaced him.

Jeff Witjas's tenure as Andy's agent also ended around this time, although in 2021 he said, "I don't know why he left . . . I think he just wasn't performing much at that point, but I never had any problem with Andy, so I don't know who called me or what happened. I don't have a recollection." Jeff would remember his time with Andy fondly, if with a tinge of sadness. "I had a blast with him. I mean, we had a good little run, and I really thought we had something going, but . . . he just couldn't take it to the next level." Nevertheless, Jeff reflected, there was "nothing that I really can say bad about him. Most of my experiences, if not all, were positive with Andy."

Band members, too, began drifting away. For Rick Robbins, it was not an easy decision to leave Andy, whom he and Cathi had come to think of as a real friend, as they showed when they visited him several times while he was at the Betty Ford Center. But the combination of Andy working less often, and not always being reliable about showing up for concerts, made it challenging (and costly in terms of lost earnings) to continue to stick with him. Rick reluctantly moved on to join the band of Earth, Wind, and Fire vocalist Philip Bailey, who was embarking on a solo career at the time. "But I can certainly tell you," Rick said in reflecting upon his time as Andy's guitarist, "that leading up to that point, from the very first day that I sat in rehearsal with that band and that rhythm section and played that music, the honor of playing those beautiful songs with a great guy like that, that was an *honor* for me and it will always be a great memory." Rick and Cathi subsequently lost track of Andy, but they would attend his funeral.

While Andy was still talking about getting back into the recording studio with Barry, in the meantime he wanted (and, financially, needed) to resume touring and performing in the casinos. At the end of July 1985, guitarist Rick Lotempio received a phone call from Joey Carbone. Lotempio and Carbone had known each other for years, and they had played together as session musicians on Air Supply's first American album, *Love and Other Bruises*, which had been recorded in Los Angeles in 1977. Now Carbone was asking Lotempio if he wanted to become Andy's guitarist. It would be on short notice. Andy was booked for two shows per night on August 1st and 2nd at the Valleyfair Amusement Park outside of Minneapolis. There wouldn't even be any time for Lotempio to rehearse with the band. "I learned the show on my own," he recalled, and he met Andy and the rest of the band at the Los Angeles International Airport (LAX). "I started right on stage that night and then he [Andy] offered me the job." Soon Lotempio would be performing onstage with Andy in Las Vegas and in Reno—the one casino city of the day where Andy had not yet performed—at the Sparks Nugget, where he was booked for two weeks in the latter half of September 1985.

Andy's engagement in Reno was as the star of a "Showcase" revue, sort of a variety show of comedy, dancing, and then a 30-minute performance by the headliner, who would change every couple of weeks or so. For Andy, this meant shorter performances—a good thing, to some extent, since his band members had noticed that the grind of two full shows a night, six nights per week, seemed to take a toll on him, even affecting his voice in some instances. On the other hand, though, giving shorter performances as part of a show like this meant less money, too.

Critic Mel Shields thought that Andy still merited his own full booking: "It's all very fine that the dancing and specialty acts take up so much time when the headliner is weak, as was the case with Barbara Eden recently. But when the headliner is strong, or at least interesting, the 30 minutes or so provide no time to prove versatility or build much momentum. What we get, then, with Andy Gibb at the Nugget is a taste, a snippet—certainly not enough." Shields, who noted that "Gibb has one of the more varied backgrounds in pop music," was hoping to hear Andy sing something from *The Pirates of Penzance* or *Joseph and the Amazing Technicolor Dreamcoat*. Instead, Shields lamented, "There is only time for the hits, plus a tribute to Gibb's brothers, the Bee Gees, 'without whom I wouldn't be here.'" (Shields obviously had never seen Andy's full-length show, which never included any songs from *Pirates* or *Joseph*.) Still, he concluded, "It's . . . good to see Gibb rebound from his personal problems and take those first steps toward revitalizing a career."

Andy did indeed seem to be taking at least small steps toward reviving his career. He had resumed making television appearances shortly after completing his six-week program at the Betty Ford Center. Two of those involved his old friends the Osmonds: first, in May 1985, almost immediately after Andy had completed rehabilitation, he appeared as a guest star on a two-hour television special, *Through the Years: The Osmonds' 25*th *Anniversary Special*, on which he lip synced "Shadow Dancing" and "(Our Love) Don't Throw It All Away." The show aired in syndication beginning in September. Then at the beginning of June, Andy returned to the Osmond Entertainment Center in Orem, Utah, for a live performance on the annual Children's Miracle Network Telethon.

Andy also seemed to be reliable as he returned to work; he wasn't canceling concerts or missing television appearances. Rick Lotempio quickly became close with Andy, and he said he never saw any evidence of Andy using drugs, although he admitted that he knew Andy would never "do any of that stuff in front of me because he knew I wouldn't approve of it." He could see though that Andy was "kind of a sad, lonely person." Sometimes Andy, living in Redondo Beach, would call Rick, who lived in Santa Monica, and ask him to come down. One time, Rick remembered, "I went over there, he wanted pizza. I brought him a pizza, [but] he just broke down and was crying in my arms about something . . . something broke him up." Rick saw that Andy was prone to bouts of depression, and knew that he sometimes drank while taking antidepressants. "I *loved* Andy, man, he had the greatest heart . . . [but] he was heartbroken over the Victoria thing . . . *crushed*." Rick was puzzled. "He could have anybody he wanted, I mean, the women *loved* him. I mean, it was nuts!"

Rick finally asked Andy one day, "Andy, what are you so upset about, why would you cry over her when you could have anybody you want?" "I'll never forget this," Rick said about 35 years later. "He told me, 'Once you've had fillet mignon, you can't eat at McDonald's.' That's what his exact words were." Rick was stunned. "'*Alright*,' I said. 'You're right.'"

Rick also soon discovered that Andy's relationship with his brothers, particularly Barry, played a major role in his state of mind. "He was hurt inside.

I think maybe he felt kind of left out from his brothers and he felt like he had messed up so many times that he wasn't welcome back and then he'd dig a bigger hole and, I don't know, man. It's hard to figure out. If I would have been able to figure it out, maybe things would've been different . . . we all tried." Rick saw that Barry sometimes took a stern approach with Andy but also tried to boost his lacking self-confidence. "Barry used to say [to Andy], 'Hey you're not coming in until you straighten things up,' or 'I'm not doing anything for you, I'm not helping you.' And it really did depend on how he was being treated by Barry, a lot of times, how his mood would go. And Barry used to tell him, 'Hey, you don't get it. You're singing two shows a night, you're going out there alone—we can't do that. We have three of us, but look at what you do. It's incredible.'"

Rick and Cathi Robbins had witnessed Barry giving Andy a similar pep talk, in which Barry also said that he could never be a successful television host or theatrical performer like Andy had been. Barry often told Andy that he had a better voice than any of the Bee Gees—an opinion shared by many of Andy's band members, including Joey Murcia, one who had performed with Andy and the Bee Gees—but no matter how much Barry praised Andy, the youngest Gibb brother never seemed to believe it. "Whatever I'd say to reassure him," Barry said in 1989, "he would still go away and hide in the depths of depression."

About three weeks after his stint at the Sparks Nugget, Andy took a ten-night engagement at the Imperial Room of the Royal York Hotel in Toronto, where he replaced Roy Orbison, who had canceled his scheduled run there. Here, too, Andy stuck to the schedule, and drew good-sized, enthusiastic crowds. On opening night, though, one obnoxious audience member kept chanting "Victoria, Victoria" as Andy sang "Me (Without You)," and according to a review of the concert in the *Toronto Sun*, "Gibb seemed a tad on edge and many of his jokes had a bullying quality." He dropped "Me (Without You)" from the set list for the rest of the engagement.

After the shows, Andy graciously met with fans, mostly young women, posing for photographs with them and signing autographs, while his mother also spoke to some of them. One member of the hotel's hospitality department, who happened to be an Andy Gibb fan, got to attend all of these meet-and-greets, and she noticed that Andy looked very thin and tired during one of them as the ten nights rolled along. He also in one instance made critical remarks about his own appearance, which to him didn't measure up to Barry's. Rick Lotempio noticed, as did many others who knew Andy, that the youngest Gibb brother "just idolized" the oldest.

The Toronto engagement went well, overall, but Andy became upset when a newspaper critic called his show a "Bee Gees show." To Lotempio, the characterization didn't seem inaccurate, though. "If you'd go see Andy perform, you would basically see a poor man's Bee Gees show," he suggested. "He would sing the shit out of those songs. I mean, when he was in the zone performing, he was just . . . incredible. That's what made everybody hang in there, just, 'God, there's so much potential with this kid.'"

Lotempio said that Andy "loved the music part" of touring. "Even after we would do shows, after we did two shows, he would invite us all up to his room, and he would sit there with his acoustic guitar and play all night . . . and that's how he would combat, probably, the demons. I think he was kind of lost when he wasn't singing, because it took his mind off stuff."

While in Toronto, Andy appeared on the radio show of a popular local DJ, Bob Durant, and gave an interview. By now, it was clear that the Barry Gibb-produced Andy Gibb comeback album would not be recorded in 1985, even though Lotempio recalled that Andy "would say stuff quite often about that, that that was in the making." Andy told Durant that "Barry is talking about producing me in May [1986] now that I am on the straight and level. All the three brothers want me to join them as a Bee Gee . . . and now I take that as it comes, you know, because they are busy and don't know when that will be . . . but that is the plan and hopefully that will be at the end of '86." When Durant observed, "You are obviously happy about that," Andy replied, "Yeah, quite happy about it. There was a time when I wanted to maintain just a solo career, but now I feel . . . we get a good feeling when we all sing together. It feels complete." (A couple of weeks later, a California newspaper reported that "Andy Gibb has agreed to join his three older brothers and become the fourth member of the Bee Gees. The new Bee Gees will embark on a tour beginning in February.")

Andy also told Durant that he was "clean now," and added, "I think the biggest thing that really helped me is that I'm in love at the moment, intensely in love. I have found the girl of my dreams, and we're talking marriage . . . and she's a *Solid Gold* dancer. If you see them on TV up here, she is one of the dancers and I am just crazed, crazed about her. She . . . only, only adds to my sobriety." Andy mentioned his new romantic interest in another interview toward the end of December 1985, describing her as someone with whom he was "very, very much in love and would like to marry."

Andy had met Nicole Romine, twenty-three at the time, in June during the Children's Miracle Network Telethon, on which the *Solid Gold* dancers had performed. "He introduced himself," Nicole recalled in 2020, "and he was quite shy really, we both were." (Indeed, for Andy to do this was rare, according to Jeff Witjas. "He wouldn't walk up to a girl and say, 'Hey, I'm Andy Gibb.' He didn't want to be rejected.") "He was such a gentleman, very kind, generous, and a pleasure to talk to," Nicole remembered. "He was a deeply kind man. And beyond gifted. He came once to visit me at a friend's house, a very humble home, and sat down on the couch and played the guitar and sang. He was incredible. I'll never forget that. It was so pure, and magical really."

But as much as Nicole liked Andy, there was a problem. "It was really more of a friendship on my end, though he felt quite differently, and he was so wonderful, I just never had the heart to tell him. I adored him; I was just never in love with him. If only I could have told him. He was very sensitive, and I was so afraid of hurting him." They kept seeing each other into 1986, and Andy remained enamored of her.

In mid-December 1985, Andy went to Miami to participate in the second annual Barry Gibb Love and Hope Tennis Festival. By this point, Andy had resumed playing his favorite sport. "He was into playing tennis every day," said Rick Lotempio. "That was his thing." After playing tennis and singing alone and with Barry at the charity event, Andy returned briefly to California, and then headed off for a short tour of the Far East.

The tour had some memorable highlights. Andy played a Royal Command Performance in Bangkok, Thailand, where the Crown Princess joined him onstage to sing "All I Have to Do Is Dream," and in Singapore he had a brief, nice reunion with his ex-sister-in-law Lulu (someone who Lotempio heard Andy mention often), who was also on tour. When it came time to take the stage in Singapore, however, Andy insisted that the promoter give him a Rolex watch before he would go on, and then made the promoter bring him marijuana. In Hong Kong, ecstatic members of an audience of 12,500 pulled Andy off the stage, giving him a bumped head and a dislocated thumb. He then canceled the second show, though; his mother told reporters that it was because his voice had given out, but Lotempio believed that Andy canceled simply because "he just didn't want to do it." Newspapers reported thousands of angry fans and a furious promoter.

Andy then went onto finish the tour in Taipei, Taiwan, before an estimated audience of 11,000, although he was two hours late, supposedly due to a canceled flight. The promoter withheld a big chunk of money from Andy, though, which in turn meant lost earnings for his band members. "We lost all that money that we were counting on," Lotempio lamented, "and you know, musicians, we don't really have anything to fall back on." "At that point Andy, on some of those occasions," Lenard Allen sadly recalled, "was so out of it that he really just didn't have any empathy for anybody else."

Andy had also canceled a show at Caesar's Tahoe in early December 1985; in that case it was a second show after the first had been marred by problems with the sound system, but still, canceled shows were once again becoming a problem for Andy's band members. It got to the point where, Lotempio remembered, "The conversation on the plane isn't, 'I hope we give a great show, can we go over some stuff?' The conversation on the plane is, 'Man, you think we're gonna get paid?'" Lotempio had toured as a member of Helen Reddy's band over a period of nearly ten years, "and that was like working at Kodak. Paid on time, travel on time, itineraries . . . so I went from that to like, 'Uh oh, I'm worried about this.'" Drummer Moon Calhoun, who had been in Andy's band since early 1984, quit shortly after 1986 began. When Andy quickly decided to fire his replacement, Jack White, a veteran of Rick Springfield's band with whom Andy apparently didn't get along, Calhoun agreed to return, but only briefly, and Andy then hired Casey Scheuerell, formerly of Gino Vanelli's band. By this point, the only holdovers from the band that Andy's management had helped him assemble in mid-1983 were bassist Bryan Garofalo and, intermittently, backup singers Chris Emerson and Jim Photoglo.

Having found himself reduced to shorter performances at a lower salary during his engagement at the Sparks Nugget a few months earlier, after Andy returned to the United States in January 1986 he found himself relegated to opening act status. Comedian David Brenner had opened for Andy during some casino shows in 1983-84, but now Andy was opening for Don Rickles at the Sahara in Las Vegas and Joan Rivers, the family friend who had heckled him about Victoria Principal on national television and a commercial airline flight a little more than two years earlier, at Caesar's Tahoe. Rick Lotempio remembered that as Andy and the band were about to take the stage at the Sahara one night, Rickles walked by and noticed Andy's open shirt revealing his hairy chest. "Hey, nice carpet, kid," Rickles quipped. Lotempio recalled that Andy was well received, and performing two twenty-minute shows per night was a lot easier for him than two hour-long shows, but opening act status also meant a huge pay cut compared to headlining status. Opening acts got paid by the headliner; when Natalie Cole opened for Andy during a week-long engagement at the Riviera in Las Vegas in the fall of 1983, Andy paid her 10 percent of his $100,000 purse. By the time Andy paid commissions and his band and crew, he wasn't earning much working as an opening act.

Andy returned to headlining status in late February, albeit at a venue that, despite a rich history, was not of the same caliber as the Sahara or Caesar's Tahoe. Rick Swig Jr., whose family owned and whose father ran the small luxury chain of Fairmont Hotels, was responsible for booking the entertainment in the hotels' showrooms. These showrooms were old, elegant (if fading), and expensive supper clubs. The Venetian Room at the San Francisco Fairmont had frequently booked Tony Bennett, Ella Fitzgerald, and the Mills Brothers, but Swig was trying to bring in younger performers who would attract younger patrons. Even most of these younger performers were older than Andy, such as Donovan, the Mamas and the Papas, and just before Andy's gig there began, James Brown, who, much to Swig's good fortune, was riding high on the charts with his first big hit in over a decade, "Living in America." Swig booked Andy for two-week engagements (two shows a night, six nights per week) at the San Francisco Fairmont from February 25 through March 9, 1986, and at the Dallas and New Orleans Fairmont Hotels in April.

For Joel Selvin, longtime music journalist for the *San Francisco Chronicle*, the fact that Andy was performing at the Fairmont was "a sign of him being totally washed up and not being able to get work for real money." Selvin reviewed Andy's opening show and wrote that "money and his brothers . . . seemed to be much on Andy's mind. Introducing one of his hits, he noted—twice—the pecuniary rewards of chart success: 'Made me a lot of bucks. Wish I had another one.'" Andy told another local music journalist, Larry Kelp of the *Oakland Tribune*, that he was taking any gigs he could get so as "to keep the money coming in" until he could make the "comeback" album that, he told Kelp, Barry would be producing for him.

Selvin also wrote that Andy "cloaked . . . caustic comments about his older brothers—the estimable Bee Gees—in the guise of good humor, but the laughter sounded a little transparent. Nobody is ever 'just kidding.'" "He wasn't kidding," Selvin said in an interview for this book. "He was broke, and he was jealous of his brothers, and he knew exactly what he was doing." Aside from Andy's comments about money and his brothers, one incident that occurred during the show stuck in Selvin's mind. "I remember . . . [during] the second number, the fuckin' second number, he stops the band, just like in the middle of nothing . . . and drops to his hands and knees to look for his fucking bracelet [one that he had bought from Liberace's jeweler], and looks up and realizes that the audience doesn't know what's going on. He goes, 'I'm looking for my bracelet. It cost me ten thousand dollars!' I've never heard of anything like that in all of my days of going to shows!" Selvin also recalled that Judy Landers was at the show, sitting at a table near the stage with Andy's mother. "She would show up at weird times," Lenard Allen laughingly remembered, "and I would just go, 'Okay, this is a booty call, we're not going to see Andy floating around tonight.'"

While Selvin was not at all impressed with Andy's Fairmont debut, Philip Elwood of the rival *San Francisco Examiner* took a more favorable view, writing that Andy's show "overall, isn't of the James Brown block-buster variety, but it's certainly more tasty, and less nasty." Elwood deemed Andy to be "a steady and solid ballad man, and, I imagine, most attractive to young women." The leader and namesake of the house band, the Dick Bright Orchestra, remembered some highlights from the shows. "He had a beautiful voice. He did 'You Don't Know Me' by Ray Charles [singing it for Barbara, for whom the song was a favorite]. He killed it. It was really cool." One night Andy coaxed Barbara onstage to sing an old ballad, and on another night, Hugh, who had arrived sometime after opening night, sat behind the drums and accompanied the Dick Bright Orchestra on "In the Mood." Andy also made use of Bright's horn section on some of the songs that he performed—"everybody [who performed there] got a free horn section," Bright recalled.

Still, it was not an easy engagement for Andy. "He is not Fairmont material," noted Larry Kelp, "and was obviously uncomfortable in a setting where the audience is older than he is, doesn't scream at every pelvic twitch or the removal of his jacket to reveal hairy biceps encased in a silver tank-top and the tightest pair of pants in the entertainment world." Bright was sympathetic but agreed. "I felt for him. He was super sweet, super nice, but . . . he didn't know how to talk to that crowd. I always felt he was uncomfortable in the room." Bright and Swig both knew that Andy had been at the Betty Ford Center the year before, and they got the impression that his mother was there "to babysit him." But Andy "never missed a show" during the two-week engagement. "He seemed totally reliable." This was despite the fact that, as can be heard on a recording of one of these shows that was released as a bootleg CD in 1999 (with ridiculous arena crowd applause added), Andy's voice was not in the best of shape. He had contracted a virus of some sort on the Far East tour and, in what was yet another sign that he was not in the best of health, he had not been able to shake it.

Yet another local journalist who attended one of Andy's shows at the San Francisco Fairmont couldn't help but notice that he didn't seem to be very well, physically or emotionally. *San Francisco Chronicle* film critic Mick LaSalle, who was a year younger than Andy and had just joined the newspaper's staff the year before, went to see Andy perform after reading Selvin's review. "Selvin," LaSalle wrote in a column in 2021, "panned Gibb's Venetian Room show, but something about the way he described it made me think that maybe there was another story there—perhaps a column. So a couple of nights later, I went to the Fairmont smelling blood." Once the show started, LaSalle quickly figured that Selvin had been "kind" in his review. "Gibb's show was a pathetic spectacle. His confidence was gone, and he was playing to a half-full crowd of maybe 75 people. At one point, between songs, he said, 'The last time I was in the Bay Area, I played the Oakland Coliseum. Now I'm playing here.'" As the show continued, LaSalle began to eagerly anticipate writing a column telling his readers "that if they wanted to see a teen idol fall apart before their eyes, this was the show. The column would be funny and, at least for a day, everyone would be talking about it. Anticipating this, I could hardly keep a straight face."

LaSalle never wrote the column though. At one point in the show, Andy, as he often did in nightclub performances, walked among the audience while he sang into a wireless microphone. When he reached LaSalle's table, the writer was struck at how small, thin, and fragile Andy seemed, and he had an epiphany of sorts. "In that moment," he wrote nearly three dozen years later, "I realized this was a young man, working hard, who was barely holding it together. And I knew I didn't want to be the person that made him come apart." Elaborating further to the author of this book in a subsequent email, LaSalle wrote, "By the way, the thing I left out of the article—I didn't mention this because I didn't think anyone would believe me—is that when I was close to him, I thought he might die soon. He looked like if you picked him up and dropped him from three feet off the ground, he'd break into pieces."

Yet, despite being hoarse and sick, Andy continued one of his longtime post-concert traditions. A fan, Marty Hogan, recalled that when he visited Andy's suite with backup singer Lenard Allen after the second show one night, Andy stayed up until five o'clock in the morning singing Bee Gees songs while accompanying himself on a guitar that Barry had given him as a birthday gift. (Andy turned twenty-eight during the engagement.) The guitar, according to Rick Lotempio, was a natural finish Guild Switch Crafter, "Andy's favorite guitar."

After wrapping up the two weeks in San Francisco, Andy traveled to Florida, where he played a benefit concert in Kissimmee for the Adam Walsh Foundation and the Russell Home for Atypical Children. From there, he returned to the Sparks Nugget for two weeks starting on March 17. Andy's engagement there as the star of a revue six months earlier had gone very well—he had been, according to a newspaper account, "the only entertainer last fall to fill the room to the balcony." Now he returned as a headliner. But, as critic Mel Shields, who had reviewed Andy quite favorably then, noted, the "Singapore bug" that he still had not shaken had rendered his voice "a wreck" by opening night. "He had no control over it at all," Shields observed. "He tried to compensate through volume, high-energy physical presentation and lots of yakking, but the audience was very cold." Shields's opinion of Andy's performance was summarized in the headline of his review: "Someone should tell Andy Gibb the show doesn't always go on." In a twist of supreme irony, Andy, who had been pilloried in the press in the past for failing to show up for concerts, television appearances, and stage performances, was now being criticized for taking the stage while ill, even knowing that his voice was in bad shape. "That was the worst show I've done in my life," he told Shields backstage afterwards. "I was so embarrassed."

Like Selvin, Shields couldn't help but notice that Andy seemed conflicted when it came to his brothers. "He doesn't much like his strong association with the name of his brothers, the Bee Gees, yet he plays off it, uses it and alternately says, 'Look at me, I'm the youngest brother of Barry, Maurice and Robin.' Then, 'Look at me, I'm Andy Gibb,' launching into an extended attack on some Toronto critic who said he did a 'Bee Gees show.'" Of Barry, whom Andy said would be the executive producer of his upcoming, "long overdue" album, Shields wrote that it was obvious that Andy both idolized him and envied his success, "given the fact [that] he makes uncountable references to Barry during a show, including how much his home costs." When Shields interviewed Andy and brought up the recent reports that the four Gibb brothers would be making a Bee Gees album, Andy seemed a bit irritated. "That's all very speculative. That's a fantasy, a nice fantasy. We're planning and talking. My family is very strange. We decide one thing and the next day, no. That's gotten out of hand in the press, all that about their bringing Andy in to add youth to the group. But we're talking, that's for sure, and if it's done it will go away from the Bee Gee sound."

It was all a bit too much for Shields. "Gibb does not know where he's going," the review concluded. "Somebody is not advising him well, or steering his career in a clear direction. He appears to be as frantic and disoriented offstage as on. Part of it may be because of a virus, but part of it isn't going to be healed by an antibiotic."

Andy was indeed becoming dissatisfied with Michael Gardner as his manager, although, as Rick Lotempio pointed out, Andy wasn't the easiest client either. "You think about it on paper," Lotempio observed, "it's like, 'Man, this should be easy.' But when you deal with the person it may not be easy. It might be a nice account to have if you can get him booked, but then the word gets out that he's not showing up for shows and people don't want to book him." The on-and-off again nature of the talk about Andy becoming the fourth Bee Gee had to be weighing on his mind, as much as he had long wanted to join his brothers' group. Something else was on his mind, too. After months of telling interviewers that he wanted to marry Nicole Romine, he finally decided to propose. Although she would be unclear about the exact date years later, it was probably as the Sparks Nugget engagement (of which Andy canceled only one show out of twenty-four) was wrapping up on Easter weekend that he flew to Kansas City, Missouri, where she was visiting her family in the house that she grew up in. He made the visit, she recalled, "to ask my father for my hand in marriage."

The proposal, particularly in the presence of her family, put Nicole on the spot. "My family adored him, and I loved his mother, Barbara, with whom he was quite close. I felt this enormous pressure from everyone to say yes, and I did very much like him . . . but as a friend. We had fun together and enjoyed one another's company, but never romantically. . . he was a gentleman. And so, I said yes. Andy was thrilled, called his brother Barry (whom he worshipped) right away, and then a week later, after I had agonized and cried over it, I called him and told him I couldn't marry him. It was an excruciating phone call. To have married him would not have been fair to him, and I knew that, and I truly wanted the best for him. It still hurts my heart to think about it," she said in 2020. But, she added, "He found a way to forgive me. That was Andy."

In an interview at the beginning of June 1986, Andy mentioned that he and Nicole had "split up about a couple of months ago." "It really has been hurting," he said, although he also said that "I'm over the major part of the hurt now." He and Nicole stayed in touch, and he phoned her from England during the final days of his life. "I loved who he was as a man, as an artist, I loved his kindness and sensitivity," Nicole would reflect. "He was so alive and full of beauty."

Something else was troubling Andy, too, during the spring of 1986. As suggested by some of the comments he had made during his Fairmont gig in San Francisco, his years of declining earnings and extravagant spending were catching up with him. Before he and his band and crew left the Sparks Nugget, Rick Lotempio had to "sign to get one of the paychecks so I could get it and pay everybody." Andy's creditors were trying to garnish his earnings. "So I signed for . . . those funds," Lotempio recalled, "not realizing I was now liable for the taxes. But they worked it all out. It wasn't easy, but they worked it out. It was like, '*Okay*, I'm not doing *that* again.'" Rick thought that may have been why Andy canceled one show at the Nugget, the fear that he might not receive his pay. "So yeah," Lotempio lamented, "that was another issue, so there were quite a few issues that I felt sorry for him [for], and that he was just going against, man, and it was hard. It was an uphill battle. But it was all 'cause he caused it . . . it didn't even have to be like that, a lot of this stuff."

Andy soldiered on, meanwhile, through six solid weeks of performing two shows nightly six nights per week. From Sparks he went to New Orleans and Dallas for more Fairmont Hotel gigs. He missed some shows in New Orleans, although the reason, according to both Rick Lotempio and Jim Photoglo, was poor attendance. "If [Andy] went and looked and there was nobody at the first show," Lotempio remembered, "he wouldn't do it. He wouldn't play for empty. And I said, 'Well, man, why don't you wait till *they* cancel the first show, and then you don't have to give back money.' But . . . he didn't want to do it. That's an ego thing . . . he couldn't believe there weren't people in line waiting to get in."

The Dallas engagement went better, with no cancellations, and Andy's voice had recovered by then despite his demanding schedule. "It was a very successful engagement," Fairmont publicist Deborah Cartwright told a local reporter after Andy died. "He was received unusually well. He hadn't had a hit in a while, but he still had a lot of enthusiastic fans." Cartwright recalled Andy sitting by the hotel pool every afternoon eating caviar from the hotel restaurant. "He was a very pleasant, cordial guy," she added, a sentiment shared by the hotel's manager, Peter Scanlan. Scanlan remembered that Andy "still attracted a lot of younger girls. He was still their heartthrob."

Jerry Jeff Walker came to one of the Dallas shows, and Paul Shaffer caught one of Andy's shows that spring as well. Decades later, Lenard Allen couldn't remember Shaffer being in the audience at any shows, while Rick Lotempio could but wasn't sure where it happened. At the beginning of June, though, Andy told interviewer Kenny Hodges about his meeting with the bandleader of *Late Night with David Letterman*. "He came to see one of my shows, and he was so blown away by it. He came up to my suite, and we talked for a few minutes. We went to the bedroom and talked, and I told him about the beginning of this . . . second chance. 'Listen,' he said, 'most people don't get second chances.' And he said, 'Do one thing for me, Andy.' And he meant it very lovingly. 'Don't screw up because you won't get a third.' And you know, he's right. He said, 'I don't know many people who get a second.' He said, 'You have, because you're so talented.' You know, he gave me these compliments, it was *wonderful*. He said, 'But one thing I will tell you, not even you will get a third. You're lucky to get a second. Use it and don't blow it. Be a good boy this time.' And I've used his advice."

Andy did indeed seem to be using Shaffer's advice. He fired Michael Gardner, telling singer-songwriter Stephen Bishop, while sipping fruit punch at an airport in Burbank, California, at the end of May 1986 that Gardner "didn't do a whole lot for my reputation." Andy and his fellow 1977 Grammy Best New Artist nominee were both among the group of entertainers who were waiting to board a flight to Utah to perform at the annual Children's Miracle Network Telethon. More significantly, Andy had completed—with no publicity this time—a shorter but, for him, more effective rehabilitation program at a clinic in Santa Barbara. According to several of Andy's friends, Beri, by now twenty-one years old but still very close to him, played a major role in convincing him to take this step (while Barry paid for the treatment) and to join Alcoholics Anonymous as well. "Beri was around a lot when we performed in Las Vegas," recalled Rick Lotempio, "occasionally showing up when we were on the road as well." Rick believed that Beri "was very determined to help Andy get better; they were very, very close. I always had the feeling Andy felt better mentally when Beri was around and with him on the road or wherever."

By the time Andy traveled to Utah, where he and Marie Osmond would sing together for what turned out to be one last time on the telethon (performing the Bee Gees composition "Islands in the Stream"), he had hired Dana Miller, best known as having been Rick Springfield's manager, to replace Gardner. Andy seemed to be bubbling over with enthusiasm. He told Kenny Hodges, who interviewed him at the Osmond studio, "Right now . . . is a very exciting time for me. It's what I am calling a turning point in my career." Andy excitedly explained how Miller was on the verge of getting him signed to either one of two record labels (Andy wouldn't reveal their names) and was helping him procure new songs from outside writers, including one from Phil Collins. Andy said that he had an album's worth of material ready and that he would be recording demos in about a week-and-a-half. Andy added that Miller had secured him a role in a movie to be filmed in the south of France, a comedy. "Plus, quite possibly, I'm opening up on Broadway again at the end of the year . . . so it's quite an exciting time for me."

Andy also, of course, talked with his old flame-turned-friend Marie Osmond while in Utah for the telethon. She recounted the conversation, almost tearfully, in the 1997 VH-1 *Behind the Music* episode on Andy. "He said, 'You know what, Marie . . . I'm a member of AA and I love it. I know I'm an alcoholic, and I know it's a problem, and I know I can beat it.' He said, 'I can do it . . . I'm off drugs. I'm clean . . . it feels so great, I'm so happy."

Andy gave a lot of the credit for his newfound optimism and what he saw as yet another comeback in the making to Miller. "He's turned my life right around," he told Hodges. But Miller, meanwhile, was soon complaining to one of his best friends, repeatedly, that he found Andy's insecurity to be "crippling."

Chapter NINE

Hell or High Water

"When I was with him, he looked terrific. He was happy. He said to me, 'My life is finally coming together.' He said, 'I am growing up. I know what I want to do with my life. I want to entertain people.' And I'll tell you, I looked in his eyes, and I really believed him." Cousin Brucie Morrow had interviewed Andy for the television program *PM Magazine* in August 1986, and when Andy died a little over a year-and-a-half later, the legendary DJ and radio host was stunned. Of course, he was hardly alone.

Andy had once again seemed to be making some progress in getting his career back on track in the summer of 1986. He sang "An Everlasting Love" on a Bob Hope-produced television special (although Hope left most of the hosting duties to Glen Campbell), *An All-Star Tribute to General Jimmy Doolittle*, which commemorated the World War II hero's ninetieth birthday and aired in August in syndication. Andy also headlined at the Hacienda in Las Vegas for a week in late July, and photos in a fan club newsletter showed him clearly enjoying himself at the city's Wet 'n' Wild water park during several afternoons he spent there, something that would have been virtually impossible for him to do half a dozen years earlier. In August he performed for two nights in the Catskill Mountains of New York, first at the Nevele Country Club and Grand Hotel in the town of Wawarsing, where Cousin Brucie and a crew from *PM Magazine* caught up with him, and then at the Raleigh Hotel in South Fallsburg, where famed entertainers such as Sammy Davis Jr., and Milton Berle had performed.

But aside from the insecurity that Dana Milller had by now become aware of, Andy's latest comeback plans faced another problem as well. As the attempt to garnish his earnings at the Sparks Nugget in March and then months later the run-in with the process server at Kezar Stadium in San Francisco had made all too clear, Andy's financial problems were becoming insurmountable. While Barry had been willing to pay for Andy to enter rehab, Andy's brothers refused to bail him out of the hole he now found himself in, at least in part because they feared that giving him money would lead to him buying drugs and/or alcohol (which, according to some accounts, he had sometimes done when his mother gave him money, although after his death, Maurice seemed to deny that that had ever happened). Yet signing a recording contract, or signing to appear in a movie or on Broadway, would have surely attracted the attention of creditors as well as the Internal Revenue Service, which was also after Andy. Even performing in Las Vegas might have been too high profile to escape such notice; Andy's booking at the Hacienda had been as a last-minute replacement, which likely meant that his creditors and the IRS couldn't find out about the gig in time to take his earnings.

In other words, for the most part, Andy's work opportunities would be confined to one-night stands such as the two in the Catskills or another at the Front Row Theater in Highland Heights, Ohio, near Cleveland, until his he got his financial mess straightened out. This, of course, meant that he wouldn't be able to support himself, since he was broke. With his brothers unwilling to rescue him, the only solution would be to declare bankruptcy.

Andy, however, didn't want to file for bankruptcy. He told James Dayley of his disappointment that even his parents wouldn't help him at all. "I remember him telling me," said Dayley, "that when it [the bankruptcy] was happening, he was kind of freaking out . . . he went to his dad [and told him], 'The tax man's after me.'" Andy told Dayley that he had asked Hugh if he would sell the Jaguar that Andy had bought him and let the money be used to pay the IRS. "No," Hugh told his youngest son. "You owed this to me." Andy, according to Dayley, "was really kind of upset about that." Andy also told

Dayley that he had asked Barbara if she would mortgage a houseboat that he'd bought her, but she, too, turned him down.

Furthermore, Andy faced another serious problem. Even though he had finally kicked his cocaine habit and was at least keeping his drinking in check, the mounting heart problems that had been plaguing him since 1978 persisted. His friend Pam Rossi said that she never "really knew about his heart condition" until September 1986. Barbara Gibb called her and said that "Andy wanted me to come visit him in the hospital in West Hills [in the San Fernando Valley]. And it was the same night that Barry was singing at a fundraiser over at Barbra Streisand's house [in Malibu] . . . and Andy was supposed to be there, but he said that he had to go to the hospital because his heart was flaring up, and they were trying to figure out what was happening. So when I went to the hospital to go visit, Barbara was there . . . and I hung out with Andy a little bit. They said his heart was inflamed, it was pericarditis, and that they were just trying to get it under control."

His brothers urged him to move back to Miami. They promised to help support him while he went through his bankruptcy, and Barry also promised that he would write songs with Andy and take him into the Bee Gees' Middle Ear Studio to record demos so that he could finally get a new recording contract. Moving to Florida would also be helpful for his bankruptcy case, given that most of his largest creditors were based in California and that Florida had more favorable bankruptcy laws for debtors than California did. As the summer gave way to autumn, and after six years of living a somewhat nomadic existence in the Los Angeles area (in addition to Malibu, he had also lived in the Hollywood Hills, Beverly Hills, Redondo Beach, and Marina del Rey, in addition to frequent absences for work), Andy returned to the city where had lived from 1977 to 1980.

He no longer had the money for a houseboat or a rental house along the coast, but he still managed to soon find equally agreeable housing. ("Andy," observed Rick Lotempio, "never did live a poor man's lifestyle during this time.") He moved into the 41st floor penthouse of a brand new condominium, the Venetia, at 1717 N. Bayshore Drive, overlooking Biscayne Bay.

Developer Tibor Hollo, a fifty-nine-year-old native of Hungary who had survived interment at the infamous Auschwitz concentration camp in Nazi-occupied Poland during World War II, had completed the ambitious project at an inopportune time. "By the time his huge Venetia condominium hit the market," journalist Tim Elfrink would later recall in the *Miami New Times*, "Miami was on the down end of one of its worst boom-and-bust cycles since the 1920s." Hollo made a deal with Andy: he could live rent-free in the penthouse in exchange for making four promotional appearances per year, essentially meets-and-greets with perspective buyers of units in the complex at which he would mingle and sing a couple of songs while playing an acoustic guitar. The penthouse included a wet bar (perhaps not a welcome luxury for a recovering alcoholic), Roman tub and shower, and wall-to-wall plush white carpeting. By the beginning of 1988, according to Hollo, the rent would have been $2,600 (just over $5,900 in 2021 dollars) had Andy not been living there rent-free under their deal.

Nevertheless, Andy was still virtually penniless upon his return to Miami. Until then he had managed to at least maintain a cash flow through nightclub performances and the occasional television booking, but now with his creditors and the IRS hounding him, he was barely working. Scott Glasel, who worked with the Bee Gees as a recording engineer at Middle Ear Studio from 1985 until 1993, met Andy shortly after he moved back to Miami. The Bee Gees, Glasel recalled, gave Andy a car to drive and "set up an account for him at Epicure Market [an upscale market and deli which served South Beach from 1945 until its closure in 2017]." Andy's sobriety still seemed a bit shaky at first, so the Bee Gees (or perhaps their personal manager, Dick Ashby) made it clear to the management of Epicure that Andy should not be allowed to charge alcohol to the account. The Bee Gees also helped Andy furnish his apartment and soon began giving him a $200 weekly allowance. "He was supposed to go to AA meetings once a week, which Mo had set up for him," said Glasel. "And to the best of my knowledge, he was doing that . . . he was going to meetings. Every time I saw him he was sober, clear-eyed."

Glasel soon found Andy to be, as did many who got to know him, "one of the sweetest people that I've ever known." He remembered that Andy would play tennis almost every morning with Barry, spend time with Barry and his family at Barry and Linda's pool, and show up at Middle Ear when the Bee Gees began work on their album *E.S.P.*, which was released in 1987. "He was just really great, a really great guy." As an example, Glasel told the story of how when studio manager Tom Kennedy, a longtime employee of the Bee Gees, began feeding a stray cat at Middle Ear that soon gave birth to a litter of kittens, Andy adopted one and took it home to his penthouse. "He *loved* that cat. That's the kind of guy Andy was." (Eventually, Andy would give the cat to Tom and his wife Stephanie for safer keeping.)

As he had at the first two of the annual Barry Gibb Love and Hope Tennis Festivals, which were always concluded with a charity auction ball that included a concert by whichever Gibb brothers were present, Andy played tennis and sang at the third one in mid-November 1986. He also served as the auctioneer for the sale of two t-shirts signed by all three Bee Gees for $2,400. In the tennis tournament, Andy was paired with Alan Thicke, and they narrowly lost a doubles match to Barry and Florida Governor Bob Graham.

Aside from singing (and playing tennis) at charity events, which Andy did frequently during his second stint as a Floridian, he continued, for a while, to take the occasional nightclub engagement. He also performed at a wedding in Atlanta. On New Year's Eve, 1986, he performed at the Indiana Roof Ballroom in Indianapolis. On January 17, 1987, he and Maurice attended the fourth annual Pig Bowl, a charity football game between the City of Miami Police and the Metro-Dade Police played at Miami's Tamiami Park, and Andy sang "The Star-Spangled Banner" before the game. About a week later, Andy returned to Las Vegas, where he had performed often over the previous three-and-a-half years, for an engagement at the Sahara's Congo Showroom, two shows per night, six nights per week from January 27 through February 8. An advertisement in the *Los Angeles Times* said that the show would "feature [Andy's] Top 10 hits and an all-new Bee Gee's [*sic*] medley." "I believe those were the last" of Andy's concert bookings, guitarist Rick Lotempio remembered.

Most of the other musicians who had been performing with Andy in recent years did not rejoin him for this last stint in Las Vegas, and he had to put together an essentially new band. He had been playing the recent one-night stands without his band and backup singers, as he was no longer performing enough to retain a band and couldn't afford travel and lodging costs to bring in musicians for one or two shows. "I was loyal to Andy," Lotempio said. "He was my friend and I didn't want to jump ship especially when he had an opportunity to work and maybe help his situation."

By then, however, Andy realized that, as much as he disliked the idea, he had no choice but to file for bankruptcy. He hired a young Miami lawyer named John Kozyak, who began the lengthy process of putting together Andy's filing. Kozyak would have a number of interactions with Andy during 1987 and early 1988, and he, too, would come to regard Andy highly. "I can certainly confirm Andy caused a stir when he came to our law firm a few times," Kozyak recalled in 2021. "The staff, especially the women, seemed more attentive than when bankers and more typical businessmen were scheduled to be in the office. Andy was always polite and gracious."

One episode in particular made a lasting impression upon Kozyak. "When Andy Gibb's Chapter 7 petition was filed," he explained, "a Trustee was automatically assigned to his case. Jeanette Tavormina was the Trustee and she called to set up an inspection of Andy's apartment to verify the possessions listed on his schedules. This is very routine, but there was a twist. She asked if she could bring a relative (a son, I believe) who had some mental disabilities. She explained that the young man was a big fan of Andy Gibb's and she would appreciate it if he could come. She promised he would not bother Andy or interfere. Andy consented and was actually quite gracious with the young man. He showed him his gold records and a few other mementoes. I suspect he gave him an autograph and might have done it on a record. The young man and Ms. Tavormina were beaming. It was a kind gesture that made me feel good too."

Kozyak's law partner Chuck Throckmorton met Andy once, accompanying him at a court appearance while Kozyak was out of town. He could still recall that meeting more than three decades later: "I remember that Andy was very friendly and open, without any edge or guile. He exuded a kind of innocent and optimistic charm. He gave off absolutely no self-aware or condescending 'star'/celebrity vibe."

Throckmorton also got a glimpse of Andy's lack of familiarity with the average working adult's reality that others had noted in him. The court appearance was brief (and not plagued by any fans or members of the press, which Throckmorton had feared might be the case) and over before 9:30 a.m. "The thing that I most remember," Throckmorton added, "is our conversation as were leaving the courthouse and preparing to go our separate ways. Andy said that he was off to play tennis. I told him that my workday was just beginning and that I had probably another ten hours to put in at the office. Andy looked at me with shock and sympathy, as if I had just told him that one of my close friends or relatives had just died. The reality of the 'long day in the office' routine seemed unfamiliar and distasteful to him, something to be (sympathetically) pitied. He thanked me for my help, shook my hand, and was off. I never saw him again."

Andy admitted that it was his own fault that he was now broke. In the fall of 1985 he told interviewer Bob Durant, "I was buying cars, yachts, and looking back, I suppose I could blame a few people 'cause I was too young to know any better, but nobody advised me. Maybe I wouldn't have listened if they had thinking back, 'cause I was pretty head strong, but nobody advised me how to invest it, what to do with it. And before I knew it they were starting to monitor it and saying cut back here, cut back there, and I wasn't used to that."

According to his friends, though, Andy was also quite generous with his parents, his friends, and, especially, his girlfriends. Victoria Principal benefited the most from his generosity, but he also bought Tony Messina a Porsche 924 shortly after Tony joined him in the United States in 1977. Andy later gave another personal assistant, John Cappadonna, the money to buy a 1965 Ford Mustang convertible.

Other friends saw this side of Andy, too. "If I said, 'Boy, that's a beautiful motorcycle you got there,'" Rick Lotempio recalled, "he'd go, 'Oh man, you can have it.' He was so generous, it was unbelievable." Jeff Witjas concurred. "He was the nicest guy," Witjas said. "He would give you anything. Material things didn't really make that much difference to him." Andy's friend George Recupito (Pam Rossi's husband) was also struck by Andy's generosity. George was on a visit to his hometown of Philadelphia during one of Andy's engagements at Resorts International in Atlantic City. George went to see Andy, and he asked him if it would be okay if he had his parents come down for the night. "He said, 'George, it's more than okay.' He gave my mom and dad the Frank Sinatra suite for the night, and he got me a room and got himself a room. So that's the kind of person he was. He always took care of everyone . . . as big [a star] as he was, that's how nice he was." George and Pam also saw how thankful Andy was when someone gave him a gift; they went to a party for his twenty-fifth birthday at his parents' house and gave him a shirt, and Andy immediately took off the shirt he was wearing and put that one on.

Andy's mounting financial problems had been ongoing, in a way, since 1982. His friend and former business associate Joe Shane, with whom he had recently renewed contact, told a reporter at the beginning of January 1988, just as Andy's bankruptcy case was wrapping up, that "from '78 to '81, he was able to live off $5 million." But by the middle of 1982, as Andy admitted to Joan Lunden on *Good Morning America*, most of that money was gone. When he quit showing up for *Solid Gold* following the split with Victoria Principal but continued living in the rented house in the Malibu Colony and began spending more than he ever had on cocaine, he had to sell jewelry and other valuable items to raise cash. Once he got back to work, his cash flow resumed; he earned over half a million dollars in 1983. But after that, as he worked less (and gradually made less and less money when he did), he went broke and fell into debt.

Several months would pass before Kozyak had Andy's bankruptcy case ready to file. In the meantime, Andy was at last ready to return to the recording studio. (Reports that would surface online many years later that Andy had recorded demos in Los Angeles in May 1986 or at Maurice's garage studio [Panther House] in September 1986 were false. Andy made it clear in the interview that Kenny Hodges did with him at the beginning of June 1986 that he had not made any demos recently, and Scott Glasel, who would know, said that "Andy never recorded at Mo's garage studio.") For several years Barry had been telling Andy that he would write with him and produce recordings for him again if Andy could kick his addictions to drugs and alcohol, and by the spring of 1987, it seemed that he finally had. Barry and Andy began writing together for the first time in years, and they were joined by Maurice, who had rarely written with Andy in the past.

"The fact that we'd done it together in the first place was what brought him back," Barry said in the 1997 *Behind the Music* episode. "You know, 'Let's do it again, let's go into the studio again and this time, I'll keep my grip, I'll hold on and I won't slip again.'" The fact that Barry was finally willing to work with Andy again made it clear that he was convinced that his youngest brother was finally clean and sober, for he had long refused to do so until he was certain that that was the case.

One day in June 1987, Maurice told Scott Glasel, "Hey, Andy's coming in tomorrow [to the Middle Ear Studio]. We're going to record some demos." Andy, Barry, Maurice, and Scott spent the next four or five days recording four songs: "Man on Fire," "Hell or High Water," "The Price of Fame," and "Arrow Through the Heart." Glasel thought that "Man on Fire" and "Arrow Through the Heart" were both strong, that "Hell or High Water" was "okay," and that "The Price of Fame" was a "great song" that "Barry didn't want to release for some reason." "My friend Jeff," Glasel recalled, "played guitar on all four of those tracks, and I don't think he ever got credited for them, but it doesn't matter. . . . I think Alan Kendall [longtime Bee Gees lead guitarist] may have played on one or two of those songs." Robin later came into the studio and added backing vocals to "Arrow Through the Heart," making it only the second recording (after "Desire") to feature vocals by all four Gibb brothers. "Robin," Glasel observed, "could smell a hit."

Glasel was quite impressed with Andy. "You didn't have to fix his vocals . . . he was a *great* singer, I mean, really, really talented . . . *man*, the guy could sing." Glasel and the Bee Gees felt confident that Andy would make a strong comeback once his bankruptcy was settled, at which time he would be free to sign a recording contract.

Longtime friends who saw Andy around this time also thought that he had turned a corner. Andy was still spending some time in the Los Angeles area, visiting his parents and Beri as well as friends, and in the summer of 1987 he visited Joey Murcia, Andy Murcia, and Ann Jillian at Andy and Ann's home. Even though Joey hadn't performed with Andy since 1980, they remained friends and saw each other periodically after that, and Andy also continued his friendship with Andy Murcia and Ann after meeting them in 1982. "We loved Andy very much," Ann remembered. "He was a very sweet, sweet gentle soul. He had a way about him that when you met him, it was like, you wanted to protect him." When Ann and the Murcia brothers saw Andy for what turned out to be the last time, he seemed well to them. "He said he was clean," Joey told a reporter just after Andy's passing. "He looked the best I'd ever seen him. He had even gained some weight." Andy said that he would be making an album soon, and he asked Joey to play on it, which Joey gladly agreed to do.

In September 1987, Ron and Howie Albert, Miami record producers and avid fisherman who had known Andy for just over a decade, took him on a fishing trip. "He was in very good spirits," Howie told a reporter after Andy died, "good health and straight as an arrow. He was happy and optimistic about life. He definitely wasn't having a drug problem at that point."

Barry further demonstrated that he was convinced of Andy's triumph over his drug and alcohol addictions when he agreed during the summer to pay for Andy to fulfill a longtime dream: learning how to fly airplanes and earning a pilot's license. Andy had taken some lessons at the Santa Monica Airport during his first brief stint as Californian a decade earlier, but his rather hectic schedule and, eventually, his substance abuse had thwarted his dreams of flying then. In October 1987, Andy finally achieved his goal. Maurice, in an unfortunate example of the Gibb brothers' penchant for exaggeration, said, "Twelve months ago he couldn't even walk onto a plane, let alone fly one." Barry, though, would later say of Andy, "For two years he was straight before he died." Andy told a reporter that piloting an airplane "is what has taken the place of drugs for me." He was also delighted when he got to ride along on a Blue Angels flight.

Apparently no one, however, had taken the place of Victoria Principal for Andy. After he died, *People* reported that Andy had "dated fellow Miamian Donna Rice a couple of times before the Gary Hart affair [which torpedoed the Democratic senator's presidential aspirations] broke" in early May 1987, but it wasn't serious. Scott Glasel introduced Andy to an attractive female friend of his who was visiting Miami from Los Angeles, but she soon told Scott that Andy had phoned her in the middle of the night, sounding as though he might have been drinking, and told her that he was still in love with Principal. Dick Ashby would say that during the final year or so of Andy's life, "He read a lot. He was quite a loner in a lot of ways."

While Andy seemed cheerful and enthusiastic to those who saw or spoke to him during this period, some of those who knew him well sensed that he was still troubled. Robert Stigwood saw Andy not long before he died and recalled, "He seemed fine, but he wasn't the young, lively person that I knew." When the Bee Gees discussed Andy on *Entertainment Tonight* on the first anniversary of his passing, Robin said, "He was great, he was clean, and things looked good to everybody else. But inside, there was a void, there was a vacuum. He just didn't, the things everybody had told him that was gonna be there once he gave all this stuff up wasn't there to fill the void, to him, and he had great expectations."

Barry began to suspect that Andy wasn't as healthy as he looked either. "I used to play tennis with him and I'd noticed that by the second or third set he would become very red in the face," Barry told reporter Beth Neil in 2009. "Even after drinking water he didn't look right." Although Hugh and Barbara almost certainly were aware that Andy had an inflammatory heart condition, given how many times they had been with him in a hospital room while he was being treated, neither they nor Andy ever told his brothers. "We didn't know about [Andy's heart condition]," Barry told Neil.

Andy's comeback plans couldn't come to fruition until his bankruptcy was settled, and in September 1987, John Kozyak had his case ready for filing. Once again, newspapers and tabloids had a field day with Andy's misfortune. Headlines screamed, "Bee Gee Brother Broke." Newspapers across the country published a UPI report that began: "Lawyers, cars and taxes have driven singer Andy Gibb to bankruptcy. Gibb, 29, younger brother of Bee Gees Barry, Maurice and Robin Gibb, filed a personal bankruptcy petition in Miami saying he has less than $50,000 and more than $1 million in debts, which his attorney says are mostly business-related."

These figures were revised considerably in papers that were filed with the court one month later, which listed his debts at $187,041 and his assets at only $1,432.79. These figures, too, were splashed all over the newspapers, along with the revelation that the furniture, video equipment, and guitars in his apartment had been loaned to him by the Bee Gees, their wives, and Middle Ear Inc. "Stage clothing and a velvet jacket," reports added, "are on loan from Barry Gibb." Andy's income for 1985 was listed as $24,727, and for 1986, only $7,755. Andy also filed a bankruptcy petition in October for his company, the Andy Gibb Organization Inc., which was listed as having $46,289 in debts and only $236 in assets. The two bankruptcy cases were consolidated. News reports noted that the businesses Andy owed money to included four hospitals, yet another hint that his health had been a brewing problem.

The reason for the considerable downward revision of Andy's debt from the September filing to the October filing had to do with Robert Stigwood. Andy owed his former manager about $1 million, but when Stigwood learned that Andy was going bankrupt, he wrote off the debt. James Dayley, however, heard Stigwood complain about it. "He was upset," Dayley said. "I was like, 'Robert, you made money off of Andy.'" But despite the bellyaching, Bill Oakes said that Stigwood "wouldn't have held that against him [Andy]. He was generous." Plus, Oakes pointed out, Stigwood thought of Andy and the Bee Gees "like family."

Andy put on a brave face as his bankruptcy was splashed across the newspapers and tabloids, even though the latter took the opportunity to recount all of his problems going back to his split with Victoria Principal five-and-a-half years earlier. During the first weekend of October, he held the Andy Gibb Sword of Hope Celebrity Tennis Tournament, in which Barry also participated, in Vero Beach, raising over $10,000 for the American Cancer Society. In November, *Entertainment Tonight* ran a segment on the Bee Gees and Andy that was taped at the annual Barry Gibb Love and Hope Tennis Festival. (This turned out to be both Andy's last public performance and the last time he appeared on US television; he would introduce the Bee Gees performing "You Win Again" on the BBC's *Top of the Pops* in December.) "All of my problems are behind me," Andy told an *Entertainment Tonight* reporter. "I'm about to sign my new record deal, which I can do now with no pressure. And everybody seems to think that, you know, I am really suffering through all the headlines [but] it's great for me. At last I can get on with my career. At last."

Barry wasn't fooled, though. "I think that [the bankruptcy] was a crippling blow to him," Barry sadly recalled in 1997. "I don't think he survived that. I think he was embarrassed by it." As Andy was filing for bankruptcy in September 1987, Barry tried to finally bring him into the Bee Gees, something that he had been discussing since 1979, and which he had told Andy would happen if Andy could conquer his substance abuse problems. But Maurice and Robin had always been resistant to that idea, and the fact the Andy had gotten clean and sober didn't change their minds. "Six months before his death," Barry told an interviewer in 1989, "I campaigned to get him included. It was put to the vote and I'm afraid I was outvoted two to one." Barry pondered the possibility that this disappointment was another factor in Andy's demise. "But I don't really think so," he said. "Andy's attitude was, 'Well, I'd like to have some more hits on my own before I join anyway!'"

Near the end of the 2020 documentary *The Bee Gees: How Can You Mend a Broken Heart*, white letters on a black screen declare, "In 1988, the Bee Gees announced Andy Gibb would join the group as an official member." No source is given for this statement, and none of the stories about Andy that were published after his death, even in reputable music industry sources such as *Billboard* and *Rolling Stone*, mentioned any such announcement. Scott Glasel, who was working regularly with the Bee Gees at Middle Ear at the time, not only couldn't recall them saying they had decided to add Andy to the group, but he also said, in 2021, "The Bee Gees were the three of them. I mean, they loved Andy, Andy's dream was to be a Bee Gee, but I think because of the age difference, he was never actually going to be a Bee Gee. . . . That was *never* going to happen, man." "If Andy [had] lived," Glasel said, "he would have been the opening act for the Bee Gees on the *One* tour," the trio's 1989 tour which might have begun in 1988 if Andy hadn't died that year.

Barry and Maurice would both later say that Andy would have become a Bee Gee for both the *One* album and tour. Even as late as 2002, though, Robin sounded less certain. "I mean, the door was open for him," Robin said when Larry King interviewed the Bee Gees on his CNN talk show that year. "But we were hoping that he recovered."

With Andy's admittance into the Bee Gees off the table, Barry set about getting him a recording contract as a solo artist. The Bee Gees, their wives and children, Hugh and Barbara, Andy, and Beri would all be spending the Christmas of 1987, which no one had any idea would be Andy's last, in England. (The correspondent in the November *Entertainment Tonight* report suggested that the Bee Gees felt more "appreciated" there, given that *E.S.P.*, their first complete new album in six years, had flopped in the United States but reached the top five in Great Britain.) Barry was by now acting as Andy's de facto manager; Dana Miller and Andy had parted ways earlier in the year, after his last Las Vegas engagement at the Sahara. With Andy doing no paid work for the rest of the year, there wasn't much need for a manager, nor, of course, any commissions either.

Given both the rejection by American pop music fans of the new Bee Gees album and the negative press coverage that Andy had been getting in America on-and-off since 1982, Barry decided that it would be best to shop for a recording contract for him in London. "The European market seems best," Barry told a journalist. "There isn't the negativity." Barry seemed confident and optimistic about his youngest brother's comeback. "He's recorded four demo tapes which he wrote with me [and Maurice]. He'll be fine. He's gone through the biggest battle."

Just after Christmas, Barry took Andy to the London headquarters of Island Records (which had become renowned for its superstar act U2, a group that RSO Records had rejected the opportunity to sign in 1979). The brothers played Andy's demo tape for Clive Banks, the head of the label's London division. Banks didn't sign Andy, but a tentative agreement was reached, and Andy was reportedly encouraged. Upon returning to Miami just after the start of the new year, he told Tibor Hollo that he would start paying rent for his condo at the Venetia, even though the agreement by which he lived there rent-free in exchange for making four annual promotional appearances for the complex was not set to expire until late in the year. A Miami bankruptcy judge discharged Andy's debts that month, although the judge filed an order in February stating that creditors would have until May 9 to file claims in the case. (None ever did so.) Andy's assets were sold to pay off a portion, albeit only a small one, of his debts, and the bankruptcy settlement left him with only $1,000 worth of personal property. The bankruptcy discharge did not, of course, relieve Andy of his $15,000 debt (equivalent to just over $34,000 in 2021) to the IRS. Andy never did pay rent to Hollo; when he died, a spokesman for the Venetia said that he had been "due in Miami next week to make some appearances."

Also upon his return to Miami at the beginning of 1988, Andy gave what turned out to be his last interview. Malcolm Balfour, who had written for years for the *National Enquirer* and by this point was working as a freelance journalist, had done "many stories about the Gibb brothers over the years" and knew them all. An experienced pilot, the Florida-based Balfour had heard that Andy had just gotten his pilot's license and that he was on the come-back trail. Balfour arranged to meet Andy at the Fort Lauderdale Executive Airport, and he flew there from Lantana, Florida, in his own airplane. Andy brought Barbara and Barry's three-year-old son Michael with him.

At first, Balfour found Andy not particularly talkative, but when he took him up "for a short flight in my plane" and let Andy—whom Balfour thought looked like "a real pro" as a pilot—take the controls, he subsequently opened up. Balfour remembered the years when "he and Victoria wanted desperately to be pictured in the *Enquirer*," and Andy spent quite a bit of the interview bemoaning his lost love. "Frankly," he told Balfour, "I still love Victoria. And I guess I always will. I wonder if I'll ever have the courage to give myself so completely to another human being." "There is still a large piece of Victoria in me," he added, "I feel her there inside me. She will be with me until the day I die."

While the interview gave credence to what Andy's friend Hayley Small, a music writer, said shortly after his death—that Andy "never got over [Victoria], he was obsessed with her and couldn't let go"—at the same time he exuded optimism. "It's great to be back," Andy told Balfour, "to have my life together. You have to hit rock bottom to know what it's like to reach the top. But thanks to the love and support of my mum and my dad and my brothers, I'm definitely back." "The future has never been brighter," Andy told Balfour. "I just know inside me that things will be fantastic for me when I go to live in England. . . . Honest, my voice has never been better. I can just feel it inside me—I'm on the verge of a hit record." Andy also told Balfour that Barbara would be accompanying him to England, where Andy would be staying at Robin's estate in Thame, Oxfordshire, "to look after me and play mum."

On January 27, 1988, Andy left America for the last time and arrived in England at London's Heathrow Airport, where he was photographed looking happy but was unaccompanied. Contrary to what he had told Balfour, Barbara did not come with him. The reason may have been the presence of a guest in the two-bedroom cottage at Robin's estate where Andy would be staying: the accomplished British scholar and Egyptologist James Terence

"Terry" DuQuesne. DuQuesne often stayed in the cottage; as an obituary noted in 2014, one of the small group of mourners at his London memorial ceremony was "his fellow Pagan and oldest friend Dwina Murphy-Gibb—widow of Bee Gee Robin Gibb."

Whatever the reason was why Barbara didn't go to England with Andy, several friends of his, in interviews for this book, said that for Andy to leave Miami and go to England alone for an extended period of time was a big mistake. "That was the *absolute* wrong move [for him] to go to London alone," Jeff Witjas said. "That was just, I don't know why he did that, but, some people I guess could be good being by themselves and just getting themselves together, but that was not Andy's thing. He needed people around him." "He spent most of his life alone," Witjas reflected, "but he didn't like being alone."

Barry, too, later said that Andy would have been better off staying in Miami. "He didn't really need to be away from his family," Barry recalled in the 1997 *Behind the Music* episode, "and we didn't really want him away from us. And I think he went into a decline because of that."

Of course, Andy wasn't truly away from family, as he was living on Robin's estate. Initially he often dined with Robin and his family, and he and Robin watched videotapes and listened to recordings of old British TV and radio comedy programs. "He was great fun," Robin recalled, "and we shared our sense of humor." Andy also bonded with Robin and Dwina's five-year-old son, Robin-John (RJ). "They had a deep connection," Dwina said in 2012. "They'd watch the film *Watership Down* together and Andy would sing him the theme song, 'Bright Eyes.' After Andy died, RJ drew a picture of him as an angel soaring into the sky, surrounded by the words, 'I Love You.'" Robin-John shared these memories himself in a Facebook post on what would have been Andy's sixty-third birthday in 2021.

Nevertheless, as Barry implied, Andy had a closer relationship with him and his family, and with Maurice and his family, who also, unlike Robin and his family, were essentially full-time Miamians. Still, Robin was the one who took Andy, upon his return to England, to the London headquarters of Island Records, this time to meet with the company's founder and president, Chris

Blackwell, and sign a contract. Robin told Blackwell that the Bee Gees would bring Andy along as an opening act on their upcoming world tour. "Andy called me up," remembered Scott Glasel, "and he was like, 'Mate, I'm gonna be signed to Island,' and it was supposed to be an eight-album deal. I mean, I don't know if Andy was exaggerating. I'd never heard of an eight-album deal." Surely, Andy was indeed exaggerating; Island didn't even give him an advance payment.

Blackwell and others at Island had plans for Andy that he didn't necessarily agree with, but he went along with them, or at least tried. Someone at the record company insisted that he needed to get a haircut in order to look more contemporary. He complied but complained about it in phone calls to some friends in America, who more than thirty years later could still remember him being quite upset. Island also assigned Andy to work with two songwriters chosen by the label to help him write the remaining six songs for the album, which were to be added to the four Barry-Maurice-Andy compositions that were on the demo tape that had landed Andy the contract. In the fall of 1987, Andy had written two more songs with his brothers: "Naked Feelings," which all four brothers wrote, and "I'm Not Wearing Make-Up," which all the brothers except Robin wrote together. These songs, though, were intended not for Andy but rather Beri, who for a time pursued a singing career herself. She recorded both of these songs, although only the latter was released, and not until 1994.

According to a report that was published in *Rolling Stone* a month after Andy's death, "Tentative plans called for a Gibb single to be released in Europe this spring, followed by another in summer and a complete album for worldwide release in the fall." The album, according to Scott Glasel, would have been recorded at the Middle Ear Studio in Miami Beach. "He [Andy] wanted me to co-produce with him, so I was really looking forward to it."

When Andy first arrived in England in late January 1988, he seemed to still be upbeat and optimistic. "He was happy and full of bounce at first," said Terry Connor, a family friend who ran a hotel near Robin's estate. "He seemed like a new man, looking forward to working again. He certainly was not doing cocaine anymore." Andy did start showing up, alone, some nights at two nearby pubs, but according to witnesses he never had more than one or two drinks. But he soon appeared to be troubled. He began sitting outside St. Mary's Church, across the street from Robin's estate, during the morning, even though he had never been a religious person. (In fact, he had once joked to Scott Paton that he would never be able to have a relationship with Marie Osmond because the Gibbs were "heathens.") The nuns invited Andy inside and served him tea and fed him. When he stopped showing up, they brought meals to his cottage, leaving them at the door when he wouldn't answer. By then, during the last three weeks of his life, Andy was also avoiding Robin.

According to what his family later said, Andy's chronic insecurity came back in full force once it was time for him to start writing and recording again. "The biggest thing on his mind," Barry said in 1989, "was 'Can I make it back to the top?' That's what he really wanted to do—and under all the pressure his mind and heart gave way." Robin said, "I had to keep reassuring him of his talent, you know, and build up his confidence. It actually affected his mind that he really had to start again. I don't think he could feel like he wanted to start again." Andy began missing appointments with Island and the songwriters he was supposed to be working with.

"He was finding it a bit of a shock getting down to work," Dick Ashby told a *Miami News* reporter after Andy died. "I think his heart was in the States, be it in California with his mum and dad or down here with his brothers." Ashby, who had started working for the Bee Gees in 1967, had known Andy well.

By the beginning of March, Barbara, who kept in touch with Andy through phone calls, was worried about him. "And I got onto Robin, and Robin said, 'Don't come, mum, you're babying him too much. He's fine.' But I was on that plane the next day because I knew *something* was wrong." She discovered at least one reason why Andy had become depressed. "You can't just make yourself write [songs]," she said in 1997. "You know, it's not something you can make yourself just sit down and do because somebody tells you to. And he couldn't. He got a block and he couldn't write. And that upset him. That upset him very, very much."

Robin and Barbara both said that Andy had begun drinking heavily again. According to Barbara, Andy "was ringing the little liquor store in Thame at two o'clock in the morning for a bottle of vodka. Those people [were] in bed, they close at ten o'clock. . . . Andy thought this was terrible, he was going back to America. He couldn't stand it." Robin said that Andy was drinking so much that "he wasn't even aware of his existence anymore." Robin also claimed that Andy fell and "smashed his face against the wall and lost all his teeth." This was yet another unfortunate exaggeration made at Andy's expense by one of his brothers (and an absurd one at that, since it is rather difficult to imagine someone losing "all" of his teeth by smashing his face against even a stone wall such as the kind in the buildings on Robin's medieval estate). Andy, as a few of his close friends knew, had, as Scott Paton put it, "lost a tooth or two in his rough-and-tumble days. He occasionally got into a fight in his 'skinhead days.'" As such, Andy had had bridgework done shortly after he came to America in 1976. In the incident that Robin referred to, Andy broke a dental bridge, and Robin's personal assistant, Ken Graydon, subsequently took him to Robin's dentist.

Barbara and Andy celebrated his thirtieth birthday, on March 5, 1988, by themselves. "He kept walking in and out and saying, 'I might as well be dead, there's nothing going on.' Because there was nobody there, you see." When Maurice phoned, Robin told him that Andy was too drunk to come to the phone. "I said, 'Oh, well sod him then,'" Maurice recalled in the VH-1 *Behind the Music* episode, "and I put the phone down, and I never spoke to him. So I never forgave myself for that for a long time. I thought, [and here Maurice sort of sighed] 'I should have spoken to him.'" Barry did have a final conversation with Andy just before his youngest brother's final birthday, but it did not go well. "The last thing that happened between me and Andy was an argument, which is devastating for me, because I have to live with that all my life," Barry said on *Behind the Music*. "And there was a phone call between him and me and I was sort of saying, you know, 'You've really gotta get your act together' and 'This is no good.' Instead of being gentle about it, I was angry, because someone had said to me at one point, 'Tough love is the answer,' you know? So, for me, it wasn't, because that was the last conversation we had. That's my regret. That's what I live with."

Yet Andy continued to talk to friends on the phone during this period and sounded fine. He called Susan George, who was also back in her native England, about a week before he died, and they made plans to meet and celebrate the resumption of his career. "He sounded very positive about life and terribly excited," she told a reporter following his death. Andy also phoned his friends Pam Rossi and George Recupito. "Andy called us a couple of weeks before he passed away; maybe it was a week before he passed away. It was kind of early in the morning," Pam recalled. (She and George were eight time zones behind Andy.) "He called and was very, very excited about his record deal and some new songs and getting back on track. He sounded really good. We were really happy. And he said, 'I'm coming to Malibu. We're gonna get together, we're gonna go out.' And I said, 'That's fantastic.'"

On Andy's birthday, he phoned his longtime backup singer Lenard Allen. "He was like, 'Hey Len, Lenny, it's Andy,'" Allen remembered. "And I'm like, 'Andy! What are you doing, what's going on?' He goes, 'Hey, it's my birthday.' And I said, 'Today's your birthday?' And he goes, 'Yeah, it's my birthday.'" Allen sang "Happy Birthday" to him over the phone, and Andy thanked him. "So what are you doing today?" Allen asked Andy. Andy told him that he was at Robin's estate in England. When Allen asked him what he was doing for his birthday, he replied, "Oh, nothing, I'm just over staying in one of the houses on the property." Allen found it sad and puzzling that Andy was alone on his birthday, but as Andy told him about his recording contract and played him some of "Arrow Through the Heart" and another song, he thought that Andy sounded optimistic. "He was hopeful," Allen thought, "and interested in trying to make another stab at a career." Andy also told Allen that he was straight and clean, and then he asked him, "Will you still work with me if I get it back together again?" Allen told him that he would be happy to, "absolutely." "And then," Allen sadly remembered, "I was surprised that he was dead a few days later."

On March 8, 1988, just two days before he died, Andy called another yet another friend in California, Rick Lotempio, who had remained in Andy's band right through his final engagement in Las Vegas the year before. Andy told him, "I can't promise you anything, but I'd like you to come to England . . . I got some action going on, some stuff I want to write and record." Thinking back thirty-three years later, Lotempio said that "I actually think I got the [airline] ticket to go there. . . . I think I got that ticket that he sent me, and I returned it [after Andy died], but I can't remember. But he did tell me he wanted me to go work on this Island recording that he was gonna be doing." Rick, too, thought that Andy sounded well. "When I talked to him that last time, it was the best he ever sounded," he said.

Andy didn't tell any of these friends that he had been having any health problems. But as Robin later revealed, "A week and a half before he died, in fact"—on February 29—"he had gone into [the] hospital suffering from severe chest pains but checked himself out [the same day] before doctors could do tests." Andy neglected to tell any of the hospital staff that he had been diagnosed with pericarditis by cardiologists in California. One of those cardiologists, Dr. William Shell, later said, "I thought that the physicians in London would have been well served by talking to some of us, because some of these events were pretty frightening. They probably could have aborted one of these events if they had known what the treatment was."

On March 7, he went back into the hospital (the John Radcliffe Hospital in nearby Oxford) for the same reason. Before Andy left Robin's estate that evening, Robin had a brief conversation with him that, twenty-one years later, he said "still haunts me." "It was a rainy night and I was stood there with an umbrella and I said, 'Andy, if you keep up what you're doing, you will not see forty-seven.' I don't know why I said forty-seven and not a rounded figure. But I said it." Once again, Andy left the hospital without staying overnight. Then on the evening of March 9, he collapsed in the cottage on Robin's estate.

According to a report in the London *Guardian* newspaper on March 11 as well as what Robin later said, Andy apparently suffered one or more seizures.

An ambulance rushed Andy, accompanied by his mother, back to the John Radcliffe Hospital. Barbara wanted to stay by his side all night, but the hospital rules wouldn't allow it. "So I had to go," she recalled in 1997, "and I said, 'I'll be back in the morning.' Well, she [the nurse] said, "Well, you better go because he'll sleep all night now, we've given him something to sleep.' And he was, he was fast asleep." Nearly a year later, Barbara and Hugh appeared on *Entertainment Tonight* to discuss Andy's life and death. Interviewer Mary Murphy asked Barbara, "What was the last thing that Andy said to you?" The answer was, "You can't die from this, can you?"

At 8:30 the next morning, March 10, Andy's doctor came into his room and asked him if he could draw some blood so that more tests could be done. Barbara had not returned to the hospital yet. Andy replied, "Fine," but that was the last thing he ever said. As Barbara recounted in the VH-1 *Behind the Music* episode, "And in the time the doctor turned around and went, he [Andy] gave one big sigh and he was gone." At 8:45 a.m., Andy was pronounced dead.

Exactly how Robin relayed the tragic news to his father and siblings was not made clear to the public. Some accounts say that he made phone calls; others say that his assistant Graydon did. Perhaps both men did. Barry, who was in Miami Beach at the time, later said that "Dad called me about six o'clock in the morning," which would have been three o'clock in the morning in California, where Hugh was at the time. "That has to be the saddest, most desperate moment of my life, when I heard he had gone," Barry told a journalist in 1989. "Since then, I've asked myself a thousand times, could I have done more or said more to help him?"

Epilogue

"MUM SEES ANDY GIBB COKE DEATH." "ANDY GIBB DIED AFTER BOOZE BINGE." Such were the headlines that British and American tabloids rushed to publish after Andy's sudden death. *People Weekly* published a longer but only slightly less sensationalized headline on the cover of its March 29, 1988 issue, alongside a photo of a smiling Andy in his heyday: "The short, turbulent life of fallen teen idol Andy Gibb. A superstar at 19, the 'baby Bee Gee' had it all but couldn't handle it. A generous, likeable kid, he blew his fortune on cocaine and blamed his troubles on a breakup with Victoria Principal. Trying for a comeback, he died, bankrupt, at 30."

On March 11, the day after Andy died, the John Radcliffe Hospital issued a statement: "Mr. Gibb died from inflammation of the heart of the sort commonly caused by a virus. There is no evidence that his death was related to drink or drugs." Coroner N.G. Gardiner conducted the postmortem investigation and found only one cause of death to list on the death certificate: myocarditis, or inflammation of the heart muscle. Andy's Beverly Hills cardiologist, Dr. William Shell, told *People Weekly* that he, too, had thought Andy's heart inflammation to be "viral in nature."

An article published in the *Palm Beach Post* on March 16, 1988, however, which quoted Dr. Azorides R. Morales, chairman of the pathology department at the University of Miami School of Medicine, and Dr. Eugene Hurwitz, a Centers for Disease Control (CDC) medical epidemiologist, suggested that Andy's history of drug and alcohol abuse may have made him more likely to contract and die from myocarditis, a condition "so rare" that, according to Morales, "as few as one person per 1,000 is afflicted" with it. When Hugh and Barbara Gibb appeared on *Entertainment Tonight* as the first anniversary of Andy's death approached, Barbara told Mary Murphy that "I was with him in England when he died, and they assured me at the hospital that there was no anything [no drugs or alcohol] in his bloodstream at all. He was clean." In another interview in 2004, though, Barbara said, "But the damage had been done. The doctors told me that was drugs."

Less than a day after Andy died, Hugh and Beri flew from Los Angles to London. Robin picked them up at Heathrow Airport. Of course, reporters were there to ask him about his youngest brother's passing. In response to the lurid tabloid reports, Robin told the press, "There was no question of Andy using drugs. I don't know where that story came from, but there is absolutely no truth in it. He was not using cocaine again." Of Andy's death, Robin said, "It was so unexpected. Andy had been ill with stomach pains for about four days."

Hugh saw to it that Kim and Peta learned of Andy's death before they could hear about it from the press, and they flew from Sydney to London and went to Robin's estate, where the family held a private memorial service at the chapel on the grounds. "He said he didn't think it would have been right," Kim said, "for me to read about it in the paper. I'll always be grateful to him for that."

Her reunion with Andy's parents, though, by her own account, did not go smoothly. Kim told London *News of the World* reporter John Lisners that "the first thing Andy's mother Barbara told me as I walked in was that if Andy was not dead I would not even be allowed in the house! We then had a row over Andy's wedding ring—she refused to let me have even this tiny memento of my dead [ex-]husband." Nor did Hugh give Kim and Peta a warm welcome. "Hughie," Kim told Lisners, "said there was not enough room for me in the main house—which has *nine* bedrooms—but I must sleep in the gatehouse where Andy had died [collapsed]. He sneered,

'That's the closest you will ever get to him now.'" After Kim and Peta entered the cottage, Marion Hawkes, an employee of Robin's whom Kim referred to as "a creepy old woman . . . who is always with the Gibb family," showed her a stain on the carpet in the bedroom that had been occupied by Andy. Kim said that Marion told her, "You can still see the patch on the carpet where he'd vomited up all the poisons his poor little body was trying to dispel."

Andy had phoned Kim in January, asking if Peta could come to England for a visit. Andy had only met Peta once, on her second birthday eight years earlier, and their contact over the past few years had been limited to, according to Kim, as few as two phone conversations per year. Kim told Andy that it wouldn't be possible for Peta to come visit him in England, so he told her that he would come to Australia in September.

After Andy died, Kim seemed to blame him and his family for his lack of a relationship with Peta. "Quite simply," she told British journalist Sue Carroll, "Peta and I were outcasts from the Gibbs. I longed to write to Andy sometimes, but I wasn't allowed to. I once sent him some pictures of Peta, but I had to do it through the fan club." Barbara, however, later said that "Andy wanted to see Peta, but her family wouldn't [even] let him write to her or send a Christmas present. It hurt." During the mid-1980s, Andy had told Peta on the phone that he would like for her to visit him in California, but it never happened.

Despite the tensions, Kim and Peta stayed at Hugh and Barbara's house when they traveled to Los Angeles for Andy's funeral, which was held on Monday, March 21, at Forest Lawn Memorial Park. Rick Lotempio, one of many former band members of Andy's who attended, remembered it as "a very bright, sunny spring afternoon." About 100 people attended the funeral in all, including, of course, Hugh and Barbara, the Bee Gees and their wives, Lesley, and Beri. Olivia Newton-John, who had last seen Andy less than one year earlier in Miami, was there as well, visibly shaken. Notably absent was Robert Stigwood. "Barry was a little bit pissed off with me," recalled James Dayley, who was still working for Stigwood then, "because Stigwood wasn't there. He said, 'Where's Robert?' I said, 'Well, he's under doctor's orders not to travel right now. He's in London. But I'm here.'"

Kim and Peta continued to be treated like outsiders even as the family buried Andy. "None of the family or anyone approached Kim," Dayley observed. (Of course, other than the family, many of the attendees had never met her, though.) Even though she and Dayley hadn't always gotten along well, he walked up to her to greet her. "I kind of put my arms out to give her a hug of condolences, and she put both her fists together and punched me in the chest. I took a step back and nearly fell . . . I was like, 'Whoa, what just happened here?'" By then the funeral service had concluded, so Dayley left and "went straight to a bar." "About a week later," said Dayley, "my mother calls me and tells me that she got a call from Kim. It was the only way that she could reach me; she didn't have my numbers. She said that she felt really bad about what happened at the funeral and that Peta [had] told her, 'Mom, you can't do that. You can't react like that. Not today.'"

At the conclusion of the funeral, as the other mourners left, the family stayed behind. Maurice, who had dreamt that Andy had died shortly before it actually happened, felt overwhelmed. "The loneliest feeling I felt," he later recalled, "was when his coffin was left outside . . . the wall where they put the coffins inside . . . and we were driving away and I looked at the wall . . . and I saw no one else was there, just his coffin lying there against the wall. *And I felt like he'd been abandoned.* And we all wanted to go back and just stay with him. Because he was by himself, with these strangers in green coats that are coming up. And it was so eerie."

Those who knew Andy well felt that he had "had an inferiority complex," as his mother said in 2004. "He didn't think he was as good as his brothers. He felt that he couldn't measure up and I think drugs filled that ache." Some of those who worked with Andy saw that, too, but they found it puzzling. "I don't think he felt like he measured up [to his brothers]," said Rick Lotempio. "When actually, he was the better talent than all of them." Joey Murcia concurred: "To me, he had the best voice of all the brothers." Olivia Newton-John thought that "Andy had it all—the voice, the looks, charisma—right up there with his brothers."

Andy's friends also recalled his humility fondly though, as well as remembering him for his sweet nature. "Even with his sudden, enormous success," Olivia said, "Andy remained humble and sweet as always." Another longtime Gibb family friend, Marion Adriaensen, who first met the Gibbs in 1973, described Andy in very similar terms. "He . . . was always very kind and humble," she recalled nearly five decades after she had met him. Joe Walsh, whose slide guitar added so much to "(Love Is) Thicker than Water," told a reporter upon hearing of Andy's death, "He was a quiet guy, extremely humble, extremely shy and as [talented] as any of his brothers. I will miss him." Walsh was hardly alone in the latter sentiment. Julie LaMagna, who had known Andy well during the late 1970s, recalled in 2021 that "it took me over twenty years to listen to his records without crying. I can't say why it hurt so much losing him. I feel there are many of us who would love to tell him how much he still touches our souls." "I was one of the lucky ones," she added, "who got to experience his wonderful spirit, voice, humor, love of animals and his ability to conquer anything he desired."

Yet for all his kindness, humility, charisma, and good looks, Andy never found an enduring companion, and that, his family and friends felt, haunted him. "Andy was unhappy that he had nobody," his mother reflected. "He hadn't got a girl and a family like his brothers." "He had girlfriends," Robin Gibb said in 1989, "but [his] relationships were 'hae a penny' because there was another one tomorrow. Yet when the chips were down, nobody was there, and he couldn't deal with that." Cathi Robbins had sensed this, too, during the period from 1983 to 1985 when she and her husband Rick became close friends with Andy. "He was just so kind and so generous," Cathi recalled, "and just always seemed to really need love and attention, and he was not good at being alone. He was so looking for that relationship that he didn't have that his brothers had and his parents had." Pam Dawber thought that Andy had "died of a broken heart. . . he just checked out. He couldn't do it anymore."

Andy's meteoric rise to fame and fortune and tragic demise became a warning of the dangers of "too much, too soon," as his father put it in 1989, for pop stars. When teen idol Justin Bieber started having some brushes with the law and was arrested in 2014 (at age nineteen) in Miami Beach and charged with driving under the influence, Barry Gibb couldn't help but note some parallels between Bieber and Andy. "Well, what I see with Justin Bieber is sort of what I see with Andy, you know," Barry said during an appearance on CNN's *Piers Morgan Tonight*. "You're heading for a brick wall. And that's a shame, because this is a great talent. This kid's got great gifts, you know. I would like to do the things he does . . . I just think it's time to grow up. It's time to grow up and—and be what—all these young girls love you, be a good example."

At the time of Andy's death, his music had practically disappeared from the radio and record stores. All of his albums were out of print. Polydor, which took over control of the RSO Records catalog after that label folded, released a best-of compilation on compact disc and cassette, simply titled *Andy Gibb*, in 1991. The album included one of Andy's 1987 demo recordings, "Man on Fire." In November 1997, VH-1 made Andy the subject of an episode of its *Behind the Music* series; it drew the highest ratings of any episode of the series to that point. Polydor then reissued all three of Andy's full albums—*Flowing Rivers* (1977), *Shadow Dancing* (1978), and *After Dark* (1980)—on compact disc in January 1998. Two more greatest hits CDs (neither with any previously unreleased songs) came out in 2001 and 2018.

In a way, Andy posthumously achieved his wish to become the fourth Bee Gee. On November 14, 1997, at the MGM Grand in Las Vegas, the Bee Gees performed a concert billed as "One Night Only," which was filmed and recorded. During the show, the Bee Gees performed "(Our Love) Don't Throw It All Away," while footage of Andy was shown on the big screen behind them. At one point, the three brothers stopped singing, except for backing vocals, while Andy's lead vocal from his recording of the song played. The hybrid Bee Gees-Andy Gibb version of the song appeared on the video and album releases of the concert, both of which were certified platinum by the Recording Industry Association of America. The Bee Gees went on to repeat the "One Night Only" concert in Dublin, London, Buenos Aires, Pretoria, Auckland, and Sydney during 1998-99. In 2010, Reprise Records released a 4-CD box set, *Mythology*, which was essentially a Bee Gees compilation with a twist: each disc focused on the recorded legacy of one Gibb brother, and the fourth disc drew from Andy's catalog. Peta selected the nineteen songs included on that disc, including the last song that her father had ever recorded, "Arrow Through the Heart." A portion of that poignant song, with its ironic chorus in which Andy practically cries out that he is too young to die, had been played to great effect in the *Behind the Music* episode, but this was the first time that it had ever been released.

By 2020, Andy Gibb had been dead longer than he had lived, yet interest in him remained strong. On what would have been his sixty-second birthday, Reelz aired an episode of its popular *Autopsy* series that examined Andy's death. In 2021 the Foo Fighters, calling themselves the "Dee Gees," covered "Shadow Dancing" along with several Bee Gees classics on album titled *Hail Satin.* At the same time an independent record label based in Portland, Oregon, called Curry Cuts, released a various artists tribute album consisting of cover versions of Andy's songs, titled *Higher Than a Mountain: The Songs of Andy Gibb.* Perhaps Andy's old friend Tony Messina, who had worked for him and spent so much time with him over the course of nearly an entire decade, assessed his legacy as well as it could be in 2021: "The music will never die. He has a really, really strong fan base, still to this day, all over the world."

Selected Bibliography

A&E Television Networks. *The Bee Gees: This Is Where I Came In*. Documentary. 2000.

"Album Reviews." *Cash Box*, May 27, 1978.

Andrews, Liz. "Why Andy Gibb grew up too fast." *Australian Women's Weekly*, February 7, 1979.

"Andy Gibb." Long Island (NY) *Newsday*, December 12, 1982.

"Andy Gibb, In the Shadow of the Bee Gees." Bee Gees Fan Fever. Website. March 5, 2011, https://beegeesfanfever.blogspot.com/2014/12/andy-gibb-in-shadow-of-bee-gees.html.

"Andy Gibb: It's Solid Gold or Bust! He's Got to Make it This Time." *16 Magazine*, February 1982.

"Andy Gibb on stage at Sahara's Congo Showroom." *Los Angeles Times*, January 25, 1987.

"Andy Gibb, pop singer, dies at 30." White Plains (NY) *Journal-News* (AP), March 11, 1988.

"Andy Gibb Rare Candid Fan Interview (part 1 of 2)." June 21, 1983, https://www.youtube.com/watch?v=SDrODzaNFOw.

"Andy Gibb Rare Candid Fan interview (part 2)." June 21, 1983, https://www.youtube.com/watch?v=3FIdus6Mgis.

"Andy Gibb treated for cocaine addiction." United Press International, April 4, 1985, https://www.upi.com/Archives/1985/04/04/Andy-Gibb-treated-for-cocaine-addiction/8424481438800/.

"Andy Gibb wounded in sex battle." *Red Deer Advocate* (Red Deer, Alberta, Canada), *TV Spotlight* section (syndicated article), April 10, 1980.

"Andy Gibb's last interview: 'I'm such a lucky guy' (1988)." Bee Gees Days. Website. https://en.beegeesdays.com/799-andy/.

"Andy Gibbs [*sic*], after split from wife, bounces back with Susan George." *The Star*, n.d. Reprinted in the *San Antonio Star and Travel Guide* (a supplement to the *San Antonio Express*), December 25, 1977.

Apter, Jeff. *Tragedy—The Ballad of the Bee Gees*. London: Jawbone Press, 2016.

Ardmore, Jane. "Victoria and Andy." *Sacramento Bee* (syndicated article), December 27, 1981.

Arnold, Christine. "The Pirates of Penzance." *Miami Herald*, October 10, 1982.

Awesome Aussie Songs Podcast. Interview with Col Joye, January 23, 2020, https://www.stitcher.com/show/all-australian-music-stories/episode/ep9-i-just-want-to-be-your-everything-andy-gibb-66937952.

Barile, Louise A. "The Bee Gees: Fame, Family & Tragedy." *Closer*, May 3, 2021.

Baron, Alexander. "Pagan Funeral for Terence DuQuesne," https://www.infotextmanuscripts.org/djetc/av-duquesne-pagan.html.

Baxter, Robert. "Andy Gibb conquers a broken heart." Camden (NJ) *Courier-Post*, October 23, 1982.

Beck, Marilyn. "Four 'Brothers Gibb' will be in concert." *Pensacola* (FL) *Journal* (syndicated column), January 26, 1980.

_____. "Julie Andrews plans to try hand as film maker." Rochester (NY) *Democrat and Chronicle* (syndicated column), March 25, 1982.

_____. "Martin Takes Role in Simon Film." *Burlington* (VT) *Free Press* (syndicated column), March 18, 1982.

_____. "Ross and Gibb are teaming-up for an album." *St. Petersburg Times* (syndicated column), January 16, 1985.

"Bee Gees' brother weds, but he wants to stay solo." *Sydney Morning Herald*, July 12, 1976.

"Bee Gees Talk About the Death of His [*sic*] Brother Andy Gibb, Rare." YouTube, https://www.youtube.com/watch?v=SyKhh6FPNeU&t=46s.

Bennetts, Leslie. "The show must . . ." *Windsor* (Ontario, Can.) *Star*, March 19, 1983.

Benarde, Scott. "Pop singer Andy Gibb dies in London at 30." *Palm Beach Post*, March 11, 1988.

Bernstein, Fred. "The Bee Gee & Sandy." *People Weekly*, April 21, 1980.

_____. "Journalism That Isn't (letter to the editor)." *New York Times*, May 22, 1998.

Bey, Rick. "We're Haunted by Ghost of Sad Andy." London *Sun*, May 15, 1989.

"Billboard's Top Album Picks." *Billboard*, May 27, 1978.

Biography Channel. *Biography: Andy Gibb*. Documentary. 2008.

Blackwelder, Carson. "Marie Osmond Recalls Relationship with Andy Gibb and How Their Split Was 'a Wakeup Call' for Him." *Closer*, October 25, 2019.

Boyer, Peter J. "Brother of Bee Gees Is 'Sort of a Loner.'" *Fort Lauderdale News*, June 10, 1977.

Braun, Liz. "Andy Gibb Opens at Imperial Room: Listening is easier than looking." *Toronto Sun*, October 24, 1985.

Bream, Jon. "Andy Gibb—Vegas transforms teen idol." *Minneapolis Star and Tribune*, November 14, 1983.

Brenna, Tony, and Reginald Fitz. "Docs Warn Andy: Quit Booze & Drugs or Die." *National Enquirer*, April 16, 1985.

Brennan, Joseph. Gibb Songs. Website. http://www.columbia.edu/~brennan/beegees/.

Bronson, Fred. *The Billboard Book of Number 1 Hits*. 5th ed. New York: Billboard Books, 2003.

_____. *Billboard's Hottest Hot 100 Hits*. 4th ed. New York: Billboard Books, 2007.

Brown, David. "Andy Gibb's career is ready to take off again . . . with some help from Barry, Maurice & Robin." *TV Week* (Australia), December 12, 1987.

Brown, G. "Andy Gibb: New Life, New Circuit." *Denver Post*, July 28, 1983.

Bryon, Dennis. *You Should Be Dancing: My Life with the Bee Gees*. Toronto: ECW Press, 2015.

Byrne, Robert, ed. *The 2,548 Best Things Anybody Ever Said*. New York: Touchstone Books, 2004.

Byrom, Sue. "The Current Scene." Scranton (PA) *Tribune* (Pop Scene Service), December 30, 1978.

Campbell, Mary. "Andy Gibb branches out to stage and TV stardom." *Fort Lauderdale News and Sun-Sentinel* (AP), December 11, 1981.

_____. "Newton-John Enjoys Being at Home." Lafayette (LA) *Daily Advertiser* (AP), October 30, 1981.

Carroll, Sue. "The Little Girl Andy Gibb Shut Out of His Life." London *Sun*, March 14, 1988.

_____. "Star treatment in the U.S. sucked him down." London *Sun*, March 15, 1988.

Chandran, Kannan. "Andy gets back on his feet." Singapore *Straits Times*, December 31, 1985.

Christensen, Dan. "Gibb: Heart inflammation, natural causes cited." *Miami News*, March 11, 1988.

Cohen, Howard. "Bee Gees' mom inspired sons to musical greatness." *Miami Herald*, August 16, 2016.

Cook, Hector, Andrew Môn Hughes, and Melinda Bilyeu, with assistance from Joseph Brennan and Mark Cohan. *The Ultimate Biography of the Bee Gees: Tales of the Brothers Gibb*. Rev. ed. London and New York: Omnibus Press, 2003.

Cowan, Ron. "Andy Gibb makes it to the fair." Salem (OR) *Statesman-Journal*, August 25, 1984.

_____. "Andy Gibb making own career." Salem (OR) *Statesman-Journal*, January 3, 1982.

Cox, James. Comments on "1406 Grave of Andy Gibb What Happened? The Bee Gees | Forest Lawn - Jordan The Lion Vlog (11/20/20)." YouTube, https://www.youtube.com/watch?v=7IIZPTBTY1k.

Coz, Steve, and Larry Haley. "Andy Gibb's Tragic Last Days." *National Enquirer*, March 29, 1988.

Cuskelly, Richard. "Youngest Gibb May Still Become Fourth Bee Gee." Nashville *Tennessean Showcase* (Pop Scene Service), November 19, 1978.

Darrow, Chuck. "Andy Gibb (at age 25) starts a comeback at Resorts." Camden (NJ) *Courier-Post*, August 26, 1983.

Davis, Ivor. "Millionaire Andy Gibb Tells 'I Was Spoiled Rotten.'" *TV Week* (London), April 3, 1982.

Deeb, Gary. "Warwick shoved aside for Gibb on 'Solid Gold.'" Tucson *Arizona Daily Star* (Chicago Sun-Times service), September 1, 1981.

Diliberto, Gioia. "AWOL from Broadway Once Too Often, Andy Gibb Is Ordered to Turn in His Dreamcoat." *People Weekly*, January 31, 1983.

Doyle, Erin. "Daryl Braithwaite spills on love, THAT romance with Olivia Newton-John and his iconic song 'Horses.'" *Now to Love* (Australia), June 10, 2020.

Duncan, Susan. "I Want Justice for Our Daughter says Andy Gibb's Ex-Wife Kim." *Australian Women's Weekly*, August 1989.

Durant, Bob. Interview with Andy Gibb. *Bob Durant's Night Music*. Canadian radio show. 1985. Transcript at https://beegeesfanfever.blogspot.com/2014/04/interview-andy-gibb-1985.html.

Edgar, Henry. "'Working' Intrigues Barry Bostwick." Newport News (VA) *Daily Press*, April 11, 1982.

Eells, Josh. "Barry Gibb: The Last Brother." *Rolling Stone*, June 5, 2014.

Elfrink, Tim. "Developer Tibor Hollo Helped Build Miami." *Miami New Times*, January 29, 2009.

Elwood, Philip. "Andy Gibb tries the Venetian Room on for size." *San Francisco Examiner*, February 27, 1986.

Estrin, Eric. "There's an Iron Fist in Brother Barry's Velvet Glove." *San Francisco Examiner* (Pop Scene Service), February 4, 1979.

Famous Lost Words. Interview with Andy Gibb, 1977. Episode 202, September 14, 2018, https://www.iheart.com/podcast/962-famous-lost-words-28822975/episode/ep-202-tina-turner-andy-29847257/.

Free, Cathy. "Movers' and Shakers' Party Makes for a Flighty Night." *Salt Lake Tribune* (Salt Lake City, UT), June 11, 1986.

Gardner, Marilyn, and Hy Gardner. "Glad You Asked That!" *Pittsburgh Press*, October 28, 1978.

"Gibb to re-enact rock nightmare." Toronto *Globe and Mail* (CP [Canadian Press]), September 27, 1983.

Gilbert, Bob, and Gary Theroux. *The Top Ten, 1956-Present.* New York: Fireside/Simon and Schuster, 1982.

"Glib Andy Gibb." *Philadelphia Daily News*, June 5, 1978.

Gold, Aaron. "Tower Ticker." *Chicago Tribune*, September 2, 1980.

"Gold & Sneed Inc." *Chicago Tribune*, August 1, 1982.

"'Grease' sequel." *Staunton* (VA) *News-Leader* (syndicated article), June 1, 1980.

Grein, Paul. "Chartbeat." *Billboard*, September 19, 1981.

Gritten, David. "Pam Dawber Casts Off from Mork to Crew with Andy Gibb and 'The Pirates of Penzance.'" *People Weekly*, June 29, 1981.

_____. "Victoria Principal, The 'Dallas' Good Girl with the Party Girl Past, Regrets Nothing." *People Weekly*, March 30, 1981.

Grossman, Doris. "Gibb tries again." *Asbury Park* (NJ) *Press*, July 29, 1984.

Hall, Carla. "The Fame Game." *Washington Post*, July 31, 1980.

_____. "Stars and Austerity at Ford's Theatre Gala." *Washington Post*, March 23, 1981.

Harrington, Richard. "The Bee Gees, After the Fever." *Washington Post*, August 3, 1989.

Harrison, Ed. "Talent in Action: Andy Gibb." *Billboard*, October 8, 1977.

Harrison, Karl. "Small-town stereotype shouldn't put limits on energy, Shane says." *Paducah* (KY) *Sun*, January 3, 1988.

HBO Max. *The Bee Gees: How Can You Mend a Broken Heart*. Documentary, 2020.

"Heart Inflammation Killed Pop Singer Andy Gibb." Associated Press, March 11, 1988, https://apnews.com/article/342cd746398e5fc913bcd dd2f4411251.

Hoffman, Ken. "Gibb Family 'Stages' Reunion." *Fort Lauderdale News*, July 10, 1978.

Hogan, Marty. "A Night with Andy Gibb." Essay posted on *Words & Music: Fans of the Brothers Gibb* Internet Mailing List. No longer archived. Screenshot in author's possession.

Huddy, John. "Andy Gibb Buys for a Good Cause." *Miami Herald*, April 25, 1979.

Hughes, Mike. "After six shaky years, 'Gold' stands on solid ground." *Fort Myers* (FL) *New-Press* (Gannett News Service), November 15, 1985.

Hugus, Jennifer K. "Tai Babilonia: Story of Survival on and off the Ice." *Los Angeles Beat*. Website. February 5, 2014, https://thelosangelesbeat.com/2014/02/tai-babilonia-story-of-survival-on-and-off-the-ice/.

Hume, Martha. "Introducing the Pee [*sic*] Gees." New York *Daily News*, April 22, 1979.

Hunt, Dennis. "Andy Gibb: He Just Wants to Be a Singer." *Los Angeles Times*, September 4, 1977.

_____. "A Chat with the Parents Gibb." *Los Angeles Times*, May 31, 1979.

Hunter, Colin. Interview with Victoria Principal, 2008. *UtlimateDallas.com*. Website, http://ultimatedallas.com/victoriaprincipal/victoria5.html.

Jerome, Jim. "It's Singles Time for Bee Gee Baby Andy Gibb: He's Got 1977's No. 1 Hit and a Marital Split." *People Weekly*, November 14, 1977.

Josie. "Between the Lines: The Story Behind the Stories You Read About Celebrities." Scranton (PA) *Times-Tribune* (syndicated column), August 29, 1982.

Kaye, Roger. "Singer Andy Gibb, Bee Gees' brother." *Fort Worth Star-Telegram*, March 11, 1988.

Kelp, Larry. "Gibb takes a shaky step on the comeback trail." *Oakland Tribune*, February 27, 1986.

Kinser, Jeremy. "Maxwell Caulfield On Gay Parties, Aging In Hollywood, His New Play And 'Grease 2.'" *Queerty*. Website. March 4, 2015, https://www.queerty.com/maxwell-caulfield-on-gay-parties-aging-in-hollywood-his-new-play-and-grease-2-20150304.

Krum, Sharon. "Barbara Gibb: My Boys 'The Bee Gees.'" *Australian Women's Weekly*, 2004, http://www.brothersgibb.org/reports-barbara-gibb.html.

LaSalle, Mick. "The night in 1986 at the Fairmont that Andy Gibb looked so fragile." *Datebook (San Francisco Chronicle)*, July 19, 2021, https://datebook.sfchronicle.com/movies-tv/the-night-in-1986-at-the-fairmont-that-andy-gibb-looked-so-fragile.

Laube, James. "Sedaka Is Back—Gibb Is with Him." *Colorado Springs Gazette Telegraph*, August 31, 1977.

Levin, Eric. "Death of a Golden Child." *People Weekly*, March 28, 1988.

Lewis, Barbara. "Here's the Answer." Scranton (PA) *Tribune* (Pop Scene Service), May 12, 1979.

Lipson, Norm. "Pop idol Andy Gibb's wife says: I'm broke while he lives in luxury." *The Star*, n.d. Reprinted in the *San Antonio Star and Sunday Magazine* (a supplement to the *San Antonio Express*), October 9, 1977.

Lisners, John. "Battle Over Bee Gee Andy's Body." *News of the World* (London), March 29, 1988.

Litsch, Joseph. "Front row." *Atlanta Constitution*, January 9, 1983.

Lloyd, Jack. "Gibb is over his loss." *Philadelphia Inquirer*, August 22, 1983.

Lucoff, Morton. "Andy Gibb has no income, borrows guitars, papers say." *Miami News*, October 27, 1987.

Lynch, Ray, and Deborah Wilker. "Singer Andy Gibb, brother of the Bee Gees." *South Florida Sun-Sentinel* (Fort Lauderdale), March 11, 1988.

Malone, Pat, and Bob Smith. "Andy Gibb: Lost, Lonely, and Lovelorn." *The Star*, March 29, 1988.

"Marilyn McCoo and Andy Gibb; Hot Duo Sizzle in 'Solid Gold.'" *Jet*, February 11, 1982.

Meyer, David N. *The Bee Gees: The Biography*. Boston: Da Capo Press/Hachette Books, 2013.

Mitchell, Greg. "The Act You've Known For All Those Years," *Crawdaddy*, August 1978.

Monette, Denis. "The Palace of a Goddess of the Small Screen." *Lundi*, March 1985, English translation, http://www.landerssisters.net/Articles/Lundi385/.

Morgan, Sally. "Wife of Bee Gee Robin, Dwina Gibb, On How His Music Helped His Miracle Recovery." *Hello!* (UK), May 7, 2012.

Morse, Steve. "Bay City Rollers—'cute and cuddly.'" *Boston Globe*, December 19, 1977.

_____. "Farewell to a teen idol." *Boston Globe*, March 11, 1988.

Mullen, Rodger. "From Silliness to Tragedy, Voet Sees the Stage Life." *Fayetteville* (NC) *Observer*, November 21, 1988.

Neil, Beth. "Bee Gees week: We'd give up all our success to have our brothers back again." London *Mirror*, November 2, 2009.

"New role for Andy Gibb." Regina (Saskatchewan, Canada) *Leader-Post* (CP [Canadian Press]), August 14, 1982.

"'Oh Brother, You're Famous' Says Andy Gibb." *Fabulous 208 Magazine* (UK), April 1969.

Oldenburg, Ann. "Barry Gibb: Justin Bieber is 'heading for a brick wall.'" *USA Today*, January 30, 2014.

"One-night stands out." Cherry Hill (NJ) *Courier-Post,* December 29, 1978.

"Osmonds unite for possible last time." Newburgh-Beacon (NY) *Evening News* (AP), October 14, 1985.

Parker, Lyndsey. "'Punky Brewster' star Soleil Moon Frye recalls being 'so in love' with first crush Andy Gibb." *Yahoo! Entertainment*, February 15, 2021, https://www.yahoo.com/entertainment/punky-brewster-star-soleil-moon-frye-recalls-being-so-in-love-with-first-crush-on-andy-gibb-223404168.html.

Paton, Scott. Comment on *AT40 From the Inside* website, September 17, 2013, https://thjkoc.net/2013/09/16/at40-from-the-inside/#comments.

Petridis, Alexis. "The Bee Gees' Barry Gibb: 'There's fame and there's ultra-fame—it can destroy you.'" London *Guardian*, December 7, 2020.

Phillips, Guy. "Barry Gibb Tormented by his Brother's Death." *Woman's Day* (Australia), September 1989, https://spicksspecks-archiv.blogspot.com/2012/01/von-guy-phillips-womans-day-september.html.

"Picks and Pans Review: Andy Gibb." *People Weekly*, December 29, 1980.

Piscino-Keosky, Donna. "Andy Gibb finds his pot of gold." Yonkers *Herald Statesman*, February 14, 1982.

Pollock, Bruce. "Gibb's journeys as a wandering Joseph." White Plains (NY) *Journal-News*, January 16, 1983.

"Pop Quiz." Escondido (CA) *Times-Advocate North County Magazine*, November 14, 1985.

"Pop singer collapses, cancels part of tour." United Press International, August 18, 1984, https://www.upi.com/Archives/1984/08/18/Pop-singer-collapses-cancels-part-of-tour/4227461649600/.

"PR for Musicians—George Dassinger." *Music Biz 101 & More* podcast, https://soundcloud.com/musicbiz-101-more/pr-for-musicians-george-dassinger-music-biz-101-more-podcast.

Price, Hardy. "Local band 'discovered.'" *Arizona Republic* (Phoenix), October 27, 1978.

"Raggedy Andy." *People Weekly*, August 16, 1982.

Redd, Jayne. "Principally, Gibb." *Us Weekly*, April 14, 1981.

Reed, Jacqui. "When I Knew Andy: My Memories of Andy Gibb." *jacquireedpath* (blog). March 20, 2011, https://jacquireidpath.wordpress.com/2011/03/20/when-i-knew-andy-my-memories-of-andy-gibb/.

Reelz. *Autopsy: The Last Hours of Andy Gibb*. Documentary. 2020.

Ressner, Jeffrey. "Andy Gibb: 1958-1988." *Rolling Stone*, April 24, 1988.

"Robert Stigwood Obituary." London *Guardian*, January 5, 2016.

"Rock Tracks." *Cicero* (IL) *Life* (syndicated column), October 21, 1981.

Roura, Phil, and Tom Poster. "Now, it's Gibb & Tucker who're singing a duet." New York *Daily News*, August 2, 1982.

______. "Sharon to Kids: 'Trust Me.'" New York *Daily News*, April 1, 1983.

_____. "Tanya Without Glen: Singer enjoying the N.Y. high life." New York *Daily News*, August 20, 1982.

Saltzman, Barbara. "Persona . . . ," *Los Angeles Times*, September 11, 1978.

Sandefer, April. "For Andy Gibb, making hearts pound is all in day's work." *Reno Gazette-Journal*, September 26, 1985.

Sanderson, Eddie. "Andy and Me by the Baby Bee Gee." London *Daily Mirror*, June 19, 1982.

Sandler, Leonard. "Andy Gibb's ghost haunts Victoria Principal." *National Examiner*, May 3, 1988.

Sasso, Joey. "Through channels." Somerset (PA) *Daily American* (syndicated column), July 7, 1981.

Schnurmacher, Thomas. "Cher's coming to town—only on film, though." Montreal *Gazette*, August 17, 1982.

_____, "Insults from Joan Rivers leave Andy Gibb pouting." Montreal *Gazette*, December 6, 1983.

Scott, Vernon. "Andy Gibb to try casino audiences." United Press International, August 11, 1983, https://www.upi.com/Archives/1983/08/11/Scotts-WorldNEWLNAndy-Gibb-to-try-casino-audiences/3275429422400/.

Segarini, Bob. "Segarini: The Brothers Gibb." *Segarini: Don't Believe A Word I Say* (blog). May 22, 2012, https://bobsegarini.wordpress.com/2012/05/22/segarini-the-brothers-gibb/.

Selvin, Joel. "Saturday Night Low-Grade Fever." *San Francisco Chronicle*, February 27, 1986.

Selvin, Rick. "People." *Philadelphia Daily News*, May 3, 1983.

_____. "Replacements: II." *Philadelphia Daily News*, May 25, 1983.

Shields, Mel. "Andy Gibb's show squeezed too much by production format." *Sacramento Bee*, September 26, 1985.

_____. "Someone should tell Andy Gibb the show doesn't always go on." *Sacramento Bee*, March 28, 1986.

Silverman, David. "Bee Gees Finally Shake Disco Fever." *Chicago Tribune*, n.d. Reprinted in the *St. Louis Post-Dispatch*, October 4, 1989.

"Singer Andy Gibb, who shot to fame in the . . ." United Press International, March 10, 1988, https://www.upi.com/Archives/1988/03/10/Singer-Andy-Gibb-who-shot-to-fame-in-the/8818573973200/.

Smith, Liz. "Bridges gets green light for fast lane." New York *Daily News*, March 11, 1982.

_____. "Of busy wives and rock-'n'-roll singing 'Pirates.'" Baltimore *Sun* (syndicated column), September 22, 1981.

Soocher, Stan. "Andy Gibb hits big with help." Madisonville (KY) *Messenger* (United Features Syndicate), October 26, 1977.

_____. "The Littlest Bee Gee? Andy Gibb Is More Than Just a Clone of His Successful Siblings." *Circus*, August 17, 1978.

Spence, Simon. *Staying Alive: The Disco Inferno of the Bee Gees*. London: Jawbone Press, 2017.

Spooner, Michael. Interview with Trevor Norton, March 5, 2014, https://www.youtube.com/watch?v=htKnn1B0jJ8&feature=emb_logo.

Stecher, Raquel. "Cinema Shame: Xanadu (1980)." *Out of the Past* (blog). August 11, 2019, http://www.outofthepastblog.com/2019/08/xanadu.html.

Sternberg, Ira. "Talent in Action: Andy Gibb, MGM Grand, Las Vegas." *Billboard*, October 22, 1983.

"Susan Stewart's People." *Philadelphia Daily News*, June 15, 1984.

Tinker, Anna. "Staying Alive—For Andy." Article from unknown Australian publication, 1993. Clipping in author's collection.

Tirbutt, Susan. "Andy Gibb dies at 29 [*sic.*]" London *Guardian*, March 11, 1988.

Trott, William C. "Bee Gee Brother Broke." United Press International, September 12, 1987, https://www.upi.com/Archives/1987/09/12/BEE-GEE-BROTHER-BROKE/5838558417600/.

Tucker, Tanya, with Patsi Bale Cox. *Nickel Dreams: My Life*. New York: Hyperion, 1997.

"TV Chatter!" *Anniston* (AL) *Star* (syndicated), February 20, 1982.

United States Citizenship and Immigrations Services. Website. Andy Gibb file. https://www.uscis.gov/sites/default/files/document/foia/LIT2013000004_-_Andy_Gibb.pdf.

Van Matre, Lynn. "Andy Gibb: Doing what comes naturally—pleasant pop positivism." *Chicago Tribune*, June 11, 1978.

VH-1. *Behind the Music: Andy Gibb*. Documentary. 1997.

Vogt, Jenny. "Disease that killed Andy Gibb is uncommon, rarely fatal." *Palm Beach* (FL) *Post*, March 16, 1988.

Von Drehle, Dave. "Fallen idol Andy Gibb dies in England at 30." *Miami Herald*, March 12, 1988.

Walters, Grant. "Andy Gibb's Debut Album *Flowing Rivers* Turns 40." *Albumism*. Website. September 12, 2017, https://www.albumism.com/features/tribute-celebrating-40-years-of-andy-gibb-flowing-rivers.

_____. "Andy Gibb's 'Shadow Dancing' Turns 40." *Albumism*. Website. April 24, 2018, https://www.albumism.com/features/andy-gibb-shadow-dancing-turns-40-anniversary-retrospective.

Whitburn, Joel. *Joel Whitburn Presents the Comparison Book: Billboard/Cash Box/Record World, 1954-1982*. Menomonee Falls, WI: Record Research, 2015.

Wikane, Christian John. "Making Her Move: Olivia Newton-John's 'Physical' Phenomenon Revisited." *Pop Matters*. Website. October 22, 2018, https://www.popmatters.com/olivia-newton-john-physical-2613720727.html.

_____. "Survival and Serendipity: An Interview with Northern Soul Legend P.P. Arnold." *Pop Matters*. Website. August 8, 2019, https://www.popmatters.com/pp-arnold-2019-interview-2639691979.html?rebelltitem=1#rebelltitem1.

Wilker, Deborah. "Andy Gibb Remembered as Caring Man." *South Florida Sun-Sentinel* (Fort Lauderdale), March 18, 1988.

Woshala, Steve. "Original Interview: Andy Gibb." Allentown (NJ) *Messenger-Press*, August 11, 1977.

Wylie, Rebel. "Growing up Gibb: A complicated relationship with a very famous father." *news.com.au*. Website. March 27, 2017, https://www.news.com.au/lifestyle/real-life/true-stories/growing-up-gibb-a-complicated-relationship-with-a-very-famous-father/news-story/ed64ab40578708836cb9905a087a051a.

"$250,000 Smile." London *Daily Mirror*, April 23, 1978.

ANDY GIBB
Art(Foto) Gallery

The Gibb family (except Hugh) backstage at a Bee Gees concert in London, circa 1968. Left to right: Barry, Maurice, their sister Lesley Gibb Evans, Andy, Barbara, and Robin. (Courtesy of Tony Messina.)

Andy often told interviewers that he had grown up around people who were older than him. This photo was taken in Ibiza, probably in 1973. Andy, about 15 at the time, is standing fifth from the left, with Beri, about 8, standing directly in front on him. (Courtesy of Tony Messina.)

Another photo from Ibiza, 1973. Andy is in the center of the bottom row, wearing an RSO t-shirt. Barbara and Hugh Gibb are standing at the left end. (Courtesy of Tony Messina.)

This photo in the family album of Andy's sister Lesley shows Hugh, Barbara, Lesley, Andy, and one of Lesley's children in Australia, circa 1975. (Courtesy of Lesley Gibb Evans.)

Andy and Zenta performing with a small orchestra at the Hordern Pavilion in Sydney, Australia, on August 27, 1975, as the opening act for the British band the Sweet. (Courtesy of Trevor Norton.)

Zenta drummer Trevor Norton took this photo of Andy and Kim Reeder in the Hordern Pavilion dressing room, August 27 or 28, 1975. (Courtesy of Trevor Norton.)

Andy's first live performance on US television was on NBC's *The Midnight Special* in the summer of 1977. To his left is bassist Jerry Manfredi. (RSO Records press photo.)

Andy onstage with lead guitarist Peter Leinheiser during his first North American tour, summer 1977. (Courtesy of Peter Leinheiser.)

A worn Polaroid of Andy and secretary and fan Charlene Coppi at the immigration office in Miami, 1978. (Courtesy of Charlene Coppi.)

Flying out of Sioux City, Iowa, on August 18, 1977. L. to r.: Drummer Russell Battelene, bassist Jerry Manfredi, Andy, keyboardist/backup singer Steve George, and Andy's personal manager James Dayley. (Courtesy of Peter Leinheiser.)

Andy's passport photo, 1978. Andy was granted permanent residence in the United States in May 1979, but he never became a U.S. citizen. (Courtesy of Julie LaMagna.)

Joey Murcia and Andy in 1978. Joey played guitar on all of Andy's albums and on tour with him that year. (Courtesy of Andy Murcia.)

Marie Osmond and Andy at the Ohio State Fair in August 1978. The Osmonds performed that night, and afterwards Andy assisted Marie while she made dinner for her family. (Courtesy of Julie LaMagna.)

Andy with the six-time world champion professional rodeo cowboy Larry Mahan at the Ohio State Fair in August 1978. Andy was an avid horse rider himself, having been given a horse by Barry for his eleventh birthday. (Courtesy of Julie LaMagna.)

Allan LaMagna and Andy on Andy's houseboat, circa 1978. Allan worked for Andy from 1977 to 1980, first as his tour manager and later as his personal manager. (Courtesy of Julie LaMagna.)

Boating and fishing were both favorite pastimes of Andy's. During the late 1970s, when he wasn't on tour or away for television appearances, he often sailed between Miami and Bimini in the Bahamas. (Courtesy of Julie LaMagna.)

Beri, Andy, and Andy's longtime friend and assistant Tony Messina with Robert Stigwood's Rolls Royce as they arrived at the 21st Annual Grammy Awards in Los Angeles, February 15, 1979. (Courtesy of Tony Messina.)

In this press photo from 1980, Andy is wearing the gold record necklace that Robert Stigwood gave him in 1977. Barbara Gibb often wore it after Andy died. (Bernie Ilson, Inc. press photo)

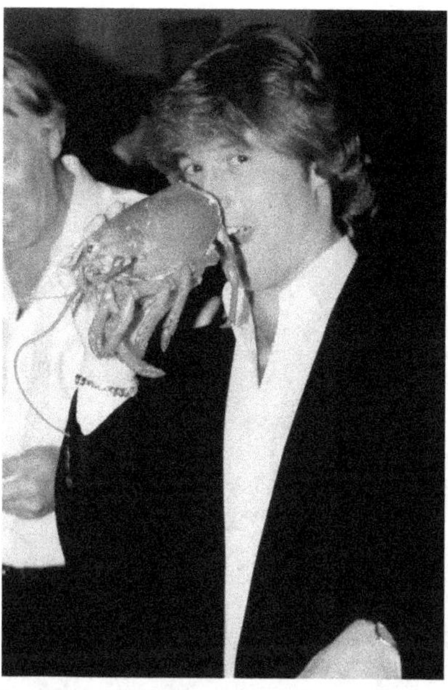

James Dayley took this photo of Andy at a birthday party in Manhattan for Robert Stigwood (partially visible) in April 1981. Andy's pose with the lobster was a reference to a routine on a Derek and Clive comedy album that he and James had often listened to. (Courtesy of James Dayley.)

Andy and Victoria Principal on the *Fourth Annual National Collegiate Cheerleading Championships*, which aired on CBS on May 26, 1981. (CBS press photo.)

Andy and one of his closest friends, Olivia Newton-John, on *Solid Gold* late in the summer of 1981. (The Garrett Company/Paramount Television Distribution press photo.)

Andy with *Solid Gold* musical director Michael Miller and co-host Marilyn McCoo in 1981. (Courtesy of Michael Miller.)

Andy guest starred as himself in the fall 1983 season premiere of NBC's *Gimme A Break!* L. to r.: Actress Lauri Hendler, bassist Bryan Garofalo, actress/singer Nell Carter, Andy, and drummer Dennis Bryon. (NBC press photo.)

Sheila Kennedy, to whom Andy is singing in this photo from a televised beauty pageant in Atlantic City in November 1983, told the author that "Andy was a total gentleman, so sweet and nice to everyone." (Courtesy of Sheila Kennedy.)

Dinner in Las Vegas in either 1983 or '84, during one of Andy's engagements at either the MGM Grand or the Riviera. Standing at the left are Andy's personal assistant, Joe Anthony, and manager, Marc Gurvitz. Seated, l. to r., are an unidentified woman, Andy, Cathi Robbins, and guitarist Rick Robbins. Leaning into the photo is lighting technician Bud Horowitz, and barely visible at the right is road manager Dan Wohleen. (Courtesy of Rick and Cathi Robbins.)

Andy and Rick Robbins at a hotel in Santiago, Chile, where Andy performed at the Viña del Mar Festival on February 12-13, 1984. (Courtesy of Rick and Cathi Robbins.)

Jeff Witjas, Andy's agent at William Morris from 1983 to 1985, didn't accompany Andy on any of his concert dates outside of North America in 1984, but, as shown in this photo from 2021, he kept the "1984 World Tour" sweatshirt that Andy gave him. (Courtesy of Jeff Witjas.)

Andy and eight-year-old Soleil Moon Frye (made up to look like an old lady for a dream sequence) on the set of NBC's *Punky Brewster* in January 1985. Andy had recently made two guest appearances on the series. (NBC press photo.)

Andy and backup vocalist Lenard Allen at the Valleyfair Amusement Park outside of Minneapolis, where Andy performed on August 1-2, 1985. (Courtesy of Lenard Allen.)

Andy's two-week engagement at the Venetian Room of the Fairmont Hotel in San Francisco during February and March 1986 drew much coverage in local newspapers at the time and was still being recalled in the *San Francisco Chronicle* thirty-five years later. Photographer Nick Rizzo took these and many other photos of Andy onstage there. (Courtesy of Nick Rizzo.)

Andy and his friend Pam Rossi, who was one of the *Solid Gold* dancers. This photograph was probably taken in 1986. (Courtesy of Pam Rossi.)

At Middle Ear Studio in Miami Beach, March 1987. Andy attended many of the sessions for the Bee Gees' *ESP* album, which they had just finished making when this photo was taken. Standing, l. to r: Andy, producer Arif Mardin, engineer Scott Glasel, Maurice, and Barry. Sitting, l. to r., are Barbara Gibb, Linda Gibb, and producer Brian Tench. Andy is wearing a Barry Gibb's Love and Hope Tennis Festival shirt. (Courtesy of Scott Glasel.)

BAD LUCK Drug free Andy Gibb said in his last interview he was fortunate to be stayin' alive. Then he died from a rare heart disease — ***page 8***

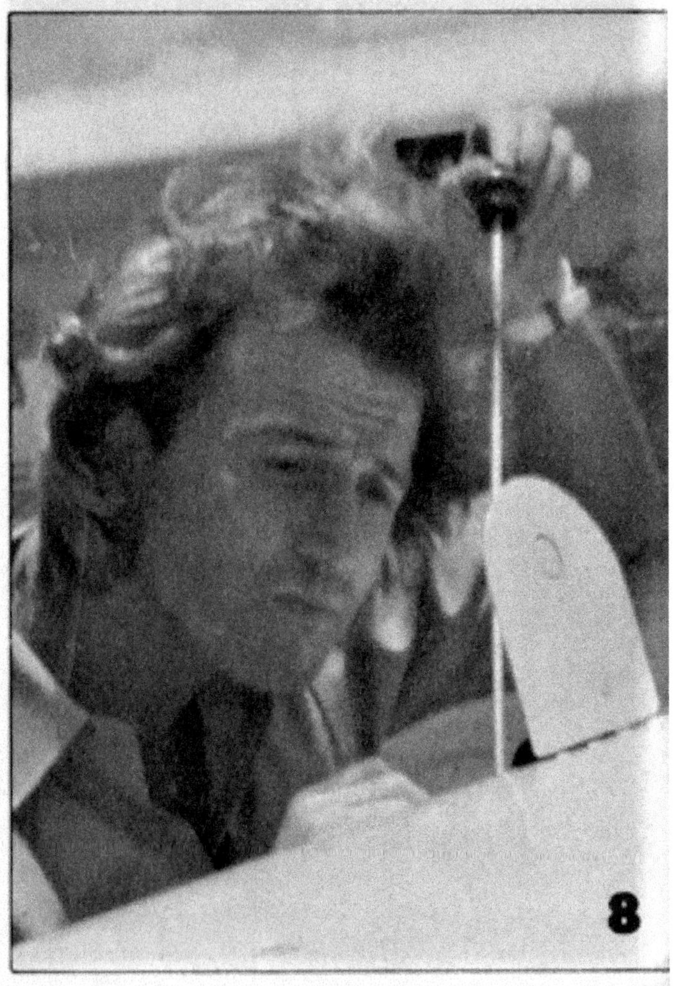

The Australian magazine *People (with Pix)* published Andy's final interview, conducted by journalist Malcolm Balfour, shortly after Andy's passing. The interview was conducted in early January 1988, at an airport and in a flight above Florida. This photo was taken at the airport in Fort Lauderdale on that occasion. (Courtesy of Bee Gees Days.)

Index

CPSIA information can be obtained
at www.ICGtesting.com
Printed in the USA
BVHW030700050722
641266BV00005B/124

9 781629 339207